The Most Reasonable Answer

*Helping Students Build
Better Arguments Together*

Alina Reznitskaya
Ian A. G. Wilkinson

HARVARD EDUCATION PRESS
CAMBRIDGE, MASSACHUSETTS

Paperback ISBN 978-1-68253-121-1
Library Edition ISBN 978-1-68253-122-8

Library of Congress Cataloging-in-Publication Data

Names: Reznitskaya, Alina, 1969- author. | Wilkinson, Ian A. G., author.
Title: The most reasonable answer : helping students build better arguments
  together / Alina Reznitskaya, Ian A. G. Wilkinson.
Description: Cambridge, Massachusetts : Harvard Education Press, [2017]. |
  Includes bibliographical references and index.
Identifiers: LCCN 2017028505| ISBN 9781682531211 (pbk.) | ISBN 9781682531228
  (library edition)
Subjects: LCSH: Inquiry-based learning. | Questioning. | Active learning. |
  Communication in education. | Student-centered learning. | Teacher-student
  relationships.
Classification: LCC LB1027.23 .R49 2017 | DDC 371.39—dc23 LC record available
  at https://lccn.loc.gov/2017028505

Published by Harvard Education Press,
an imprint of the Harvard Education Publishing Group

Harvard Education Press
8 Story Street
Cambridge, MA 02138

Cover Design: Ciano Design
Cover Photo: asiseeit/E+/Getty Images

The typefaces used in this book are Minion Pro and Myriad Pro.

Contents

APPENDICES

Foreword

How would we describe the normal course of events inside US classrooms?

- Classrooms are characterized by a lot of teacher talk and relatively little student talk.
- Classroom talk frequently focuses on information and rarely focuses on ideas.
- Students are expected to provide answers more often than they are allowed to formulate questions.
- Topics are typically selected based on the textbook or the content standards, and often remain irrelevant to students' lives and unconnected to their interests.
- When classroom discussions occur, students frequently offer opinions and rarely present well-developed arguments.

This volume, *The Most Reasonable Answer: Helping Students Build Better Arguments Together*, documents all these conditions, presents a cogent argument that they represent an impoverishment of educational opportunity, and, most importantly, presents a set of procedures and strategies that could help teachers move beyond their default practices to introduce high-quality, student-involved, goal-directed discussion into their classrooms.

The authors call the kind of discussion they are promoting *inquiry dialogue*. Inquiry dialogue is characterized as discussion in which "students search for the most reasonable answer to big, contestable questions and, if agreement is not possible, they work to clarify the basis and criteria for their disagreement." It is, in other words, directed at finding, or at least approaching, truth. Inquiry dialogue is a form of discussion focused on getting to a better understanding of an issue rather than to either agreement or victory.

Alina Reznitskaya and Ian A. G. Wilkinson, both acknowledged experts in the analysis and promotion of discussion-based teaching methods, display in this volume precisely the skills in critical thinking that they attribute to participation in inquiry dialogue. Developing what they call *argument literacy*—skill in producing and evaluating arguments—is the outcome they most value and the reason they want to see opportunities for inquiry dialogue in every classroom.

Argument literacy is not, I would contend, the only important outcome of good classroom discussion. Student levels of engagement are visibly enhanced during discussion, as are their opportunities to confront alternative perspectives on issues—alternative perspectives that are more potent precisely because they come from the students' classmates and friends.

My appreciation of this volume derives from my experience during the last several years promoting and analyzing classroom debates conducted as part of the Word Generation program (www.wordgen.serpmedia.org). Debate, a term often paired with discussion in treatments of classroom interaction, can (like Socratic discussions) take many forms, but it is distinct from inquiry dialogue in that the discussion topic is formulated as opposing positions, and in that the goal of the participants is to defend their chosen (or assigned) position as effectively as possible. One motivation for engaging in debate is to win. In other words, debate is inherently competitive, whereas inquiry dialogue is inherently collaborative.

The teachers in our projects who have implemented Word Generation, like those who have adopted inquiry dialogue, often find it an intimidating prospect at the beginning. They mistrust their skills as discussion launchers and leaders, and worry about introducing disorder, disruption, and interpersonal conflict into their classrooms. Discussion is not a practice that most of these teachers were exposed to in the classrooms where they were students, nor is it typically a practice emphasized in teacher education programs. The selection of topics and deployment of helpful talk moves that keep discussion going constitute huge challenges for many teachers. Thus, the careful descriptions of how to prepare for and support discussion that are provided in this volume, together with the concrete examples offered in the final chapters of texts and questions that can sustain discussion, constitute an invaluable resource.

Are there reasons to prefer inquiry dialogue to debate or other specific forms of classroom discussion? No one has carried out a rigorous comparison, but the available evidence suggests that any format that enables students to express their own views in carefully thought-through forms of language, with specific goals and the chance to think deeply about appealing topics, will improve student outcomes. Such opportunities are vanishingly rare in most classrooms, so adding even a brief session of inquiry dialogue or debate just a few times a week to any student's schedule would constitute a significant enhancement. Once opportunities for discussion of some sort are ubiquitous in US classrooms, it will be time to analyze in greater detail the value added of various specific formats, topics, question types, and supports.

The work described by Reznitskaya and Wilkinson is (as they note) closely allied with the Philosophy for Children Program, which provides models for effective discussion with children as young as preschoolers. A central question for research is the mechanism by which such discussions promote child skills. Is the inquiry component crucial? Or would other practices that give children more opportunity for linguistic autonomy and voicing their own thoughts work as well? It would be useful, for example, to compare the outcomes of Philosophy for Children sessions with outcomes from Story Telling/Story Acting, the narrative-authoring/theatre-directing technique initiated by Vivian Gussin Paley. Whereas Philosophy for Children is focused more directly on argument literacy, Story Telling/Story Acting gives children agency and a mechanism for exploring interpersonal conflicts. One might hypothesize that all that is really needed in classrooms is lots more opportunities for students to speak aloud about things they are interested in, an end that can be achieved with a variety of talk forms and practices. Or perhaps there are very specific affordances associated with the search for truth inherent in inquiry dialogue, with the efforts to triumph inherent in debate, and with the need to manage classmates' dramatizations characteristic of Story Telling/Story Acting. If so, then students should be given access to *all* these opportunities to promote their own and contribute to others' thinking.

A key characteristic of all the various forms of classroom talk that we see so little of and need so much more of is distributed cognition. Only if students can talk with one another can they learn from one another, can their own understandings of events and phenomena be enriched by access to others' understandings. Distributed cognition is the essence of shared learning, of teamwork, of going beyond friendly cooperation to the cognitive wrestling associated with authentic collaboration. Collaboration is the essential twenty-first-century skill, in a society encountering problems that are too complicated to be solved by individuals. Collaborative efforts are made possible by the communication skills honed in classrooms where students discuss. We need to make such classrooms the default, and *The Most Reasonable Answer* will help greatly.

Catherine E. Snow
Patricia Albjerg Grahan Professor of Education
Harvard Graduate School of Education

Preface

The Most Reasonable Answer: Helping Students Build Better Arguments Together is a book about teaching students to reach better, more reasonable conclusions by building and evaluating arguments *together*. In addition to focusing on the need to support rigorous thinking, we also place special emphasis on the collaborative nature of argumentation. In this way, our book differs from other publications that deal with arguments developed individually or with the primary goal of persuading others.[1] Our goal in writing this book is to help elementary school teachers engage students in discussions about the texts they read for the purpose of collectively determining what is more reasonable to believe or do, rather than winning over opponents.

This book is written at a time when our nation is deeply divided about what to believe or do about many important issues, ranging from climate change to health care to immigration. Moreover, there is a growing concern that we do not seem to share certain foundational norms and strategies for resolving our disagreements, or, in other words, for talking and thinking about complex, controversial issues together. At news conferences, TV shows, work meetings, and family gatherings, we see people talking *past*, not *with* each other. Often this happens when they play different kinds of conversational games and rely on different assumptions about the purpose of the discussion, the rules of participating, and the criteria for evaluating the quality of arguments. As a result, people routinely fall short of having a civil, rigorous, and collaborative discussion that brings about a better understanding of each other and the world around them.

Yet, productive engagement in argumentation may be one of the few options we have to resolve disagreements in a way that leads to better decisions and peaceful coexistence. For this reason, in 1995, an American educator and theorist named Neil Postman urged schools to teach students "how to argue, and to help them discover what questions are worth arguing about, and, of course, to make sure they know what happens when arguments cease."[2] He also explained that "when arguments cease—blood happens, as in our Civil War, when we stopped arguing with one another."[3]

Today, major policy documents, academic publications, and the popular press expect teachers to prepare their students to become independent thinkers capable of negotiating the dynamic, globalized, and information-rich environment of the twenty-first century.[4] According to the Common Core State Standards Initiative, for example, students should develop the ability to comprehend and formulate arguments through speaking, listening, reading, and writing—or *argument literacy*.[5] They should learn to "think critically and deeply, assess the validity of their own thinking, and anticipate counterclaims in opposition to their own assertions."[6] These are commendable goals, but they place heavy demands on teachers and require new approaches to instruction.

Unfortunately, despite broad agreement about the value of argument literacy, not enough resources have been made available to support teachers, as well as others concerned with classroom practice, in their efforts to foster the skills of argumentation. Currently, few research-based materials are designed for teachers who want to offer their students opportunities to experience the challenges and joys of collaborative and rigorous argumentation. Especially lacking are instructional materials made for upper elementary students. This scarcity of resources is regrettable considering that these students are developmentally ready to engage in argumentation and we know they can improve their skills through such engagement.[7] In fact, we see the upper elementary grades as an ideal context in which teachers can nurture students' emerging argument literacy skills. Lack of quality resources for fostering argumentation in elementary classrooms is also problematic given that recent educational policies, including the Common Core State Standards, describe argument literacy as an intended educational outcome for students at every grade level.[8] As researchers and teacher educators, we wanted to address this gap by developing effective instructional methods and classroom materials with and for practitioners.

This book reflects current educational theory and research on the benefits of discussions centered around argumentation to support the development of students' higher-order thinking.[9] It draws on our previous work with established pedagogical frameworks, such as *Philosophy for Children* and *Collaborative Reasoning*, as well as on our expertise with text-based discussion and argumentation.[10] But, above all, this book is based on what we have learned from a recent, multiyear program of research called "Dialogic Teaching: Professional Development in Classroom Discussion to Improve Students' Argument Literacy."[11] This research was sponsored by a grant from the Institute of Education Sciences (IES), US Department of Education, with Drs. Wilkinson and Reznitskaya serving as coprincipal investigators.

As part of this project, colleagues from The Ohio State University and Montclair State University partnered with upper elementary school teachers to design curriculum materials and activities that support teacher learning and use of new discussion practices. Over four years, a total of 49 teachers and 935 students from public schools in Ohio and New Jersey participated in this research. Participants came from urban and suburban school districts, including schools with high percentages of minority and economically disadvantaged students. Each year, we worked collaboratively with a new cohort of teachers and students to identify and organize instructional content and activities. We systematically collected data from teachers and students to assess the effectiveness of the program and inform its revisions. Our results consistently showed that by the end of the school year, teachers and students learned to use new discussion practices and engage in the critical and collaborative construction of arguments in relation to big, contestable questions raised by their readings.

Our multiyear partnership with teachers was invaluable for helping us discover what was beneficial (and what wasn't) in the classroom. In this book, we share field-tested methods, materials, tools, and activities that we developed from this partnership. We are grateful to all the collaborating teachers who helped us create what we hope to be a useful resource for practitioners concerned with helping their students become better thinkers.

PART ONE

Understanding Essential Concepts

CHAPTER 1

Why Inquiry Dialogue?

Let's listen in for a moment to a discussion in a fifth-grade classroom. The students have just read an article titled "Deadly Hits" about a boy named Zack who was paralyzed after getting a concussion during a football game. They are discussing the question, "Who was responsible for Zack's injury?"

TEACHER: So who would like to start us off this morning? Okay, Jerry.[1]

JERRY: Well, I think the one responsible for Zack's injury would be the coach, because he was the one who let Zack play when he shouldn't, because he knew that he already had an injury.

ANDREW: I disagree with Jerry because it actually said in the passage that Zack thought that his team needed help, so *he* decided to go in, 'cause the coach wasn't trained to find a concussion. So, he decided to go in on his own, without the coach telling him to. 'Cause the coach wasn't trained to see a concussion.

LILY: I agree with Andrew because . . . you wouldn't let . . . If you know we got hurt and we insisted to go back into something like that, you would at least make sure that we're okay. And I think Zack's coach probably did that . . . I think Zack's coach probably made sure that he was okay, so it's not all of his fault. He, as an adult, should say, "No, maybe you could go back in next time." But it's not only his fault.

TEACHER: So, wait, how is that agreeing with Andrew? 'Cause Andrew says it's not the coach's fault, but you're . . .

LILY: Yeah, I don't think it's the coach's fault either.

TEACHER: But you said, "As an adult he should know." I'm just . . . I want you to just clarify.

LILY: Well okay, I agree with Andrew, like everything that he said, but it's not complete. . . . Okay, I just agree with Andrew, like what he said . . . The coach didn't say, "Zack, get back in here." Zack wanted to and he went in on his own.

KATE: I disagree with Jerry. I don't find that it's the coach's fault because in the paragraph it says they, the coaches, weren't trained at that time to know what brain concussion looks like. 'Cause brain concussions are invisible injuries, it says it in this story, so, I don't find that it's the coach's fault and . . .

JERRY: But Zack was hurt . . .

KATE: Yeah, but he said he was all right, so how is the coach supposed to know?

TEACHER: Okay, so let's let him respond to that. [Teacher turns to Jerry] They challenged you, right? So now let's let Jerry respond. . . . We had a few challenges, so let's let Jerry maybe respond to that challenge. . . .

JERRY: But if you see someone fall down very hard on their head and come back to the bench, saying that they're all right, the coach should know that they've been in an injury, and the coach should not let them play.

In this discussion, the students and the teacher are engaging in a type of talk called *inquiry dialogue*. The students are given considerable control over the flow of discourse; they ask questions, participate in management of turn taking, and evaluate each other's answers. Several exchanges with consecutive student turns occur without teacher interruption. The discussion is centered around an open-ended, contestable, big question that does not have a single right answer: "Who was responsible for Zack's injury?" As students discuss their positions on the issue, they provide elaborated explanations of reasoning behind their views and refer back to the story for evidence. The teacher does not dominate the discussion, speaking less than students. Her strategically chosen questions serve to advance the inquiry further, as she asks students to clarify how their ideas connect with those of other group members ("So, wait, how is that agreeing with Andrew?") and encourages the discussion of an alternative perspective ("They challenged you, right? So now let's let Jerry respond"). Together, the discussion participants search for the most reasonable answer to the contestable question. Although not shown in this excerpt, at the end of the discussion the teacher prompts students to reflect on their progress, on both the quality of talk and on their answers to the question of who was responsible for Zack's injury.

Inquiry dialogue is quite different from a more traditional type of classroom talk, called *recitation*. During recitation, the interaction follows an Initiation-Response-Evaluation (I-R-E) pattern, in which the teacher *initiates* a question, students *respond*, and the teacher *evaluates* the responses.[2] Let's compare inquiry dialogue with recitation by examining another excerpt from a fifth-grade classroom. In the following exchange, the teacher and the students are discussing a Native American story called "Tonweya and the Eagles" about a young man who finds himself in a very dangerous situation.[3]

> TEACHER: Okay. So, now he got stuck on the cliff. So, now what? That's a big problem. . . . But, first of all, why did he want to reach the eagles? Gabriel?
>
> GABRIEL: Because he wanted to bring them back to his tribe so that everyone would have, like, a feather for everybody.
>
> TEACHER: Okay. He didn't want to bring the eagles back. He wanted to bring what back, Trisha?
>
> TRISHA: The feathers.
>
> TEACHER: The feathers. For what? What's it called? For what headgear? Who's that person? What are they called? Andrew?
>
> ANDREW: The chief.
>
> TEACHER: The chief. The . . . starts with a *w*?
>
> JACK: Warriors.
>
> TEACHER: Warriors. For the warriors' headgear. And what problem did he reach, um, when he was trying to reach the eagles again? He got what, Marla?
>
> MARLA: The rope, it was broke.
>
> TEACHER: It broke.
>
> MARLA: And he fell down.
>
> TEACHER: Okay.

Note how the teacher and her students follow the typical I-R-E pattern: the teacher *initiates* each new exchange with a question (e.g., "But, first of all, why did he want to reach the eagles? Gabriel?), a student *responds* (e.g., "Because he wanted to bring them back to his tribe so that everyone would have, like, a feather for everybody"), and the teacher *evaluates* the response (e.g., "Okay. He didn't want to bring the eagles back"). The pattern is then repeated with the next teacher question. We can see that the teacher shapes and guides the talk while the students passively recite what is known from the text. The teacher controls the direction of the discussion and has interpretative authority; she reacts to students' answers by evaluating them as right or wrong. Student answers are short, often consisting of just one or two words (e.g., "the chief, warriors, a ladder"). Students don't explain their thinking in depth, and they don't engage with each other, instead directing all their answers to the teacher.

Research studies consistently reveal that recitation, with its characteristic I-R-E pattern, emphasizing the central role of the teacher, is much more common in today's classrooms, compared to discussions that share features with inquiry dialogue.[4] At the same time, discussions that share features with inquiry dialogue are shown to be better suited for addressing more ambitious educational goals, such as helping students develop higher-order thinking and deep understanding of the material.[5]

Importantly, discussions in which students have more control over the flow of discourse, collaborate with their peers, and engage in rigorous argumentation are not achieved by simply having students gather in groups and giving them free rein. In a comprehensive review of forty-two studies on classroom discussions, the authors concluded that "it is one thing to get students to talk to each other during literacy instruction but quite another to ensure that such engagement translates into significant learning. Simply putting students into groups and encouraging them to talk is not enough to enhance student comprehension and learning: it is but a step in the process."[6] Teachers have a very important role to play in supporting students' talk.

This book is all about enhancing teachers' skills and knowledge of how to engage students in inquiry dialogue to help them develop what we call *argument literacy*. In this chapter, we explain what we mean by argument literacy and how it can be supported through students' participation in inquiry dialogue. Next, we describe the concept of inquiry dialogue in more detail and review some guiding principles for engaging students in this type of talk. We then step back and provide the big picture, discussing why classroom talk is such a powerful tool for furthering students' thinking, learning, and problem solving. We conclude with a brief preview of what is to come in the rest of the book.

WHAT IS ARGUMENT LITERACY?

One of the most significant changes in language arts instruction today is the special attention given to argument. From major policy documents, academic publications, and the popular press, we hear the call for teachers to prepare their students to make well-reasoned judgments about complex, open-ended problems.[7] Making well-reasoned judgments about such problems requires students to engage in argumentation, during which they support their positions with accurate reasons and evidence and evaluate alternative perspectives. Although this focus on argument might seem like a new direction in education, it actually reflects decades of scholarship advocating for argumentation to be an integral part of students' experience throughout their schooling.[8]

Embracing these ideas, the latest Common Core State Standards Initiative in the United States places a special emphasis on having students engage in argumentation in all grade levels and school subjects.[9] Quoting Gerald Graff, an English and education professor, the Common Core State Standards note that "'argument literacy' is fundamental to being educated."[10] With an eye toward college and career readiness, they state: "The university is largely an 'argument culture,' . . . therefore, K–12 schools should 'teach the conflicts' so that students are adept at understanding and engaging in argument (both oral and written) when they enter college."[11] A quick look at the Common Core State Standards is enough to underscore the attention given to argument. According to the grade 5 standards for language arts, for example, students are expected to

- Engage effectively in a range of collaborative discussions with diverse partners on grade 5 topics and texts, building on others' ideas and expressing their own clearly;
- Summarize the points a speaker makes and explain how each claim is supported by reasons and evidence;
- Explain how an author uses reasons and evidence to support particular points in a text, identifying which reasons and evidence support which points(s);
- Write opinion pieces on topics or texts, supporting a point of view with reasons and information.[12]

Our definition of argument literacy encompasses all these skills and more. We define argument literacy as *the ability to comprehend, formulate, and evaluate arguments through speaking, listening, reading, and writing.* As does the Common Core, we consider argument literacy to be a fundamental life skill that is "broadly important for the literate, educated person living in the diverse, information-rich environment of the twenty-first century."[13]

WHAT IS INQUIRY DIALOGUE?

Inquiry dialogue is a type of talk that offers an ideal training ground for helping students develop argument literacy and acquire deep understanding of complex issues raised by the texts they read. As we saw in the excerpt at the beginning of this chapter, inquiry dialogue is a type of talk in which participants engage in argumentation to collectively formulate the most reasonable judgments.[14] Other types of talk, such as persuasion and negotiation, also involve argumentation. The beauty of inquiry dialogue, as opposed to other dialogue types, is that it is cooperative in nature, and it is directed toward finding the truth, or as close to it as we can get, based on accurate reasons and evidence. So, inquiry dialogue is ideal for supporting students' collaborative and rigorous argumentation and promoting their deep understanding of knowledge in a variety of disciplines.[15]

It is worth emphasizing that the purpose of inquiry dialogue is to collectively think about complex problems and to formulate reasonable judgments about these problems.[16] During inquiry dialogue, participants do not simply try to win an argument—to convince each other that they are right by justifying their positions with reasons and evidence. At the same time, they are not engaging in dialogue just for the sake of uncritically sharing opinions. Instead, students take positions on the issue being discussed, they evaluate reasons and evidence for different positions, and they explore alternative perspectives—all to see which position survives this truth-seeking process.[17] The teacher's role is to support students in their collaborative and rigorous argumentation around the big questions.

During inquiry dialogue, the students and the teacher actively test each other's ideas, and they are willing to change their views in light of the new arguments considered by the group. When participants cannot agree on the most-reasonable answer, they work to clarify the basis and criteria for their disagreement. So, inquiry dialogue has a purpose, and a demanding one at that—it is directed at finding the truth. This gives the discussion much-needed forward momentum and makes it more meaningful for students.[18]

FIVE PRINCIPLES FOR ENGAGING STUDENTS IN INQUIRY DIALOGUE

The features of talk illustrated in the excerpt at the beginning of this chapter are brought together in five guiding principles for engaging students in inquiry dialogue. The sources of these principles are many, and we do not go into details here. The principles owe much to those used in *Philosophy for Children* and in other, more general approaches to teaching that capitalize on dialogue as a means of furthering students' thinking, learning, and problem solving.[19]

The first principle is that students have greater control over the flow of talk in the discussion. Typically, we, as teachers, talk about two-thirds of the time in the classroom, and our students contribute only one-third of the time. In inquiry dialogue, we seek to reverse this ratio! We want to give students space to offer and react to each other's points of view during the discussion. We need to allow students to have greater control over turn taking (who speaks and when) and greater interpretive authority for evaluating the validity and acceptability of each other's positions and reasons.

A second principle is that there is a cumulative quality to the talk. Instead of students offering their ideas detached from the ideas of others (i.e., talking in "silos"), we need to help them build on their own and each other's thinking. One way to think about this is that students' contributions need to connect with each other to form a coherent chain of reasoning.[20]

A third principle is that students offer alternative ideas and perspectives. A multiplicity of ideas and perspectives, and the tension and conflict that arises from the differences among them, can be a good thing because it helps us understand the issues at hand more deeply. When alternative viewpoints come together, we say that they help to "inter-animate" or "inter-illuminate" each other.[21]

A fourth principle is that students have a meta-level awareness about talk. They are able to reflect on their talk and their skill in using talk to further their thinking. We might add that we, as teachers, also need to become aware of, and skillful in, our use of talk. This meta-level awareness helps students internalize their skills in argumentation and transfer these skills to new tasks, such as writing a persuasive essay.

A fifth principle, and one that makes all the others possible, is that students work together as a community of inquiry to identify the best or most reasonable answer to the big question. Competition can motivate students, but when they are faced with complex, open-ended problems, collaboration works better. When students work collaboratively with each other, they can pool their resources, test their ideas against others' ideas, and hopefully, achieve an outcome that is better than any one of them could have achieved alone. Moreover, when working as a community of inquiry, students learn the social skills necessary for participation in a democratic society; they learn "to listen to each other carefully, to help each other articulate their ideas and questions, to criticize each other's ideas respectfully, to build on each other's ideas, and to identify the inquiry as the work of the group."[22] Figure 1.1 details what it means for students to work as a community of inquiry. The appendix to this chapter contains a survey you can use with your students to explore what they consider to be important practices that characterize a community of inquiry.

FIGURE 1.1

A community of inquiry

- **We respect each other.** We listen carefully to each other. We help each other express what we mean. We take each other's views seriously. We challenge each other's views respectfully. We make sure most of us are contributing most of the time.

- **We practice many kinds of good thinking.** We give reasons and evidence. We identify assumptions. We make careful inferences. We challenge each other. We look for missing perspectives. We build on each other's ideas. We change our mind if there are good reasons.

- **We help advance the line of inquiry.**

- **We think about our own thinking.**

Adapted by permission from Maughn Gregory, ed., *Philosophy for Children Practitioner Handbook* (Montclair, NJ: IAPC, 2008).

THE BIG PICTURE: THE POWER OF TALK

Most classroom instruction happens through talk. That is why we, as teachers, need to become aware of our use of talk and its power to shape student learning. So let's pause at this point to reflect on what happens when we make a choice to engage students in inquiry dialogue. When we use inquiry dialogue, we are strategically using a particular type of talk to engage students in collaborative and rigorous argumentation to foster their argument literacy and deep understanding of important topics raised by their readings. We might also use other types of talk—effective teachers have a broad repertoire of talk to draw from to achieve different instructional purposes. Robin Alexander, an influential scholar who studied classroom instruction in different countries, identified five kinds of teaching talk:[23]

- *Rote repetition.* Good for the drilling of facts, ideas, and routines (e.g., math facts).
- *Recitation.* Often good for stimulating students' recall of what they have learned previously or to cue students as to how to work out an answer to a problem based on what they already know. As we have seen, recitation tends to follow the traditional Initiation-Response-Evaluation pattern of classroom talk.
- *Exposition.* Good for telling students what to do, conveying information to them, or explaining something.
- *Discussion.* Good for furthering students' thinking, understanding, learning, or responding to literature. We define discussion as the open-ended, collaborative exchange of ideas between a teacher and students or among students for the purpose of achieving these goals.
- *Dialogue.* Good for achieving a common understanding of something. In this type of talk, students develop a genuine spirit of discovery and openness to exploring new ideas. It is marked by different kinds of questions, elaborated responses, exploration of alternatives, and building on each other's ideas.

The important thing to keep in mind is that different kinds of talk are good for different purposes and our role is to use talk strategically to accomplish the goals we have for our students. Each kind of talk has its place in the classroom, but the last two—discussion and dialogue (and inquiry dialogue in particular)—are better aligned with the goal of supporting the development of students' argument literacy and deep understanding. Ironically, discussion and dialogue are the least common kinds of talk found in classrooms.[24]

What happens when students engage in inquiry dialogue? For one thing, students learn new ways of thinking and knowing. During such discussions, students take public positions on an issue, support them with reasons and evidence, challenge other participants, and respond to challenges from others. Over time, the skills and strategies of argumentation that are made visible in the group's discussion become part of an individual's thinking. For instance, a student who says something vague during a discussion will, at first, only recognize that vagueness when someone else pushes her for clarification. Eventually, the student anticipates this reaction from her peers and self-edits her ideas before communicating them to the group. What began as *interpersonal* interaction in the group becomes an *intrapersonal* cognitive habit in the individual.[25] In other words, students internalize the knowledge, skills, and dispositions of argumentation and use them in their subsequent discussions as well as in other settings, such as when reading or writing arguments. Students' ability to transfer the skills of argumentation that they practice in discussions to new tasks can be further supported through various post-discussion activities. For example, after the discussion, students can write an essay that explains the most reasonable position developed by the group during inquiry dialogue.

Another thing that happens during the discussion is that talk becomes a tool for *thinking together.* The talk gives students a means for combining their intellectual resources to collectively make sense of experiences and to solve problems. Here, talk is used as a social mode of thinking or as a tool for "interthinking."[26] During inquiry dialogue, students interact with each other's ideas—adding detail to given reasons, qualifying general statements, or finding flaws in each other's arguments.[27] The multiplicity of perspectives generated in search of the most reasonable answer to the big question enables students to test their ideas against those of others, providing a kind of self-correcting mechanism that helps improve the overall quality of argumentation.

Note that on occasion during a discussion, the talk may shift from inquiry to other types of talk. For example, when the discussion stalls, the talk might include recitation-type exchanges, during which students are asked to recall previously learned information (e.g., "What did we say 'rites of passage' meant yesterday?"). At other times, teachers may temporarily shift to exposition when they want to explain or point out the different parts of an argument or reasoning moves to students (e.g., "Notice that Mary used evidence from the text to support her position. That really helps make her argument stronger"). However, in the discussions we feature in this book, inquiry dialogue is the overarching norm—the type of talk that is typically used—and other types of talk are used only in service of the larger goal of collectively searching for the best or most reasonable answer.[28]

A PREVIEW OF WHAT'S TO COME

The goal of this book is to support upper elementary school teachers in engaging students in collaborative and rigorous argumentation during inquiry dialogue. The book is organized into three parts. In this first part, we introduce you to key concepts and principles to be used in the rest of the book. In the next chapter, we discuss what arguments are, address why they are important, and describe key parts of an argument. In the other chapters in this section, we review important teacher dispositions and practices that are helpful for facilitating discussions, and we introduce the *Argumentation Rating Tool* (*ART*). The ART makes concrete the practices that support effective facilitation of inquiry dialogue. We then provide an overview of how to plan for and conduct a discussion centered on inquiry dialogue.

In the second part, we illustrate the entire process with four discussion plans, using two narrative fiction and two informational texts, as well as excerpts from related discussion transcripts. We chose these texts because we have found them to be helpful in stimulating inquiry dialogue. For each of the four texts, we discuss examples of effective facilitation with annotated excerpts from actual classroom discussions, and we describe effective pre-discussion and post-discussion activities.

In the third part, we focus on further advancing your use of inquiry dialogue. We describe how to choose texts to engage students in inquiry dialogue, how to foster student independence, and how teachers can reflect on and evaluate the quality of their facilitation with the ART. We conclude with a discussion of questions that teachers commonly ask as they continue to use inquiry dialogue in their classrooms.

KEY TERMS

Argument literacy is the ability to comprehend, formulate, and evaluate arguments through speaking, listening, reading, and writing.

Discussion is the open-ended, collaborative exchange of ideas between a teacher and students or among students for the purpose of furthering students' thinking, learning, understanding, problem solving, or literary appreciation.

Dialogue is a type of talk that is good for achieving a common understanding of something. In dialogue, there is a genuine spirit of discovery and openness to exploring alternatives for the purpose of achieving agreement or a common understanding.

Inquiry dialogue is a type of dialogue in which participants work to collectively formulate the most reasonable judgments about complex questions.

Appendix (Chapter 1)

What Do We Mean by Community of Inquiry?

Decide whether the statements on the left *are* or *are not* good practices in a community of inquiry.

	YES COMMUNITY OF INQUIRY	NO COMMUNITY OF INQUIRY	? NOT SURE
1. Thinking about what you want to say more than listening to the person speaking.	☐	☐	☐
2. Noticing when only a few people are doing the talking and saying something about it.	☐	☐	☐
3. Giving reasons for your positions and explaining your thinking.	☐	☐	☐
4. Providing evidence from the text and other sources to support a position.	☐	☐	☐
5. Ignoring other people's positions when they are different from your own.	☐	☐	☐
6. Agreeing with your friend's ideas because you like your friend.	☐	☐	☐
7. Challenging someone else's position by questioning the reasons or by offering a different point of view.	☐	☐	☐
8. Working hard to "win" the argument to show that you are right.	☐	☐	☐
9. Building on the ideas of others in the group to support a position.	☐	☐	☐
10. Keeping your thoughts to yourself when you disagree with other people's ideas.	☐	☐	☐
11. Not responding to someone's idea because you don't understand what they mean.	☐	☐	☐
12. Being willing to change your position after listening to reasons given by others.	☐	☐	☐

Adapted from Matthew Lipman and Ann Sharp, ed., *Ethical Inquiry: Instructional Manual to Accompany Lisa* (Montclair, NJ: IAPC, 1985).

CHAPTER 2

What Is an Argument?

This chapter is about arguments. It is based on an extensive review of scholarship on argumentation and related instructional materials.[1] We begin by explaining what arguments are, what they aren't, and why they are important. Next, we review key parts of an argument and show how these parts can be examined to build strong arguments. Finally, we describe four criteria for evaluating arguments. Learning about arguments will enable you to recognize them during discussions and will help you enhance the intellectual rigor of the discussions. We invite you to share the language of arguments with your students because doing so will allow them to develop a meta-level awareness of argumentation and help them acquire the skills to build, evaluate, and understand arguments, or argument literacy.

WHAT IS AN ARGUMENT?

A *basic argument* is defined as a position (or a conclusion) supported by reasons. Reasons are used to justify a particular position. Consider, for example, a basic argument for banning the sale of super-sized sugary drinks:

> Consuming large amounts of sugar contained in super-sized sugary drinks causes obesity. We should not sell products that have serious health risks. This is why the sale of super-sized sugary drinks should be banned.

Figure 2.1 displays this argument using the metaphor of a house to convey the idea that building an argument is like building a house: the position is the roof of the house, and the reasons serve as supporting bricks.

FIGURE 2.1

Basic argument

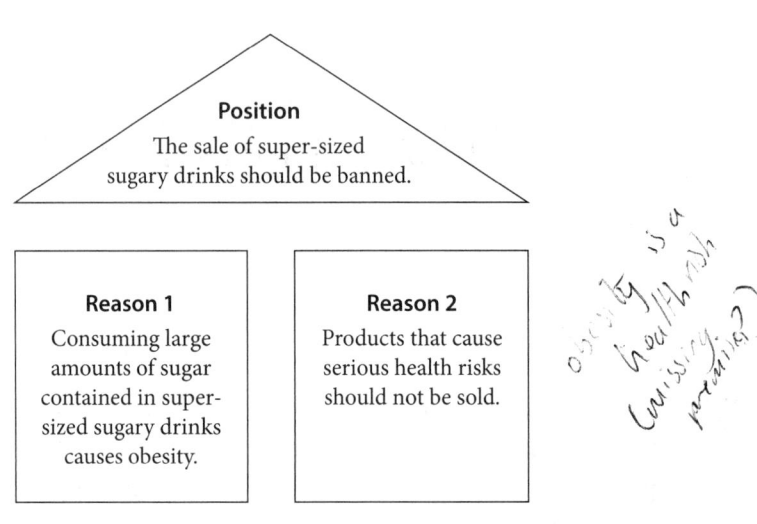

One way to assess the quality of an argument is to examine the *acceptability* of the reasons. That is, we can question whether we should believe a given reason and accept it as accurate: Is there strong evidence confirming the connection between obesity and sugary drinks, as stated in Reason 1? Should we not sell any products that cause serious health risks, as proposed in Reason 2? Using our metaphor, are the bricks (reasons) of the argument house solid or cracked?

Having acceptable reasons, however, is not enough. The reasons need to be *logically connected* to the position. "There is a movement in an argument: the position *follows from* the reasons. This movement is called *inference*; we infer the position from the reasons."[2] Looking at an argument as an inference helps us assess whether the move from reasons to the position is really justified. Are the reasons (bricks) we have enough or sufficient, by themselves, to support the position (the roof), or do we need other bricks to keep the roof from collapsing?

Asking critical questions about arguments allows us to enhance the quality of reasoning and, in the end, come up with better judgments. This is why in a *strong argument* we carefully consider both supporting and opposing reasons to come up with the most reasonable conclusion. In other words, we take into account sensible objections or challenges to our reasoning. We also try to think of compelling responses to such challenges. For example, someone who does not support a ban on super-sized sugary drinks might argue that many other products, such as pastry or candy, present similar health risks, and we do not ban those products. Or someone might argue that banning food products is wrong because it restricts individual freedom. These are compelling challenges, and we need to seriously consider them as we work toward reaching the most reasonable position on this issue.

When we are thinking through any complex problem, it is good to actively seek out people who disagree with us and talk with them! If we never test our ideas against those of others, how can we really know that we are correct or that we are not missing an important perspective? In other words, we depend on each other to help us think better and reach better conclusions because solving complex problems benefits from collective thinking that goes beyond the ideas of a single person. This kind of back-and-forth discussion with others does not need to be adversarial or unpleasant. Ideally, it takes place in a spirit of collaboration and intellectual safety.

In a similar way, when a jury deliberates at the end of a criminal trial, the members don't have a casual conversation about it or simply vote their individual opinions. They engage in a process of argumentation together—evaluating the strength of the reasons and evidence presented by each side, with the goal of arriving at a shared conclusion that is also the most reasonable (guilty or not guilty). Thus, the process of argumentation offers us a way of resolving differences of opinion in a rational manner and reaching sound conclusions.

Note that we make a distinction between an argument and argumentation, with an *argument* being a product and *argumentation* being the process of generating and evaluating arguments to come to the most reasonable position. "Argumentation is an activity—something persons do—while an argument is the product that can be distilled from that activity."[3] When we discuss complex issues with our students during inquiry dialogue, we engage in argumentation (an activity, a process), during which students generate and evaluate each other's arguments (outcomes, products).

WHY IS IT IMPORTANT TO BUILD STRONG ARGUMENTS?

Talking to others about controversial issues and considering other people's challenges to our own thinking helps accomplish three goals. First, as we have indicated, it disciplines us to carefully formulate and examine our own thinking because we need to justify our positions to others. By putting our ideas into words, we have a chance to think more deeply and clarify what we actually believe and why. In fact, it is hard to have a well-thought-out position unless we have had a chance to discuss it with others. Second, engaging in argumentation with those who disagree helps us improve our own judgments by discovering misconceptions, factual errors, and flaws in our reasoning. In other words, it serves as a natural corrective to our blind spots. Third, discussing contestable questions with others gives us an opportunity to change our minds. Changing one's mind in the face of previously overlooked evidence or faulty reasoning should not be viewed as being weak or inconsistent. It is a sign of careful thinking, intellectual humility, and openness to new insights. This is the how progress is made in the pursuit of knowledge in historical inquiry, medical research, and all other kinds of scientific endeavor.

Strong arguments are not mere opinions; they help us reach the most reasonable judgments about what to believe or do. Many of us have opinions or beliefs about matters that we have never previously studied or even thought about. Sometimes we don't even remember how we came to hold a certain opinion. It may be something that we learned as a child, or just heard repeated by people around us (e.g., "chicken soup is the best cure for a cold"). Often we have a sense that these opinions are not well examined, and we would not be able to justify them by using good reasons and citing specific evidence. At the same time, we feel that we have a right to hold an opinion on any topic, as expressed in the saying "Everyone is entitled to their own opinion." Although it is true (and commendable) that our society respects the diversity of opinions and the right to express them, that does not mean that all opinions are equally valid. Compared to unexamined opinions, *strong arguments*, which are based on credible reasons and evidence and have survived the test of public scrutiny, are more sound and provide better guidance for understanding and acting in the world around us.

One last point: in ordinary language, the word *argument* is often used to mean a fight or a quarrel. For example, when a friend says, "Let's not get into an argument over this," she probably means that we should not have a conflict. In contrast, in this book, we use the word *argument* as it is used in science, philosophy, math, law, and other academic disciplines. By argument, we mean the use of logic, reasons, and evidence on both sides of the issue to decide on the most reasonable position. Reasoned arguments lead to better conclusions, help us address disagreements in a constructive manner, and encourage us to treat each other with respect.

THE ANATOMY OF ARGUMENTS

We now look closely at the structure of an argument and identify its basic parts. We hope this will help you better follow and evaluate the arguments that your students make during discussions. Let's revisit our example about super-sized sugary drinks, but now consider a stronger argument for the ban:

> I believe that the sales of super-sized sugary drinks should be banned. The reason is that consuming large amounts of sugar contained in super-sized sugary drinks causes obesity. According to one study, an additional 12 ounces of sugary liquid per day increases the risks of becoming obese by 60 percent. We should not sell products that have serious risks for consumers, and obesity poses many such risks, including heart disease and cancer. Some people might say the ban on super-sized drinks restricts individual freedoms. However, the proposed ban applies only to very large portions and does not prevent consumers from buying sugary drinks. This is why the ban on super-sized sugary drinks is justified.

The entire argument is shown in figure 2.2 as an argument house. The argument in figure 2.2 consists of five major parts: (1) position, (2) reasons, (3) evidence, (4) anticipated or actual challenges, and (5) responses to those challenges. In your class discussions, you and your students might want to identify the different parts of an argument. Developing an ear for argument structure is part of the meta-level awareness that helps us become more adept at questioning the quality of argumentation. At the beginning, it may be helpful to focus on just one part of an argument at a time.

The roof of the house is the position. A *position* can also be called a claim, a conclusion, a judgment, or a thesis. Positions are often introduced with words and phrases, such as *I believe, I think, so, therefore, hence, thus,* or *this is why.* Note that a position can represent an initial point of view on a certain question or a judgment reached after engaging in argumentation. In argumentative writing, we usually start with stating the position and then justify it. In discussions, we try to arrive at a

FIGURE 2.2

Strong argument

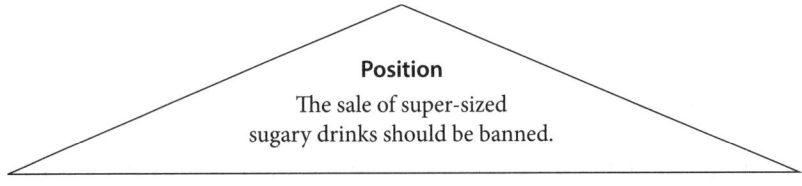

Position

The sale of super-sized
sugary drinks should be banned.

Reason 1	**Reason 2 (Link)**	**Challenge**
Consuming large amounts of sugar contained in super-sized sugary drinks causes obesity.	Products that cause serious health risks should not be sold.	Some people might say the ban on super-sized drinks restricts individual freedoms.

Evidence	**Reason 3 (Link)**	**Response to challenge**
According to one study, an additional 12 ounces of sugary liquid per day increases the risks of becoming obese by 60 percent.	Obesity poses many serious risks, including heart disease and cancer.	However, the proposed ban applies only to very large portions and does not prevent consumers from buying sugary drinks.

certain conclusion after engaging in the process of argumentation through clarifying the terms of that position and considering reasons and evidence for and against it.

The bricks supporting the roof represent the remaining four parts of an argument, including reasons, evidence, challenges, and responses to those challenges. *Reasons* are general statements that justify a position. We can often spot reasons in students' arguments by looking for characteristic words or phrases, such as *because, as, since,* or *the first reason is.* In activity 2.1, you and your students can practice identifying positions and reasons in a written argument.

Activity 2.1
Test yourself and try with your students

(answers shown in the appendix to this chapter)

1. Identify positions and reasons in the arguments below.

2. Underline typical words or phrases that indicate the use of positions and reasons.

I think young children should not be allowed to have smartphones because they start watching movies and playing games, and then they become addicted and want to do it all the time. As a result, children end up spending less time playing with their friends or reading. Another reason is that children become less active, and that's not good for their health. This is why I do not support the use of smartphones by young children.

Importantly, we can actually think of each reason as a conclusion from some other, previous argument, and so each reason can be further evaluated. The way we evaluate reasons depends on whether they represent facts or values. *Facts* are statements about *how the world is.* Factual statements can be verified through observation, such as through a scientific study or personal experience, and we can check on those facts by referring to an authoritative source, such as a textbook or an expert. In contrast, *value statements* tell us about *how the world should be.* Value statements reflect our morals, norms, rules, and conventions. For example, Reason 1, "consuming large amounts of sugar contained in super-sized sugary drinks causes obesity," is a factual statement because it *describes* reality. On the other hand, Reason 2, "products that cause serious health risks should not be sold," is a value statement because it *prescribes* what we should or should not do as a society.

As we explained earlier, one way to evaluate reasons is to ask critical questions to determine whether we should believe or accept them. This is where the distinction between fact and value statements matters. For example, to evaluate the acceptability of Reason 1 (a factual statement), we can ask questions about the amount and quality of research on the relationship between sugar intake and obesity: Have scientific studies examined this relationship? Were the results consistent across many studies? Do the results of these studies apply to all people or only to some? Should we believe these studies?

In contrast, to evaluate the acceptability of Reason 2 (a value statement), we can examine the source of the value in question, compare it to other values we have, and question how consistently we adhere to this value: Where did the idea of the government protecting one's health come from? Why should governments try—or not try—to protect the health of citizens? Is this a more important value than protecting individual freedoms? Do we ban all products that pose health risks? It is sometimes assumed that there is no way to critically evaluate value statements, since they are matters of deep personal conviction or identity, but that is not really true. Value statements can be overly vague, misunderstood, biased, or applied at times when they are not appropriate. Also, the assumption that our values cannot or should not be critically evaluated—that there is no way to reason about them—leads to either the avoidance of careful thinking about many important moral and social issues, or to discussions about them that become hostile. In inquiry dialogue, value statements are potential building blocks of sound arguments and they still need to be examined. In activity 2.2, we invite you and your students to practice identifying and evaluating fact and value statements.

Because reasons are general statements, they often need to be elaborated with more specific details. Another part of an argument, called *evidence,* is a specific statement that further supports or illustrates a reason. Evidence comes in the form of scientific facts, personal anecdotes, stories, experiences, and examples. Often evidence is introduced with phrases such as *according to, for example,* or *in the text it says that* . . .. In our example in figure 2.2, Reason 1 is supported with "according

---

Activity 2.2
Test yourself and try with your students
(answers shown in the appendix to this chapter)

1. Classify the statements below as either a fact or a value.

2. Ask one question about each statement to question its acceptability.
   - Self-driving cars cause fewer road accidents.
   - Enjoying the game is more important than winning it.
   - You should not be friends with a person who lies.
   - Taking away recess lowers student achievement in math and reading.

---

to one study, consuming an additional 12 ounces of sugary liquid per day increases the risks of becoming obese by 60 percent." This is an example of *scientific evidence*, or evidence obtained using a scientific method. We can further assess acceptability of this scientific evidence by asking critical questions about it: Who conducted the study? Was it published in a reputable peer-reviewed journal? Who were the participants? What methods did the authors use to collect their data?

In class discussions, students often use different types of evidence. For example, students might use *textual evidence* when they refer to a specific detail from the story that supports their thinking. Students might also rely on *anecdotal evidence* by making connections to and telling personal experiences or anecdotes. We encourage students to use multiple types of evidence during discussions, including scientific, textual, and anecdotal evidence. In this way, students learn about possible limitations of different kinds of evidence. For example, although scientific evidence is usually more reliable, it may also come from a poorly designed study or from an untrustworthy source. On the other hand, anecdotal evidence based on personal experience (e.g., "My brother drinks large sugary drinks every day and he never gains any weight") can be powerful and vivid, but it is difficult to verify and it may not hold true for everyone. At the same time, a quote from the text (textual evidence) might not be applicable, or its interpretation might not be accurate. Perhaps it is taken out of context, or perhaps the character in the story who made the statement cannot be trusted. In sum, we should question different types of evidence because each can be flawed and misused in an argument.

So far, we have discussed ways of questioning the acceptability of reasons and evidence. However, having acceptable reasons and evidence, or solid bricks, is not enough for building strong arguments. We also need to evaluate whether our reasons and evidence are *logically connected* to the resulting position. "Do the reasons really support the position? If we accept all the reasons, do we *have to* accept a position?"[4] To answer these questions, we need to look out for a special kind of reason called a link, represented by the middle bricks in figure 2.2. A *link* is a special type of reason that has a unique function: it works as a bridge that connects a reason to a conclusion. Sometimes called a *warrant*, a link "authorizes the inferential leap" from other reasons to the position.[5]

Links are often assumed and are omitted in an argument. Uncovering unstated links, or assumptions, helps improve the quality of arguments. Let's look at our modified basic argument, displayed in figure 2.3.

FIGURE 2.3

Basic argument with a link missing

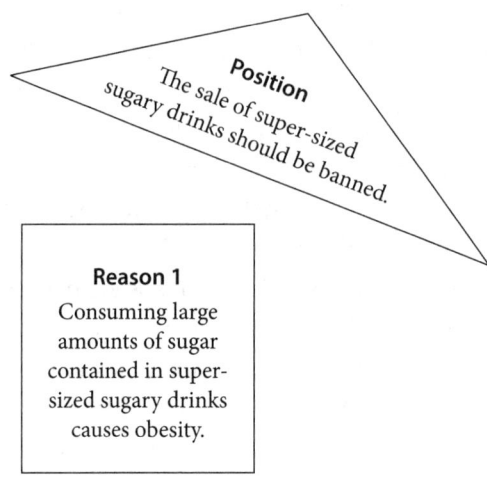

In the argument shown in the figure, the conclusion does not follow directly from the given reason. In other words, Reason 1 alone is not sufficient to logically lead to the conclusion that we should ban super-sized drinks. Something else needs to be added to authorize the move, or inference, from Reason 1 to the conclusion. Otherwise, the roof will collapse! Can you come up with the missing link? Note that more than one link could justify the move from Reason 1 to the position.

In figure 2.4, Reason 2, which functions as a link, connects Reason 1 to the conclusion, making the conclusion logically follow from the reasons. Figure 2.5 further illustrates the movement from the two reasons to the conclusion. Here, we show how the link (Reason 2) serves as a bridge that reinforces the leap from Reason 1 to the conclusion.

You can see that the link makes the house more stable. Yet, students often forget to clearly show how their reasons are connected to a position. So we may need to help students uncover their unstated links during the discussion by asking questions, such as "What are we assuming here? Is your reason enough to warrant the position? So, are you saying that any product causing health problems should be banned?"

FIGURE 2.4

Basic argument with the link

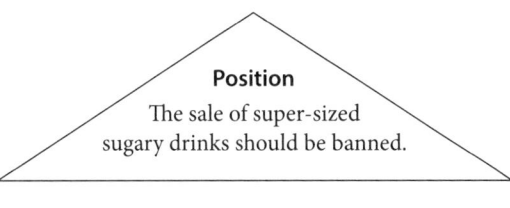

Position
The sale of super-sized
sugary drinks should be banned.

Reason 1	**Reason 2 (Link)**
Consuming large amounts of sugar contained in super-sized sugary drinks causes obesity.	Products that cause serious health risks should not be sold.

FIGURE 2.5

Linking Reason 1 to the position

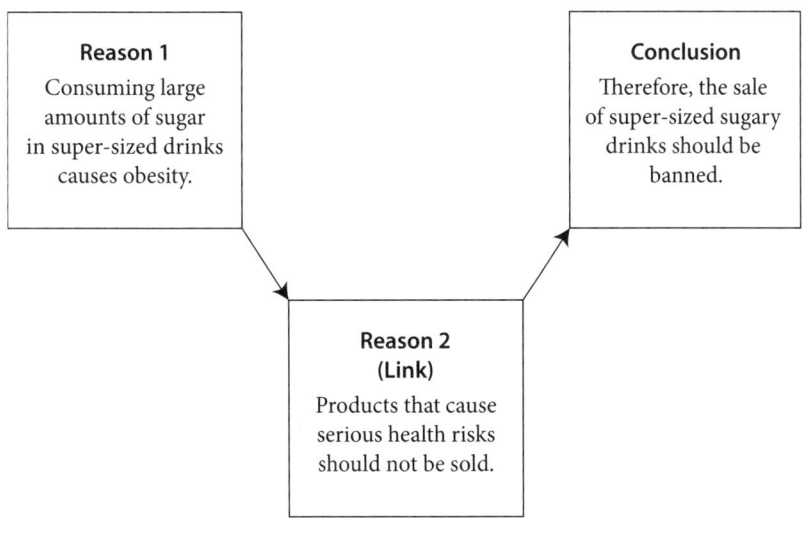

Reason 1
Consuming large
amounts of sugar
in super-sized drinks
causes obesity.

Conclusion
Therefore, the sale
of super-sized sugary
drinks should be
banned.

Reason 2 (Link)
Products that cause
serious health risks
should not be sold.

It is easier to spot missing links if we agree with a given reason but disagree with the position. For example, suppose we cannot find any problem with Reason 1, "Consuming large amounts of sugar contained in super-sized sugary drinks causes obesity," since it is a widely accepted fact. However, suppose that we also feel strongly against banning super-sized drinks. This means there is likely an unwarranted leap made from the reason to the position. During discussions, this leap is often revealed with a statement "But you are jumping to a conclusion!" In other words, the logic of an argument makes us uncomfortable; something was probably assumed, implied, left unstated. What was it?

After Reason 2, or the link, is uncovered and clearly articulated, it becomes available for public scrutiny. For example, during a discussion someone can point out that we allow the sale of other products (i.e., cigarettes) that cause serious health risks. So making implicit links *explicit* helps us challenge our assumptions and expose problems with arguments. See whether you can find the missing links in the arguments shown in activity 2.3.

Challenges and responses to challenges are necessary parts of a strong argument. A *challenge* is a statement questioning any part of an argument: the position, the reasons, the evidence, or the connections among them. In discussions, we often hear students introduce a challenge with "Yeah, but . . ." Other ways to challenge include words and phrases, such as *however, on the other hand, at the same time, it can be argued,* or *some people might say.* In figure 2.2, the challenge is, "Some people

---

Activity 2.3
Test yourself and try with your students
(answers shown in the appendix to this chapter)

Identify missing links in the following arguments:

- Young children should have smartphones because they need to learn about technology.
- People should not go to college to study art because it is hard to find a job as an artist.
- School libraries should have videogames because students enjoy playing them.

---

might say that the ban on super-sized drinks restricts individual freedoms." Note that, as teachers, we prefer to use the phrase "some people might say" to introduce challenges because it diminishes teacher authority and power to steer the discussion in a particular direction. This phrasing is more likely to invite students to come up with responses to a challenge, rather than to passively agree with the teacher's point of view.

A *response to challenge*, sometimes called *rebuttal*, is a reason offered in an attempt to disprove or invalidate the challenge. For example, the response to the challenge in figure 2.2 is, "however, this ban applies only to very large portions and does not prevent consumers from buying sugary drinks." It is often signaled with the same words and phrases as a challenge, such as *however, but, on the other hand, at the same time.*

If it is not possible to rebut a challenge to a reason, then that reason should be revised or even removed, which would mean that our position is no longer supported—the roof of the house might collapse! So we must either find another reason that can withstand the challenge or else be willing to change our position. You can now see why considering and responding to challenges is such a crucial part of argumentation. When we address valid objections—either by refuting them or by revising our initial reasons and positions—we construct stronger arguments and arrive at sounder conclusions because we have tested our reasoning against possible flaws, misconceptions, fallacies, or blind spots.

Will adding more parts—more reasons, evidence, challenges, and responses—make an argument in figure 2.2 even stronger? The answer depends on the quality of these parts and the connections among them. Just having more argument parts does not necessarily lead to stronger arguments. Next, we discuss four criteria that teachers can use to evaluate the quality of argumentation and help students build stronger arguments.

CRITERIA FOR EVALUATING ARGUMENTATION QUALITY

Inquiry dialogue is a type of talk in which participants work together to move toward the most reasonable judgments about complex questions. During inquiry dialogue, students need to (1) collaborate with each other and (2) engage in rigorous argumentation. Unfortunately, as teachers and researchers, we know only too well that collaborative and intellectually rigorous discussions do not automatically happen when students gather in groups. Teachers play a crucial role in supporting productive student engagement by helping students evaluate the process of argumentation and the resulting products—their arguments.

Student argumentation and their arguments during a discussion can be evaluated using the four criteria presented in figure 2.6. The first criterion is called *Diversity of perspectives*, and it reflects the importance of equally distributing responsibilities for the discussion among all participants to share a variety of viewpoints. When no single voice (not even the teacher's!) dominates the discussion, students have more opportunities to propose multiple positions, reasons, evidence, challenges, and responses to challenges. Importantly, sharing control over talk with students does not imply that anything goes, or that all ideas will be accepted as equally valid. It means that the responsibility for judging what is reasonable is now given to all group members, who contribute diverse perspectives and hold each other accountable to rigorous thinking.[6]

The second criterion, *Clarity*, addresses the precision of the language we use to express our ideas and the clarity of the structure of our arguments. In a typical

FIGURE 2.6

Four criteria for evaluating argumentation and arguments

1. Diversity of perspectives	We explore different perspectives together.

2. Clarity	We are clear in the languages and structure of our arguments.

3. Acceptability of reasons and evidence	We use reasons and evidence that are well examined and accurate.

4. Logical validity	We are logical in the way we connect our positions, reasons, and evidence.

discussion, students rarely speak with great clarity or precision. There are many reasons for this. One is that during inquiry dialogue students are still exploring and creating their thoughts, and thus, don't yet have a complete control of their expression. In fact, students are often unaware of vagueness in their speech until someone asks them, "What did you mean by that?" Also, words that the students use may have multiple meanings, which may often lead to ambiguity, vagueness, and resulting misunderstandings. Consider, for example, the word *theory*. The word can mean an initial insight into something, as in "I have a theory about why she left so abruptly." It can also mean a coherent system of principles supported by scientific evidence, as in "Learning about the theory of evolution makes students well prepared for college." A discussion in which students use the word *theory* to mean different things will quickly become confusing. It is impossible to have a productive discussion without developing a clear, common understanding of the intended meanings of the words that participants use.

In addition to misinterpreting each other's statements, students often miss connections between their own thinking and the ideas of others. We all have the experience of being in a discussion in which people continue to argue without fully understanding how their ideas are similar to or different from those expressed by others. For example, students may fail to realize that they share the same position, but disagree on the strength of evidence used to support it. In fact, a lot of frustration during argumentation happens because participants lose track of where they stand in relation to each other. Lack of clarity in understanding the connections among arguments made by students breeds confusion and impedes the progress toward the most reasonable answer. Yet, it can also be a rich opportunity for learning because every effort to resolve confusion by clarifying an idea and connecting it with other ideas is a new act of meaning making. In any case, confusion is an unavoidable part of resolving differences of opinions! As teachers, we should expect confusion to be part of the learning process: if students are never confused, they may not be challenged enough to think deeper and learn something new. So, instead of avoiding confusion, we should help students learn how to work through it. That is, students need to recognize problems with the clarity of the language or structure of their arguments and see them as opportunities for deeper thinking. And we, as teachers, can support students through carefully chosen prompts to help them clarify what they are saying and how it fits into the overall line of inquiry.

We began discussion of the third criterion, called *Acceptability of reasons and evidence*, earlier in the chapter, when we explained the importance of having well-informed and accurate reasons and evidence to support advocated positions. When questioning the acceptability of reasons, we are asking ourselves, "How do we know this? Why should we believe this? Is this really true? Is it only true in some cases? Are there times when it doesn't apply?" By addressing the acceptability criterion, we are helping students build arguments with solid, credible support (the bricks of our argument house). We also are helping them question their own and each other's factual and value statements by critically evaluating their sources and accuracy.

Finally, *Logical validity* refers to the quality of inferences, or the legitimacy of the logical move from reasons to the position. We addressed this criterion earlier in the chapter when explaining the importance of a *link*, a special kind of reason that provides a bridge to connect reasons to the chosen position. "We say that the conclusion *follows from* the reasons, and the whole question of logic is, 'Does this really *follow*?'"[7] As we discussed earlier, students often omit links from their arguments, which may lead to making unwarranted conclusions. Yet, links, when stated, often contain ideas that can be challenged and even dismissed (see activity 2.3 for examples), which would weaken the strength of the argument. As teachers, we can help students uncover missing links and make them available to group scrutiny.

In this chapter, we introduced many important ideas about argument and argumentation and explained key criteria for evaluating their quality. Even though knowing about the parts of an argument and the criteria for evaluating an argument is necessary, it is not sufficient to effectively support students in constructing and evaluating their own arguments. In the next chapter, we show how the knowledge we have built in this chapter connects to classroom instruction—how we can encourage students to rely on the criteria for evaluating arguments during inquiry dialogue through the strategic use of various facilitation practices and related talk moves.

KEY TERMS

Argument is a series of statements in which a position is supported by reasons and evidence. A strong argument includes consideration of opposing reasons and evidence.

Argumentation is a process of generating and evaluating arguments to come to the most reasonable position.

Challenge is a statement that questions any part of an argument: the position, the reasons, the evidence, or the connections among them.

Evidence is a specific statement that further supports or illustrates a reason.

Fact is a statement about how the world is. Facts can be verified through observation.

Link is a special type of reason that has a unique function: it works as a bridge that connects a reason to a position.

Position is a point of view on a certain question. It may be an initial insight, formed without much thought, or it may be a judgment reached after engaging in argumentation.

Reason is a general statement that justifies a position. It may be a factual statement or a value statement.

Response to challenge is a reason that is offered in an attempt to rebut a challenge.

Value is a prescriptive statement about how the world should be. Value statements reflect our morals, norms, rules, and conventions.

Appendix (Chapter 2)

Answers to Activities

Activity 2.1
Test yourself and try with your students

1. Identify positions and reasons in the arguments below.

2. Underline related text markers.

   <u>I think</u> young children should not be allowed to have smartphones *[Position]* <u>because</u> they start watching movies and playing games *[Reason]*, and then they become addicted and want to do it all the time *[Reason]*. As a result, children end up spending less time playing with their friends or reading *[Reason]*. <u>Another reason</u> is that children become less active *[Reason]*, and that's not good for their health *[Reason]*. <u>This is why I do not support</u> the use of smartphones by young children *[Position]*.

Activity 2.2
Test yourself and try with your students

1. Classify the statements below as either a fact or a value.

2. Ask one question about each statement to question its acceptability.

   - Self-driving cars cause fewer road accidents.
     Factual statement.
     Are there studies comparing the number of accidents between self-driving and regular cars? Who conducted these studies?

   - Enjoying the game is more important than winning it.
     Value statement.
     If this were true, why do we often reward winners with medals and trophies?

   - You should not be friends with a person who lies.
     Value statement.
     Does this depend on the type of lie? What if a friend lies in order to not hurt someone's feelings?

   - Taking away recess lowers student achievement in math and reading.
     Factual statement.
     What is the evidence to support this statement? How do we know this?

Activity 2.3
Test yourself and try with your students

1. Identify missing links in the following arguments:

   - Young children should have smartphones because they need to learn about technology.
     Link: Smartphones can teach children about technology.

   - People should not go to college to study art because it is hard to find a job as an artist.
     Link: The only reason to go to college is to find a job.
     Link: The only job you can have after studying art is to be an artist.

   - School libraries should have videogames because students enjoy playing them.
     Link: School libraries should have all things that children enjoy.

CHAPTER 3

How to Facilitate Collaborative and Rigorous Argumentation?

Inquiry dialogue is a type of talk in which participants work to collectively formulate the most reasonable judgments about complex questions. During inquiry dialogue, students need to work on two major goals: (1) to collaborate with each other and (2) to engage in rigorous argumentation. These are ambitious goals, and they are not achieved by simply having students gather in groups. In our work with teachers learning to facilitate inquiry dialogue, we sometimes see discussions in which students fail to effectively interact with each other. Instead, they just report about their own ideas, essentially disregarding contributions of their peers. One teacher called this "popcorn talk"—student voices pop up in a random and disconnected manner, resulting in a discussion that is repetitive and unfocused.

We also see discussions in which students collaborate well with each other, but their exchanges lack intellectual rigor. Students discuss each other's opinions, but they do not engage in critical evaluation of different points of view. As a result, students are failing to meet the second goal of inquiry dialogue: to engage in rigorous argumentation. During such discussions, anything goes: students misrepresent textual evidence, make logic errors, rely on unwarranted assumptions, and fail to build on one another's ideas. Because participants in the discussion miss opportunities to challenge and support each other's reasoning, the quality of argumentation is low. Students are left with the impression that they have not made any progress toward answering the big question or, worse, that there is no way to make progress.

The good news is that, as teachers, we can do a lot to support students in their efforts to engage in collaborative and intellectually rigorous discussions. In this chapter, we discuss the role of the teacher during inquiry dialogue and describe teacher practices that are helpful for supporting argumentation. These practices are made concrete in the Argumentation Rating Tool (ART), which we introduce in this chapter. The ART connects the four criteria for evaluating arguments to specific facilitation practices and related talk moves to be used by teachers and students.

STEPPING IN, STEPPING OUT

The role of a facilitator is to help students accomplish the two goals of inquiry dialogue: to collaborate with each other and to engage in rigorous argumentation. When students are not achieving these goals independently, we need to *step in* to the dialogue to model and support collaboration and strong reasoning, and to move the discussion toward the most reasonable answer.

For example, suppose we notice that only a few students are doing most of the talking. If that is the case, we need to step in to ask for more students to participate (e.g., "It would be good if we heard more points of view about this. Let's give the next three turns to people who haven't spoken yet"). Or suppose that during a discussion all students line up on the same side of the issue. Then, we can intervene and ask students to consider alternative positions and reasons (i.e., "If another fifth grader disagreed with you, what might she say?"). During each of these interventions, the teacher uses *talk moves*, or verbal prompts that help engage students in collaborative and rigorous argumentation. The first talk move addresses the goal of effective collaboration, ensuring that every group member has an opportunity to contribute. The second one prompts students to think about opposing views that they have overlooked, thus making their arguments more comprehensive and nuanced.

Through the use of such talk moves, we can model for students the productive ways of speaking and thinking during inquiry dialogue. Importantly, we want students to pick up on and use these talk moves with each other in their subsequent discussions. In this way, the responsibility for facilitating discussions, which has been traditionally reserved for the teacher, gets shared among all participants. From research on classroom talk in collaborative discussions, we know that the talk moves of the teacher or more advanced peers snowball; in other words, they are used by more and more students in the group who observe, practice, and gradually adopt new ways of speaking and thinking.[1] In the long run, we want students to take over the facilitation practices and talk moves introduced by the teacher and to become more independent in their ability to comprehend, formulate, and evaluate arguments. We also want them to develop meta-level awareness—to think not only about their own thinking, but also about how well the group is thinking together, and to take responsibility for both. This means that we, as teachers, need to learn to also *step out* and gradually release responsibility for facilitating inquiry dialogue to our students. Gradual release implies that we reduce our support *only when* students have acquired the skills for effective engagement in quality argumentation. Although we cannot know exactly when this will happen in a classroom, we can keep in mind the four criteria for good argumentation listed in the ART to continuously assess students' progress in learning how to build stronger arguments together.

Finding the right level of involvement during inquiry dialogue is a tricky task because genuine inquiry is neither teacher-centered nor student-centered. Rather, it is truth-centered, with the teacher supporting the group's progress toward the truth, or the most reasonable answer.[2] This truth-seeking orientation changes the discussion from a mere conversation, in which participants exchange and uncritically accept each other's opinions, to an intellectually rigorous search for the best possible conclusion. Note that in many classroom discussions, students may not arrive at finding the most reasonable answer. The reason is that, when dealing with complex questions, we often don't have enough information to reach the best conclusion; several positions may be legitimately considered reasonable. There are also logistical issues; the class might run out of time when students have to switch to a different activity. Yet, having the goal of finding the most reasonable answer is crucial for discussions that go beyond simply sharing opinions: this goal directs students to engage in *testing* different positions and reasons and *eliminating* those that fail to withstand the scrutiny of the group. This is why working toward the most reasonable answer is challenging for teachers and students. It requires the ability to understand and apply the criteria for evaluating arguments.

Consider, for example, the way one teacher explained this truth-seeking process to his students by comparing argumentation to the process of building, inspecting, and eliminating argument houses:

Imagine that we arrive at some place, called the Land of the Big Question, and we need to start living there. So, we start building houses. At the beginning, everyone is just building their own house, the Argument House, and now we have a lot of them. But the next *very important* step is: we need to find out *which of these houses is the strongest*, the best place to live in. Which one has the most reasonable answer? So, we start evaluating, inspecting each other's houses, looking carefully at every brick. This is when you think, "Hold on! That's not what the story said. That brick is not going to hold up the roof! It's not a house I want to live in, it's weak." So, I just wanted to point out that so far we haven't been talking this way, but I think it's time for us to talk this way as a group. Because the goal is *to choose a house*, it is not just building and sharing what we're building: "your house is blue, my house is pink, they are both beautiful." That's great, but it's not enough! So, from now on, let's start moving forward to carefully inspect our argument houses. Let's start asking ourselves: Is this really true? Is this acceptable to all of us? Do we all agree on this interpretation? And if not, let's eliminate some bricks, or even some houses, so that we all can end up living in the strongest one.

We suggest you use each discussion as your own training ground for figuring out when to step in and when to step out. Although we do not advocate giving up responsibility for encouraging rigorous argumentation during inquiry dialogue, we invite you to try holding back and to experience the excitement of watching your students assume ownership of the discussion. This excitement can be glimpsed from a comment of one teacher after she experienced releasing some of her responsibilities for navigating the discussion to her students:

> Even if we didn't reach that [ideal discussion] and we were just touching the surface, it was still better than anything else we are doing. It's making my students think about what they read. It's making them listen and critique each other. It's making them consider other people. And how does that then affect your classroom in general? How does that affect the atmosphere of your classroom? Think about how powerful that can be across everything! Thinking about each other's answers, respectfully disagreeing with someone . . . I hear my kids saying that now, "You don't have to say it like that. Respectfully disagree." That's a big thing!

MAKING THE GOOD MOVE

When facilitating a discussion, we need to carefully observe and listen to our students, *developing an eye and an ear* for strong collaboration and argumentation. First, we need to *see* how students participate: Do they look at each other when speaking? Are they searching for evidence in the text? We also need to *hear* students' ideas, recognize their strengths and weaknesses, and share what we notice with our students to make strong (or weak) collaboration and reasoning visible to the group.[3] In other words, we should pay close attention to the quality of students' collaboration and their ideas so that we can evaluate them in relation to the four criteria for good argumentation. If students are not meeting the criteria, we might need to step in and say something. But what specifically should we say?

Unfortunately, there are no simple recipes for choosing effective talk moves during inquiry dialogue. The word *move* in inquiry dialogue is borrowed from games like checkers and chess, in which there is no way to plan your next move until you see the move of the person playing with you.[4] In dialogue, as in these games, each new move depends on, and is a response to, the moves that have been made before it. For teachers, it is a strategic choice that has important consequences: it can either open up or restrict opportunities to enhance student learning and advance the inquiry forward.

To help teachers decide when and how to step in, we created an instructional tool called the Argumentation Rating Tool (ART).[5] The entire ART is included in appendix A. Here we look at its key features. First, the ART connects each of the four criteria of quality argumentation to a set of facilitation practices. We identified these practices during our work with elementary school teachers and students, as well as through a comprehensive review of literature on the use of discussions to support high-level thinking and reasoning.[6] Figure 3.1 shows the connections between the argumentation criteria and various facilitation practices.

For example, to address a problem with *Clarity* (criterion 2), we can step in and use one of the four different facilitation practices related to this criterion. We can ask students to further explain the intended meaning of their contributions (facilitation practice 4), prompt students to identify the connections between their ideas and those of their peers (facilitation practice 5), make visible the processes of argumentation through labeling reasoning processes and parts of an argument (facilitation practice 6), or help students follow and summarize the arguments presented by the group (facilitation practice 7). Of course, the choice of a specific practice will depend on the issue with clarity of argumentation that we are trying to address.

Our work with teachers revealed that simply having a list of facilitation practices, as shown in figure 3.1, does not provide teachers with enough information about how

FIGURE 3.1

Four criteria for evaluating argumentation and the related facilitation practices

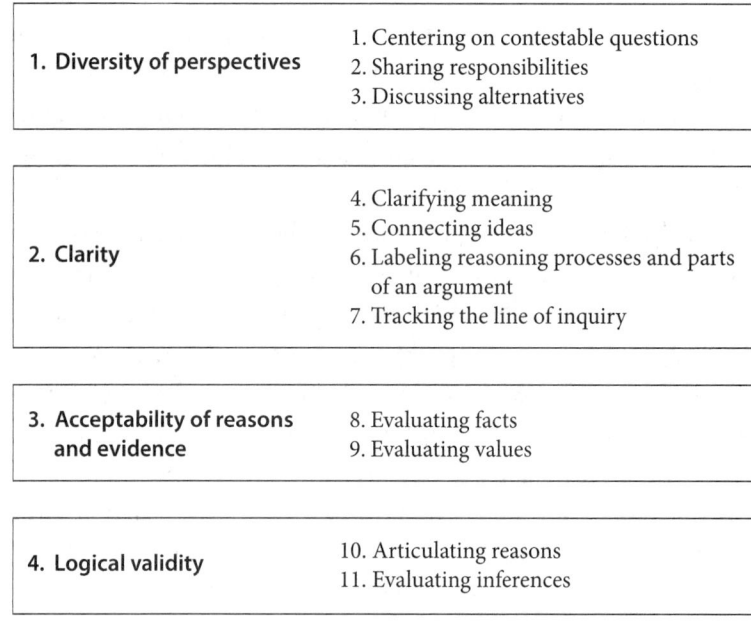

1. **Diversity of perspectives**	1. Centering on contestable questions 2. Sharing responsibilities 3. Discussing alternatives

| 2. **Clarity** | 4. Clarifying meaning
5. Connecting ideas
6. Labeling reasoning processes and parts of an argument
7. Tracking the line of inquiry |

| 3. **Acceptability of reasons and evidence** | 8. Evaluating facts
9. Evaluating values |

| 4. **Logical validity** | 10. Articulating reasons
11. Evaluating inferences |

to best intervene during discussions. This is why, for each of the eleven facilitation practices, we developed a rubric with detailed descriptions of underlying principles and examples of specific prompts, or talk moves that function to support a given practice. To illustrate, let's look closely at two selected facilitation practices (5 and 7), shown in figure 3.2. At the top of the rubric is a six-point rating scale, with three categories: Advancing, Developing, and Not Yet. In the Advancing category, we first provide a general description of a teacher effectively using this practice and illustrate it with examples of related talk moves (e.g., "Which part are you agreeing with?"). We then describe what students should do in relation to this practice. Each of the eleven practices in the ART contains a similar pair of descriptions that purposefully match teacher and student actions. This allows teachers learning about facilitation to see what they and their students should be doing for each practice.

FIGURE 3.2

ART rubric for facilitation practices 5 and 7.

CRITERION #2. CLARITY: WE ARE CLEAR IN THE LANGUAGE AND STRUCTURE OF OUR ARGUMENTS

Practice 5. Connecting ideas

	6 ADVANCING	5	4 DEVELOPING	3	2 NOT YET	1
Teacher	The teacher clarifies the group's reasoning by making visible the connections among students' ideas. The teacher prompts students to relate their ideas to what's been said by others in specific ways. He attributes student ideas and questions to specific speakers. This happens whenever students fail to build on or challenge each other's arguments. *Which part are you agreeing with? What is the difference between what you are saying and what Quincy said? How does this relate to what William said? Martin, do you want to respond to Kim? Kelly, you said you are disagreeing with Jon's point. How are you disagreeing? I don't see how your example supports Keisha's position. Can you explain more? How is this example relevant to what Marina said earlier about . . . ?*		The teacher allows students to give redundant answers that make the points already made by others. The requests for connections are often overly general. The teacher misses opportunities to connect students' ideas. *Anything else? Does anyone have something to add? Does anyone agree or disagree?*		The teacher does not relate student answers to each other. *Okay, the next question on page 12 is "Why did Morgan run away from home?" Who can give us the answer?*	
Students	Student responses are interrelated and connected to the ideas of others. The responses are chained together as students react to each other's positions and justifications, building on or challenging each other's reasoning. *As Jack said before . . . I disagree about one thing in what Brad just said . . . Jamilla's point might be true, but I have a different example. . . . What Omar said changes everything for me. Now, I think . . . .*		Students occasionally relate their answers to the contributions of other group members. Often, these connections involve sharing similar opinions and personal experiences. Thus, the degree of simple agreement and repetition may be high. *Colleen's story reminds me of one time when I got lost in the mall.*		Students simply state their answers in a sequential fashion, essentially disregarding the input of others. Their answers do not relate to contributions already made in the discussion.	

CRITERION #2. CLARITY: WE ARE CLEAR IN THE LANGUAGE AND STRUCTURE OF OUR ARGUMENTS

Practice 7. Tracking the line of inquiry

	ADVANCING 6 / 5	DEVELOPING 4 / 3	NOT YET 2 / 1
Teacher	The teacher summarizes or asks students to summarize the arguments made by the group in relation to the big questions. She does this to help students see a continuous and clear line of inquiry—moving from the big question, to generating and testing possible answers, to then narrowing down to the most reasonable answer or answers. The teacher steps in whenever there is a need to clarify confusion, improve coherence, assess progress, or help advance the inquiry further. *Where are we now? Let's retrace what has been said so far. So, it seems that we are torn between the value of learning a lesson and the chance to win a competition. How many different positions on our big question have emerged so far? Can someone now list all the reasons we gave for and against this position? Are we ready to eliminate any of them?*	The teacher may summarize or ask students to summarize key points of the discussion (e.g., to emphasize a given point). The teacher misses opportunities to summarize or asks students to summarize the arguments made by the group. *Sally, what do we know about the relationship between Carlos and Gloria? . . . So, do you see now why he wanted to impress her?*	The teacher does not summarize or ask students to summarize the arguments. She may ask students to retell specific facts and events from the text to test for basic knowledge and comprehension. There is no ongoing line of inquiry to which the students could relate their ideas. *Max, tell us what the conditions on the ship were like? . . . Good. Kim, now what did the sailors decide to do next?*
Students	Students ask for and/or offer summaries of each other's arguments by stringing together multiple strands of a discussion. They direct attention back to the big question and help each other follow the ongoing line of inquiry, keeping the discussion well focused and relevant. *I think what Lisa and Rob were saying is that . . . But then Derek disagreed and said that . . . Sounds like we are going around in circles. Can we go back to Alex's example of . . . ? We decided that Kelly should not tell on Evelyn because . . .*	Students may summarize key points of the discussion or restate their own opinion. However, students do not summarize the arguments made by the group. *I was saying that Carlos wanted to impress Gloria because he liked her. So, he got too close to the skunk.*	Students don't summarize group arguments. They may recall the events from the text, often in a sequential fashion. *First, he climbed the mountain to get the bird's feathers. But then his rope broke, and he got stuck up there.*

Another important feature of the ART reflects the need for the teacher to ultimately step out and gradually release responsibility for orchestrating the discussion to students. Eventually, we want students who participate in inquiry dialogue to become independent in their use of important practices, first introduced and encouraged by the teacher.[7] For example, we want students to learn to connect their ideas with those of others without additional prompting from the teacher. This means that at the more advanced stages of student development (ratings 5 and 6), the teacher's use of talk moves should *decrease*, to allow the students to take more control of the discussion. To reflect these changes in the levels of teacher involvement, we framed the descriptions of teacher actions in terms of *opportunities missed or taken*. For example, for ratings 5 and 6, we qualified the descriptions of the ideal teacher practice with such phrases as "whenever students fail to . . ." or "whenever there is a potential issue with . . ." This wording highlights the importance of teacher responsiveness to the development of the group's collaboration and reasoning. If students are performing at a high level, the teacher may not be missing any opportunities to intervene.

In figure 3.2, the description of each talk move has a similar structure: a six-point rating scale, elaborated with a general review of practice, and followed by specific examples of talk moves. We recommend that you familiarize yourself with each of the eleven practices in the entire ART included in appendix A. In fact, you can think of the ART descriptions in the Advancing category as sort of a facilitation textbook that explains the most common strategies used by experienced facilitators. Elementary school teachers in our professional development programs consistently emphasize the value of rereading the descriptions of the ART practices and talk moves *before and after* their discussions, as they continuously work on refining their facilitation skills.[8] For example, teachers find it helpful to use the ART when planning their discussions and when reflecting on their practice, as shown in this quote from one teacher:

> The ART is so, so valuable. I used it a lot, actually. I would look at it before and I would think, "Okay, so now I'm just going to work on this one thing." And sometimes I would tell the students, "I'm working on this." And at the end of the day, or after watching [my own] video, I would also look through it. . . . Every time I open it, I would find something I'd never read before. Even though I know I read the whole thing, but I just find it so, so rich because I would have just had the experience. . . . So, I used it a lot. I love it.

USING VERSIONS OF THE ART: ART DURING INQUIRY AND ART FOR KIDS

Evaluating collaboration and argumentation on the four criteria listed in the ART during real-time discussions might sound like an overwhelming task. Students express their ideas in everyday language that is often vague and confusing. At times, it is hard to understand what students are saying or how it relates to the discussion, let alone to evaluate the strengths and weaknesses of their reasoning! For this reason, when we are learning to facilitate inquiry dialogue, it is helpful to focus on just one criterion at a time and get comfortable with the practices and talk moves that accompany it. To further support teacher learning of facilitation practices, we created another version of the ART, called *ART During Inquiry*. It is a shorter, more practical version, since the original ART proved to be too comprehensive and detailed to be useful during discussions. This version, shown in appendix B, contains one-page reminders that teachers can refer to as they engage in inquiry dialogue with their students.

Also, remember that we, as teachers, do not have sole responsibility for supporting argumentation during inquiry dialogue. We share responsibility with the group—everyone is responsible! Often students will spontaneously find problems with group collaboration or flaws with each other's arguments. With time, they will learn to use the same facilitation practices and talk moves we use, such as inviting others to speak, soliciting alternatives, or asking for clarification. To help involve students in evaluating the quality of argumentation during inquiry dialogue, we created another version of the ART, called *ART for Kids*. This version, included in appendix C, invites students to rate the quality of argumentation in their own discussions, explain their ratings, and suggest strategies for improvement. In chapters 5 through 7, we offer examples of how the *ART* and the *ART for Kids* can be used in a classroom.

DEVELOPING HELPFUL DISPOSITIONS

Facilitating inquiry dialogue places new demands on us as teachers, often requiring us to reconsider our previously held notions about teaching and learning. Here, we list several dispositions that are useful for facilitating inquiry dialogue:

1. *Talk less and listen more.* In traditional instruction, teachers typically dominate class discussions, speaking more than students and controlling key aspects of the talk (i.e., who speaks and when, what questions are being discussed, what the

right answers are). In contrast, during inquiry dialogue, both the quantity and the quality of teacher talk need to change. First, instead of talking, try to focus more on closely *listening* to what students are saying. Listening to student talk is the key to effective facilitation: only when we are able to diagnose strengths and weaknesses in students' collaboration and argumentation can we know when and how to step in.

   In other words, our contributions during inquiry dialogue change from telling students the right answers to helping them work together, think carefully, and, as a result, arrive at the more reasonable answers themselves. During inquiry dialogue, teachers are *substantively weak but procedurally strong.*[9] That is, instead of giving students the answers, we model and support their use of talk to collaborate and reason together.

2. *Keep a "road map" of arguments.* Inquiry is a process of investigation that begins with a question; considers a number of possible arguments; tests and eliminates positions, reasons, and evidence that do not meet the criteria for quality arguments; and ends with a judgment about which position is the most reasonable. Good facilitators keep this larger picture of inquiry dialogue in mind and help students advance through it.[10] This means that during the discussion, we need to keep a road map of the group's arguments in mind and help students do the same. The ART facilitation practice 7, Tracking the line of inquiry, shown in figure 3.2, can help with this task. For instance, if a number of positions have been suggested, we can use this practice to ask the students to pause and summarize. Some possible talk moves are: "We now have a lot of ideas on the table. Can someone tell us how many different positions on the big question have been offered so far?" Similarly, when we feel lost in a discussion, we can use the same ART facilitation practice and related talk moves to ask the group for help (e.g., "Where are we now? Let's retrace what has been said so far"). This practice will help slow down the discussion, allow students to summarize each other's arguments, and model for students how to address confusion during inquiry dialogue. At different points in the discussion, it is also important to ask students to talk about the progress they have made during their inquiry. For instance, students should be able to refer to the big question, summarize the main positions they developed in response to it, and identify some of the most compelling reasons and evidence for and/or against them.

One way to keep track of students' arguments is to take notes during a discussion. For example, as you listen to your students, you can jot down each person's name, position, reasons, and evidence. It may be helpful to group student contributions into three categories of responses to the big question that often come up during the discussions: Yes, No, and It Depends. Finally, try sharing your notes with the students or involve them directly in the process of tracking arguments by having them build argument houses on the board or simply write key ideas for and against a particular position.

3. *Value what students think.* In traditional classrooms, the teacher is often viewed as the "sage on the stage." The teacher knows all the answers and delivers them to students, who then copy the new knowledge into their minds. Current research tells us that this approach is not effective for promoting meaningful learning and deep understanding.[11] To learn something well, students need to develop their own ideas and test these ideas against those of others. Classroom discussions offer an ideal environment for students to identify, examine, and modify their views, as well as to learn the process of arriving at the most reasonable conclusions—in short, to take responsibility for their own thinking and their own beliefs and values.

   During inquiry dialogue, we work with students to co-construct meaning together. We recognize that students' contributions are valuable and that they need to be heard, discussed, and sometimes challenged. Some authors call this "displaying scholarly ignorance," which means that teachers consciously open their minds to being curious about their students' ideas (even when we know the right answers), are ready to be surprised by them, and are willing to learn from their students about new ways of approaching a question.[12]

4. *Be ready for the unexpected.* Inquiry dialogue is much less predictable compared to traditional lessons that have a more established sequence of questions and activities. Each group of students will bring up unique considerations, so an inquiry about the same big question is likely to result in the group exploring different topics and reaching different conclusions. This means that we need to be flexible and spontaneous in our facilitation and be ready to follow the argument where it leads, as long as we maintain the focus on finding the most reasonable answer to the big question. In other words, we need to respond to specific ideas offered by students and not be restricted by our expectations and past experiences.

5. *Most importantly, focus on truth and insist on good reasoning.* Valuing students' thinking does not mean that we have to uncritically accept anything that students say. It also does not dismiss the authority of the teacher as a more knowledgeable and skilled member of the group. We need to help students recognize and challenge weaknesses in group collaboration and argumentation by using the criteria listed in the ART. When group members take part in challenging each other's ideas, they hold everyone accountable to standards of good reasoning. What gets challenged, however, is the process used to arrive at a given conclusion, not the answer itself. This way, students will not only develop deep understanding of complex questions, but they will also acquire the thinking skills and collaborative processes needed to come up with well-reasoned conclusions.

CHAPTER 4

What Happens Before, During, and After Discussion?

In this chapter, we provide an overview of what happens before, during, and after discussion and introduce some key ideas and principles that we use in the rest of the book. To help you get started, we begin by describing how to establish ground rules for discussion. We then introduce the *Discussion Planning Tool*, a resource to help you plan, put into practice, and reflect on a discussion.[1] Next, we review three steps for conducting a productive discussion:

1. Before the discussion: using pre-discussion activities to promote students' engagement with the text.
2. During the discussion: launching the discussion (reviewing ground rules, the general purpose, specific focus, and asking the big question), facilitating the inquiry dialogue, and providing closure and thinking ahead to the next discussion.
3. After the discussion: using post-discussion activities to help students transfer the argument skills and dispositions learned in the group to their individual efforts in speaking, listening, reading, and writing arguments.

GETTING STARTED: ESTABLISHING GROUND RULES FOR DISCUSSION

One of the most important things to do in the early stages of conducting discussions is to establish ground rules for talk. These are norms of behavior for productive argumentation that everyone agrees to follow in forthcoming discussions. Establishing the norms or ground rules will help you share control of the discussions with your students and help them regulate their own behavior. It also helps students reflect on their talk and their skill in using talk to further their thinking. So, it helps promote the meta-level awareness about language that is important for productive participation in inquiry dialogue as well as for transferring argument skills from group discussions to other contexts, such as reading and writing.

We suggest starting with a short list of ground rules (four or five) and building on them as you and your students become more familiar with what works best during discussions. Ideally, you will establish the ground rules collaboratively with your students. This is a community of inquiry after all! You may wish to ask students to suggest the ground rules by saying, for example: "We will need to think and talk together about difficult questions and to try to find the best, most reasonable answers. What are some ground rules that will help us do that?" List the rules on an anchor chart that is prominently displayed in the classroom so you and your students can refer to it during discussions. Some good rules to have in place are the following:

- We support our positions with reasons and evidence.
- We connect our ideas to what others say.
- We look at the speaker.
- We challenge each other's ideas.

Good ground rules for productive argumentation address both cognitive and social dimensions of participation. In the preceding list, supporting positions with reasons and evidence and challenging each other's ideas help achieve the cognitive goal of rigorous argumentation. Connecting to what others say is part cognitive, but it is social too; we want students to interact and collaborate with each other. Looking at the speaker is entirely social and is good etiquette when we engage in conversation with each other. It also helps focus students' attention on the ideas of others. In activity 4.1, determine whether these ground rules used by a teacher are cognitive or social (see the answers in the appendix).

A few words about the participation structure in the discussions—who gets to speak and when. Ideally, we would like to have an open participation structure in which, instead of the teacher nominating students to speak, students have control over turn taking. This open participation structure encourages the free exchange of ideas among students. This is why, in small-group discussion, we like to ask students

---

Activity 4.1
Test yourself

(answers shown in the appendix to this chapter).

Identify which rules address the cognitive dimension and which ones address the social.

What we do when we talk and listen

- Eyes on the speaker
- Listen with my whole body
- Wait for a 'space' to talk so we don't raise hands
- One person talks at a time
- We share and listen
- It's good to disagree and ask 'why?'
- Give reasons to explain our thinking
- Respect each other's ideas
- Invite others to speak

---

not to raise hands; instead, we ask them to wait until the speaker is finished before contributing. Raising hands slows down the exchange of ideas and makes the discussion a bit artificial. There is also a danger that students who are waving their hands to bid for a turn do not listen to what is being said, instead focusing on what they are going to talk about when they get the floor.

An open participation structure works well in a small-group discussion, but it can be a little unwieldy in a whole-class discussion in which students can easily talk over each other. One solution is to have students raise their hands when they want to contribute to the discussion and have the speaker choose the next student to talk. This approach slows down the pace of discussion a little (sometimes that is a good thing!), but it still gives students control over who talks next.

PLANNING THE DISCUSSION

To help you plan, implement, and reflect on your discussion, many teachers find it helpful to use the Discussion Planning Tool shown in figure 4.1. The tool is divided into three parts: on the left is a column to list what you will do *before* the discussion to prepare students for the inquiry dialogue, in the middle is a section to plan what will happen *during* the discussion, and on the right is a column to list what you will do *after* the discussion. The core of the process, of course, is the discussion itself and engaging students in inquiry dialogue, so we suggest you start planning by focusing on the middle section. After you have planned the discussion, think about pre- and post-discussion activities to engage students before and after the discussion. In figure 4.1, we filled in the spaces with prompts and reminders about what is involved in each phase. Appendix D provides a template of the tool for you to fill in during lesson planning.

Embedding the discussion within a larger framework of pre- and post-discussion activities is good practice. Most of the rigorous, intellectual work in discussion takes place during the inquiry dialogue. Nonetheless, we have found that discussions are more successful when students come to the group knowing the text well and having a vested interest in discussing it. The pre-discussion activities do just that—they help prepare students for the discussion. In a similar vein, we have found discussions are more productive for students' learning when they are followed by independent (for the most part) work that allows students to apply the skills of argumentation they practiced during inquiry dialogue to new tasks, completed individually. Post-discussion activities help support the transfer of knowledge and skills from the collective reasoning that occurred in the group to the individual reasoning we want students to use later in their independent work.

You may have a productive discussion without having students complete pre- and post-discussion activities. However, based on our experience working with students, coupled with good theory about effective teaching and learning, we strongly recommend using them. Having students complete these activities increases the likelihood of having successful discussions that foster students' argument literacy.

In the following sections, we discuss the purpose of these pre- and post-discussion activities in more detail and the general principles to keep in mind when planning and conducting them. We also provide examples of the activities you might use. Remember that these are just samples of the myriad of activities you can use. We list the examples to give you an idea of the types of activities teachers have found useful so you can develop your own pre- and post-discussion activities to suit your needs and purposes.

FIGURE 4.1

Discussion Planning Tool (with prompts and reminders)

Text:

Grouping: e.g., Small Groups, Whole Class, Fishbowl

PRE-DISCUSSION	DISCUSSION	POST-DISCUSSION
Reading: e.g., Independent reading, pair/buddy reading *Engaging with text:* e.g., Make sticky notes about your connections, questions, reactions *Reminder:* Use pre-discussion activities to get students engaged with the text and invested in discussing it. The activities should have a light touch, feeding into the discussion, rather than structuring it.	**Launch** Remind students that the *general purpose* of the discussion is to search for the most reasonable answer as a community. Review basic *ground rules* (to be revisited): • We support our positions with reasons and evidence. • We connect our ideas to what others say. • We look at the speaker. • We challenge each other's ideas. Review the *specific focus* for today. *Reminder:* Think about past discussions and focus on specific ground rules to be addressed. We can treat ground rules as an inquiry topic; that is, we can reflect on them as a way of understanding how they contribute to inquiry and revise them as needed. Pose the *big question.* *Reminder:* When choosing a big question, examine the text, looking for themes, potential dilemmas, questionable decisions and outcomes, or ambiguities. **Inquiry Dialogue** Anticipate different perspectives on the big questions, including positions, reasons, and evidence. Review facilitation practices from the ART that might help achieve the specific focus of the discussion. **Closure** *Reflect on the specific focus:* e.g., How did we do on challenging each other today? What did you notice? How did challenging each other help us make progress on finding the best answer to the big question? *Reflect on other aspects of the process:* e.g., Did we reason well? Did most of us contribute or only a few? *Reflect on the group's progress toward answering the big question:* e.g., Did we get any closer to answering our big question? Identify a specific focus for next time. *Reminder:* During the discussion, you can identify areas of strength and weakness to be addressed during closure and in the next discussion.	*Speaking:* e.g., Tell a partner whether or not you changed your initial position and explain why. *Listening:* e.g., Listen to a podcast on the same topic and identify the reasons that support the position(s) presented. *Writing:* e.g., Write your position now, and list the strongest reason for and the strongest reason against your position. *Reading:* e.g., Identify the words, phrases, or statements from a text on the topic just discussed that reveal the author's argument or point of view. *Reminder:* Use post-discussion activities to help students transfer their new skills to other speaking, listening, reading, and writing tasks.

Before the Discussion

The purpose of having a pre-discussion activity is to promote students' engagement with the text. By engagement, we mean a sustained personal commitment to understanding the topic or issues raised by the text. Engagement includes both a *cognitive* and an *affective* (or emotional) component. From a cognitive perspective, we want students to engage with the text sufficiently so they understand what it is about and have thought about the characters, events, or issues; they might have even formed an initial opinion about them. Students do not have to come to the discussion understanding everything in the text, but they should have sufficient knowledge of the content to be able to talk about it. From an affective perspective, we want the text to have touched the hearts of students—their interests, attitudes, feelings, or values. We want students to come to the discussion not only knowing what the text says but also having a vested interest in discussing it!

Of course, before the discussion takes place, students need to have read the text. Depending on the demands of the text, you might do a whole-class read-aloud, have students engage in paired reading, or have students read the text independently. It is good practice to have the students read or listen to the text more than once before coming to the discussion so they are very familiar with it. If the text is particularly demanding in terms of the background knowledge students need to understand it, you might want to help students build that background knowledge with a prereading activity, just as you would normally do with a text on a somewhat unfamiliar topic.

What makes a good pre-discussion activity? A general principle to keep in mind when planning for an activity before discussion is to *keep it simple*. We want the activity to fuel or motivate the discussion but not to replace it. A pre-discussion activity might be used to prompt students to take a position on the big question before the discussion, but it does not have to. The goal of the pre-discussion activity is simply to promote students' cognitive and affective engagement with the text.

Here are some examples of good pre-discussion activities:

- Have students take notes about the reading. They can note their reactions, thoughts, and questions using sticky notes, insert notes, or drawings. For example: "Is there anything that is confusing or surprising to you?" "Is there anything you feel strongly about?" "What connections do you see: text-to-text, text-to-self, or text-to-world?"

- Have students selectively highlight ideas or facts in the text that resonate with them. Alternatively, have students choose one sentence in the text that speaks to them. Next, have students share their sentence with a partner and explain their reasons for choosing the sentence.
- Share the big question with the students and have them write their position in response. You might also have them support their position with one reason.
- Have students summarize the story or identify the main ideas in another way.
- Have students write eight words about the issue, topic, story, or character. Then have them use the words as a tool for writing a summary statement about the issue or character.
- Have each student write ten words that describe the story, character, issue, or topic. Then have them work with a partner to eliminate five of the words; then eliminate four more to arrive at the one word that best describes the text. This technique is called the *10-5-1 strategy*. You might also have students compose a sentence using the one word that best describes the text.
- Have students write their opinion about the reading, a character, or an issue. This writing does not have to be about the big question. The purpose of the activity is to engage students with the text.
- Have students complete a *position line*. Write a Likert scale on the board from 1=strongly disagree to 5=strongly agree and a contestable statement about the topic or character in the story (e.g., "Super-sized sugary drinks should be banned"). Ask students to choose a number to indicate the extent to which they agree or disagree. Then have students turn to a partner and explain their choice. An alternative is to turn your room into a big Likert scale and have students move to the number that reflects their position. Again, have students discuss their points of view and their reasons. You might use just a three-point scale (1=disagree, 2=agree and disagree, 3=agree).
- Have students choose a controversial quotation from the text and then share the quotation with a partner.
- When using a multimodal text set with a print text and a video or podcast, have students read the print text and then watch the video. Then have them use a note-catcher to make opinion-based notes during and after viewing or listening (e.g., "zoos are fun," "zoos are cruel"). When using a video or podcast, you

might want to pause periodically for short bursts of discussion to help students identify specific facts and ideas they have heard.

A word of caution when planning and conducting a pre-discussion activity. If students make notes about a text they are going to discuss, it is best that they leave the notes at their desks or at least avoid relying on them in the discussion. The discussion is where the inquiry takes place, where we want students to collaborate with each other and to engage in rigorous argumentation. If students rely too much on their notes during the discussion, we run the risk of students seeing their role as simply to report on what they wrote rather than to collectively come up with the most reasonable answer to the big question.

During the Discussion

Launch

In launching the discussion, remind students of the general purpose of the discussions, review the ground rules, establish the specific focus of the upcoming discussion, and pose the big question. Although we have listed these steps in a certain order, they can be covered in almost any order. We want to avoid making things too routinized.

Remind students of the general purpose. Tell students the general purpose of the discussion is to search for or find the most reasonable answer to the big question. We use the phrase "most reasonable answer" deliberately. The phrase "best answer" is sometimes used, but "best" can be interpreted in different ways. "Most reasonable" implies that the answer has withstood the test of rigorous argumentation: it is logical and backed by acceptable reasons and evidence, has been tested against alternative perspectives, and has withstood the scrutiny of the group. It is oriented toward seeking the truth or as close to it as we can get to it. For various reasons, students may not arrive at the most reasonable answer by the end of the discussion. But making the goal of finding the most reasonable answer is important if we want the discussion to go beyond a simple sharing of opinions. It may be useful to sometimes tell students that you do not know the answer to the big question and that through careful argumentation, together as a group, they can search for it. As students become more familiar with the process, you might not need to remind them of the general purpose every time.

Review the ground rules. It is good practice to remind students of the ground rules and refer to the anchor chart, especially when you are starting to conduct discussions in your classroom. Of course, doing this at the start of every discussion can become tedious, so over time, you should be able to phase out revisiting the ground rules. The specific focus of the discussion provides an opportunity to revisit the ground rules the group needs to work on and to revise them accordingly.

Establish the specific focus. State the specific focus of the upcoming discussion. Keep in mind the ground rules established for the group and the four criteria for good argumentation listed in the ART. For example, in previous discussions, the group may have had difficulty connecting with each other's ideas. If so, then connecting ideas might be the specific focus for the upcoming discussion. Alternatively, the group may have had difficulty challenging each other's positions or reasons. If so, then challenging might be the specific focus. Think about past discussions and focus on specific ground rules as a corrective to improve the quality of students' talk. You can treat the ground rules as an inquiry topic in itself and have the group decide what they would like to include to improve the quality of discussions. Add to or revise the list of ground rules depending on the progress of the group.

Pose the big question. The big question sets up the overall goal of the inquiry dialogue. It ignites the discussion. It invites multiple interpretations, explanations, perspectives, or opinions about the text and encourages students to engage in well-founded, reasoned arguments supported by evidence. And it is the differences of opinion and reasoned arguments that pull students into a close reading of, and critical thinking about, the text.

What makes a good big question? A good big question is

- *Contestable.* It invites multiple interpretations and elicits reasoning.
- *Authentic.* You or your students have genuine doubt and curiosity about the answer to the question.
- *Central.* It is a meaty question about a significant issue raised by the text.
- *Clear.* Everyone should understand the question in the same way.

Choosing the big question is one of the more challenging, yet essential, aspects of inquiry dialogue. The question frames the inquiry, and the success of the discussion hinges on the quality of the big question.[2] One way to develop the big question is to start by identifying two or three key concepts or themes that are relevant to the text (e.g., friendship, fairness, coming-of-age) and to develop several big questions around those concepts or themes. Then test the questions to see which question is more contestable by thinking of possible justifications for different positions. If you find it hard to justify more than one position, or if you suspect that most of your students will adopt the same position, then it may not be a truly contestable question. Also, big questions do not have to invite only two positions (yes or no, as in a debate); students might consider several positions. Think carefully about how you word the question so it does not lead students to favor one side (e.g., "Was killing the bear a bad thing?" might lead the students to agree, whereas "Should they have killed the bear?" is more open and more likely to invite a range of responses). Questions worded with *should* that pose moral or ethical dilemmas for students make good big questions. Finally, the question must be clear and understood by all.[3] "If the question is confused or badly stated, then the inquiry will go wrong from the very beginning because those involved lack a clear understanding of the problem."[4]

Because choosing the big question for inquiry is challenging, it may be best if you, rather than your students, formulate the questions when you are beginning to have these discussions. However, with time, after students have experienced inquiry dialogue and been exposed to multiple examples of big questions, you might wish to have them suggest the big question. Asking students to generate questions offers another way of relinquishing control of the discussion to students. It also engages students in an important practice of formulating meaningful questions about their readings.[5] Of course, you may need to help students reword their original offerings so that the final question meets the key criteria of being contestable, authentic, central, and clear.

Inquiry Dialogue

The inquiry dialogue tends to follow a trajectory or arc, beginning with the big question and ending with a possible answer to the question or at least a greater understanding of the competing arguments that have survived the group's critique.[6] Along the way, students take positions in response to the big question and support them with reasons and evidence; clarify their understanding of the proposed arguments and test them against each other; and either confirm, revise, or eliminate the various positions as a result. Although you should not pressure the group to come to a definitive answer, it is important that the dialogue has forward momentum and that everyone involved sees that progress is being made toward answering the big question.[7]

During the inquiry dialogue, keep in mind the four criteria for good argumentation:

- Are students exploring different perspectives?
- Are they clear in the language and structure of their arguments?
- Are they using reasons and evidence that are well examined and accurate?
- Are they logical in the way they connect their positions, reasons, and evidence?

Depending on how well students are meeting these criteria, use the accompanying facilitation practices in the ART to support students in their search for the most reasonable answer.

It is important to help students track how the dialogue is progressing toward answering the big question. To keep track of the arguments, many teachers take notes of students' contributions and group them by the positions they take in response to the big question. You might even share your notes with the students or involve them directly in the process of tracking arguments. During the discussion, also try to note areas of strength and weakness to be addressed during closure and in the next discussion.

Closure

In closing the discussion, ask students to reflect on and evaluate their performance, both the quality of their argumentation (the process) and their answers to the big question (the product). To evaluate the process, ask students how well they think they did working on the specific focus for the discussion (e.g., "How did we do on challenging each other today? What did you notice? How did challenging each other help us make progress on finding the best answer to the big question?"). You might also have them reflect on other aspects of the group's process. Again, keep in mind the ground rules, both the social and cognitive dimensions, and the four criteria for good argumentation (e.g., "Did we reason well?" "Did most of us contribute or only a few?"). To evaluate the product, ask students to reflect on the group's progress toward answering the big question (e.g., "What do we now think about banning super-sized sugary drinks? Did we get any closer to answering our big question? What should we do next to answer the big question?").

When evaluating group performance, you might have students use a thumb gauge (thumb up for "good," thumb down for "needs work," thumb to the side for "okay"). Then follow up by asking one of two of the students why they evaluated themselves the way they did. Reflecting on the group's process and product during closure is another way of helping students develop meta-level awareness of their talk. At the end of the discussion and based on the ideas offered during closure, identify a specific focus for your next session to improve the quality of argumentation (e.g., "Next time, let's focus on giving everyone an opportunity to talk"). You may wish to do this collaboratively with students by asking them what they think about the specific focus for the next discussion.

After the Discussion

The purpose of the post-discussion activity is to help students transfer the argument skills and dispositions learned in the group to their individual efforts in speaking, listening, reading, and writing arguments. The theory is that, as students engage in collective argumentation in the group, they gradually internalize the skills to recognize, analyze, formulate, and evaluate arguments and learn to apply these skills on their own in new situations.[8] A good post-discussion activity that is related to the issue just discussed serves as a bridge between the argumentation students do in the group and the argumentation they will do on their own when faced with other tasks.

What makes a good post-discussion activity? A general principle to keep in mind when planning for an activity after discussion is *it's all about argument*. The activity should not simply prompt a general reflection from students. It should focus on argument or the parts of an argument.

Think of the metaphor of an argument as a house (figure 4.2). Does the activity focus on a position? Does it focus on reasons or evidence? Does it focus on challenges or responses to challenges? Showing students a diagram of the argument house can serve as a prompt for students to think about the different parts of an argument.

Following are some examples of good post-discussion activities. Because the goal of post-discussion activities is to promote argument literacy, we have organized these into reading, listening, speaking, and writing activities.

Reading
- Have students identify the words, phrases, or statements from a text on the topic just discussed that reveal the author's argument or point of view.

FIGURE 4.2

Argument house

- Have students reread the text just discussed and underline information that could be used to support their position. Then have them underline information in the text that could be used to argue against their position. Next, have students pair up and share.

Listening
- Have students listen to a video clip of their discussion and identify the key arguments. You might have students build argument houses to represent the key parts of an argument.
- Have students listen to a podcast on the same topic as the text just discussed and identify reasons and evidence that support the different positions.

Speaking
- Have students share with a peer whether or not they changed their position and explain why.
- Have students think of two new ideas that they heard during the discussion and explain to a partner how the new ideas affected (or did not affect) their position.

- Have students restate and discuss the strongest reason they heard against their position during the discussion.

Writing

- Have students write letters to a relevant party (e.g., a protagonist in the story or the editors of *Time for Kids*) explaining their position or their group's position.
- Have students write essays comparing their positions before and after the discussion. If their position changed or strengthened, they can explain why.
- Have students write a paragraph completing the story based on their position or the group's position. The first sentence of the students' paragraph could be their position statement (e.g., "'I think I should stay in Twin Rivers longer,' Ovatniah said to her mother."), and the rest of the paragraph could elaborate on their reasons.
- Have students write persuasive essays stating their position on the issue, the reasons for their position, and possible challenges and responses to challenges. For a prewriting activity, students can use the student version of the argument house (appendix E) to help organize their thoughts.

If you would like to grade students' post-discussion writing, you could use the guidelines in the handout showing the Argumentative Writing Scoring Rubric (appendix F). Depending on your focus, you could grade students' writing on one, some, or all of the criteria.

INTERNET RESOURCES

The following resources may be useful to help structure pre-discussion activities:

Insert notes. To help students monitor their thinking as they read. www.readwrite think.org/files/resources/lesson_images/lesson230/insert.pdf

Selective highlighting. To help students organize what they have read by selecting what is important. www.adlit.org/strategies/23332

Frame routine. To help students organize main ideas and details to summarize what they have read. www.adlit.org/strategies/22229

Notice and note. To help students monitor their thinking while reading. www. heinemann.com/shared/companionResources/E04693/NoticeNote_App5 _Bookmarks.pdf

Appendix (Chapter 4)

Answers to Activity 4.1

Activity 4.1
Test yourself

What we do when we talk and listen

- [*Social*] Eyes on the speaker.
- [*Social*] Listen with my whole body.
- [*Social*] Wait for a space to talk so we don't raise hands.
- [*Social*] One person talks at a time.
- [*Social*] We share and listen.
- [*Cognitive*] It's good to disagree and ask "why?"
- [*Cognitive*] Give reasons to explain our thinking.
- [*Social*] Respect each other's ideas.
- [*Social*] Invite others to speak.

PART TWO

Planning and Conducting Discussions

CHAPTER 5

Discussing "What Should Kelly Do?"

In this chapter, as well as in the next three chapters, we illustrate the steps involved in conducting entire lessons that are built around inquiry dialogue and aimed at promoting students' argument literacy. We put into practice the basic concepts and principles discussed in Part I by describing how to plan for and conduct discussions with literary and informational texts. For each text, we discuss examples of effective facilitation with annotated excerpts from actual classroom discussions.

We begin by showing how to plan, conduct, and reflect on a discussion using a short story called "What Should Kelly Do?" The entire story is included in the appendix to this chapter, and we suggest you read it before continuing with this chapter. Briefly, the story is about two classmates, Kelly and Evelyn, who are taking part in their school's art contest. Kelly is a gifted artist and really wants to win, but she might not be as good as Evelyn. Evelyn is probably the most talented artist in the entire school, though she claims not to care about contests and winning. Evelyn brings a beautiful painting to submit for the contest, but she gets distracted and leaves her work outside. In a few minutes, Evelyn will miss the deadline for submitting her work. More importantly, the approaching rain will ruin her painting. Kelly notices Evelyn's painting outside and has to make a decision about whether to alert Evelyn, probably losing her own chance of winning the contest. What should she do?

Based on our work with teachers, this story proved to be an excellent text to use for a first lesson centered around inquiry dialogue. We begin with how to go about planning the lesson and then look at a short excerpt, in which fifth-grade students are discussing "What Should Kelly Do?" In our analysis of the excerpt, we focus on the teacher's use of talk to support students' progress toward figuring out the most reasonable answer to the big question. We end the chapter by showing how to frame the discussion with pre- and post-discussion activities.

PLANNING THE DISCUSSION

We usually start planning the lesson by filling in the top portion of the Discussion Planning Tool shown in figure 5.1.

In the beginning, it is helpful to have both versions of this tool in front of you—the empty one and the one with the reminders (see chapter 4 and appendix D). In the top portion, we write the title of the text and decide on the grouping arrangement. We suggest using a small group with six to ten students for your first discussion. It is easier to get most students to contribute and to track their arguments in a small group. Also, discussing the same story with multiple small groups in your class offers excellent opportunities to practice and sharpen your facilitation skills.

Next, we turn to the middle section, the Discussion section of the Discussion Planning Tool. As shown in figure 5.1, every discussion begins with the *launch*, which typically includes four key practices. First, we need to introduce or remind students of the *general purpose* of the discussion: to find the most reasonable answer to the big question. Explicitly stating (or restating) this purpose helps focus students on the task at hand and alert them to different uses of talk for learning.

Second, we need to agree on the basic norms or *ground rules* for the discussion. You will probably need to revise these rules as students become more adept at participating in inquiry dialogue and as new challenges come up during discussions. For the first discussion, we suggest starting with the four ground rules listed in figure 5.1.

Third, we need to identify a *specific focus* of the discussion. The focus can be on one of the ground rules; for example, we might choose "We connect our ideas to what others say" as our specific target for this discussion. When you are choosing the focus, it helps to reflect on some challenges you often have or anticipate having with a given group of students in relation to the key tasks they will be working on during inquiry dialogue: collaborating with each other and engaging in rigorous argumentation. Do you anticipate having problems with student collaboration, such as students interrupting each other or dominating a discussion? Are there problems

FIGURE 5.1

Discussion Planning Tool for "What Should Kelly Do?"

Text: "What Should Kelly Do?"

Grouping: Small Groups

PRE-DISCUSSION	DISCUSSION	POST-DISCUSSION
Reading: Independent reading	**Launch**	*Writing:* Ask students to complete the story by writing an argument for Kelly's decision.
Engaging with text: Give students one minute to discuss in pairs their position on the big question and to state one reason to support it.	*General purpose:* To find the most reasonable answer to the big question.	
	Ground rules:	or
or	• We support our positions with reasons and evidence.	Ask students to draw argument houses using the handout included in appendix E.
Ask students to choose a position on the big question and underline one to two sentences that they can use to support it.	• We connect our ideas to what others say. • We look at the speaker. • We challenge each other's ideas.	
	Specific focus: Connecting our ideas to what others say.	
or	*Big question:* What should Kelly do?	
Ask students to draw their favorite part of the story or a painting they would submit to the art contest.	**Inquiry Dialogue**	
	Position: Yes, tell Evelyn. It's our duty to help others. The painting will be ruined. Kelly will regret not telling.	
	Position: No, do not tell Evelyn. Evelyn needs to learn to be responsible. Not telling will help Evelyn in the future. Evelyn will not be upset to lose the contest because she does not care about winning.	
	Talk moves: How do we know that Evelyn does not care about winning? Can someone suggest a reason why Kelly should not tell Evelyn? How is this connected to . . . ?	
	Closure	
	Thumb gauge: How did we do on connecting our ideas to what others say? Can someone summarize what we now think about Kelly's dilemma: Where did we end up?	

with the intellectual rigor of the discussions? Do students support their positions with reasons and evidence? Do they challenge each other's ideas?

Fourth, we need to decide on the *big question*, which is contestable (invites multiple interpretations), authentic (ignites curiosity), central to important issues raised by the text, and clear (there is no confusion about its meaning). This story's title "What Should Kelly Do?" meets all these criteria. This question brings up controversial viewpoints about ethical treatment of others, fair play, importance of rules, the value of winning, the respect for art, and the role of personal responsibility. Notice that the question is not about what Kelly *would* do, because this question is likely to encourage students to speculate about possible answers that are not truly contestable. It's hard to evaluate pure speculation or to support it with good reasons. In contrast, *should* questions prompt students to formulate and challenge each other's arguments about moral, ethical, or social issues.

Launching a discussion does not have to involve lengthy or tedious explanations. It can be done in an efficient and interactive way, as shown in this excerpt from a fifth-grade classroom:

> **TEACHER:** We are going to talk about Kelly today, but I just want to set the stage about how I would like us to talk. We already have some rules for what counts as "respectful talk," so can someone tell me one of those rules?
> **STUDENT:** Only one person can speak at the same time.
> **TEACHER:** Right, one person at a time. Now, in addition to this, when we do this kind of talk, it's important that we are not just sharing. So, our job is not just to get our ideas out so that everybody can hear them. It's actually to offer ideas up in the hopes that the group can determine *what the most reasonable answer is, the best answer, the most thought through.* So, our job is not just to share our answers, but also to consider other people's answers. And that means that we have to *build on each other's ideas* and make connections. So, the idea is to test, test each other's ideas. As a group, we should be able to think better than we can by ourselves. Does that make sense? All right. So, let's take one minute to talk with your neighbor. The big question is "What should Kelly do?" and I just want you to talk to your neighbor and begin to discuss this together. What should she do? What do you think?

Here, the teacher explains the purpose of the discussion to his students and briefly goes over some key practices that need to happen for the group to be able to make progress toward the most reasonable answer. Note how the teacher stresses the importance of going beyond simply sharing ideas, or what we earlier called "popcorn talk"—when ideas pop up in a random, disconnected manner. Instead, the teacher invites his students to build on and test each other's arguments so that together the group can come up with the best solution to Kelly's dilemma.

When you are preparing for the discussion, it is helpful to explore possible answers to the big question. For example, under the Inquiry section of the Discussion Planning Tool in figure 5.1, we jotted down some reasons for and against Kelly telling Evelyn about the painting, and we invite you to add a couple of your own reasons on each side. Thinking through possible reasons for and against a given position on the big question helps us be more prepared to react when such reasons come up during the discussion. In addition, identifying reasons on both sides is a good test to find out whether the big question is, in fact, contestable. If we cannot come up with several reasons for and against a certain position, perhaps we need to revise the big question to make it truly controversial. Another helpful way to get ready for the discussion is to review the Argumentation Rating Tool and remind ourselves of the facilitation practices and related talk moves that we are likely to use during the discussion. For example, if we anticipate that most of our students will line up on the side that Kelly should tell Evelyn about the painting, we could prepare by identifying some talk moves that prompt students to consider alternative perspectives (see figure 5.1 for examples). Also, because our specific focus for this discussion is to build on each other's ideas, we should review the sections of the ART that address this practice and related talk moves.

At the end of each discussion, we always leave some time to engage students in reflection on their progress. During Closure, students should consider both the processes and products of the discussion. In line with our specific focus for this discussion, we could have students evaluate how successful the group members were in building on each other's ideas during the discussion (the process). We could invite students to quickly show what they think using a thumb gauge. When using a thumb gauge, we usually follow up with one or two students to ask them why their thumb is up or down and what can be done to improve group performance next time. It is a good idea to write down the group's suggestions for the next time and use them as a specific focus in the following discussion.

During Closure, we also need to ask the group about the progress we made toward finding the most reasonable answer to the big question (the product). Although we often end the discussion without having a definitive answer, students should be able to recognize more comprehensive, nuanced, and careful ways of thinking about Kelly's dilemma that emerged as a result of discussing this story with others. One way to do this is to simply ask students to summarize the group's current thinking about the big question: What do we now think about Kelly's dilemma: Where did we end up?

ANALYZING AN EXCERPT OF DISCUSSION

Before moving on to review the rest of the Discussion Planning Tool (i.e., pre- and post-discussion activities), let's look closely at an annotated excerpt from a discussion about "What Should Kelly Do?" in a fifth-grade classroom. In figure 5.2, we used the first column to name the speakers and to number their turns. The second column shows an actual transcript, and the third displays our commentary. It is helpful to first read the entire transcript in the second column and later refer to specific turns when reading the commentary.

FIGURE 5.2

Excerpt of discussion of "What Should Kelly Do?" with commentary

SPEAKER (TURN)	TRANSCRIPT	COMMENTARY
Leo (1)	I think Kelly should tell Evelyn that her painting is out in the rain because . . . Well, it's nice to win competitions, but the painting [is] going to be ruined in less than five minutes, in this story. I think that Evelyn is probably going to be sad.	*In the first two turns, Leo and Jill are explaining their thinking and building on each other's ideas. Leo begins by taking a "Yes, Kelly should tell" position and supporting it with two reasons: (1) the painting is going to be ruined, and (2) Evelyn is going to be sad. Jill agrees with Leo's position and adds a third reason (i.e., it was Evelyn's best picture) to strengthen Leo's assertion about Evelyn being upset. The exchange between Leo and Jill illustrates the ART's Criterion 1, Diversity of perspectives: the students are building on each other's ideas about the big question and sharing ownership over key aspects of talk. The students are working well together, so no teacher intervention is necessary.*

SPEAKER (TURN)	TRANSCRIPT	COMMENTARY
Jill (2)	I agree with Leo because . . . It is not only about the contest because it said there that it was the best picture that Evelyn ever made and maybe she would be upset if it got ruined in the rain.	
Louis (3)	[referring to Jill] I'd like to disagree with you. In the story, it says Evelyn didn't really care if she won the contest or not.	*During turn 3, Louis brings up a new idea of Evelyn not caring much about losing the contest. He also puts himself on the opposite side from Jill. This is a bit confusing, considering that Jill's statement was about Evelyn being upset about her painting being ruined, not about losing the contest.*
Teacher (4)	So, what are you disagreeing with?	*In turn 4, the teacher uses a talk move: "What are you disagreeing with?" In the ART, this move is shown as one of the ways of addressing criterion 2, Clarity, under facilitation practice 5, Connecting ideas.*
Louis (5)	I am disagreeing with the fact that Evelyn would be sad. She would be sad to lose the painting, but she wouldn't be sad to lose the contest.	*The teacher's use of this talk move turns out to be an effective intervention: it prompts Louis to examine in which specific ways his thinking is similar to and different from Jill's.*
Teacher (6)	Oh, okay. So, you are actually agreeing about the painting, but you are challenging Jill about Evelyn being upset?	*In fact, this teacher is following one of the common strategies of effective facilitators: when we are confused about what has just been said, it's very likely that our students are confused as well. And this means that it's time to step in! Discussions can quickly become unproductive when students lose track of the group's line of inquiry and misunderstand how their thinking is similar to or different from that of other students.*
Louis (7)	Yeah.	*As the discussion progresses, we see more students joining in to make public their thinking about the big question and to react to the contributions of their peers.*

continued

SPEAKER (TURN)	TRANSCRIPT	COMMENTARY
Meghan (8)	I agree with Louis that in the story it said she painted whenever she felt like it and she did not care about prizes and contests and winning. But also, she did like to paint just for the fun of it. Plus, Kelly still could win even if she tells Evelyn that her paining is outside.	*In turn 8, Meghan retells several facts from the story to provide further evidence for Louis's reason. She also offers two reasons that could support the opposite position (i.e., Kelly should tell): Evelyn enjoyed painting (and so may be upset about her ruined masterpiece), and Kelly may still win, even if she tells.*
Jamaal (9)	I disagree with Meghan because, well, in fifth grade you should be responsible for your own things, and your friends are not always going to be there to help you. And then you have to make your own decisions. . . . And with Evelyn, she was not responsible. She *left* her painting outside and it's about to rain, so it's not Kelly's fault that it gets poured on. It's Evelyn's because she should be more responsible for what she does with her paintings.	*Jamaal (turn 9) disagrees with Meghan's (assumed) position and offers a strong argument for not telling Evelyn about the painting. The exchange between Meghan (turn 8) and Jamaal (turn 9) is another example of two students tackling the ART Criterion 1, Diversity of perspectives. This time, the students go beyond agreeing with each other and offer opposing perspectives on the big question.* *Note, that in his turn 9, Jamaal provides a lengthy, elaborated explanation of his thinking, using several reasons that focus on the importance of personal responsibility, maturity, and autonomy. However, he does not say whether he believes that Kelly should tell Evelyn about the painting, thus leaving out an important part of his argument.*
Teacher (10)	So what's your position?	*This is when the teacher intervenes to prompt Jamaal to explicitly state his position (turn 10). In fact, throughout the discussion (i.e., turns 4, 6, 10, and 20), the teacher consistently points out the parts of an argument (i.e., position, evidence) and the processes of argumentation (i.e., agreeing, challenging, connecting). This is an intentional teacher behavior that is related to the ART Criterion 2, Clarity, and the facilitation practice 5, Labeling reasoning processes and parts of an argument. This practice allows students to pick up the language of argumentation, introduced and modeled by the teacher, and use it to formulate and defend their positions.*

SPEAKER (TURN)	TRANSCRIPT	COMMENTARY
Jamaal (11)	No, don't tell.	
Daniel (12)	I agree with Jamaal's position, and I have some evidence to back it up. It says here [reading from the text] "with her painting carefully wrapped in brown paper," and she "waited on the school steps for the bell to ring." While Evelyn "propped a picture against the side of the school wall" and went to play.	*Consider, for example, the ways in which Daniel and Rosa (turns 12 and 13) use the language of argumentation to explain their thinking: "I agree with Jamaal's position and I have some evidence to back it up," "I agree with Daniel and the reason is it does say in the story. . . ." These ways of speaking demonstrate that students are developing meta-level awareness of how to use language to think through complex problems, formulate positions, support them with reasons, and refer to the story for evidence. Having meta-awareness of argumentative discourse is one of the key principles of engaging students in inquiry dialogue. Another principle is that students assume greater ownership of interactions as they both build on and challenge each other's thinking in a collaborative search for the most reasonable answer. We see these principles reflected in the ART's Criterion 1, Diversity of perspectives, and exemplified in this excerpt. For example, out of twenty-two turns, only seven belong to the teacher. Also, students' contributions are lengthy, totaling 632 words (83 percent), compared to only 126 words spoken by the teacher (17 percent). We see students exploring and formulating their own ideas about Kelly's dilemma, as well as interpreting and evaluating each other's responses.*

continued

SPEAKER (TURN)	TRANSCRIPT	COMMENTARY
Rosa (13)	I agree with Daniel and the reason is it does say in the story that Evelyn does not really care what she does. [Reading from the story] "She could turn out pictures that looked good enough to be on magazine covers, but she only painted when and what she wanted to." Which you could figure in two ways, but I am guessing it's the first way, which is a person who thinks they are so talented and they are amazing and they only paint when they want to! Because they are so good, so amazing that they deserve to do things whenever they want to. So, that's how I interpret it. . . . And just to add on to Daniel . . . Kelly wrapped hers in brown paper while Evelyn propped it against the wall of the school! Is that really respect for painting? That kind of hints to me that she does not really care about painting.	
Teacher (14)	Evelyn?	
Rosa (15)	Yeah. And she thinks she is so great she can just make another one just as amazing whenever she wants to and she does not have to follow the rules.	

SPEAKER (TURN)	TRANSCRIPT	COMMENTARY
Teacher (16)	Can I just check on this? Cause in these last two moves . . . I am just trying to understand this, so you tell me if I got this right. Are we then saying if Evelyn doesn't have respect for her work, then her work should not be protected?	*The next several turns (starting with turn 16) demonstrate one of the more complex yet useful, practices that experienced facilitators use during inquiry dialogue: helping students uncover unstated links or assumptions made during the discussion. We discuss the links as part of the ART Criterion 4, Logical validity, facilitation practice 11, Evaluating inferences. Let's now look closely at the teacher's use of this facilitation practice.*
Colene (17)	We are saying, Evelyn does not protect her work, she does not care about it.	*In turns 9 through 17, Jamaal, Daniel, Rosa, and Colene are collaboratively building an argument for Kelly not telling Evelyn about the painting. This argument is presented in figure 5.3 using the house metaphor. The position is: Kelly should not tell Evelyn (and thus let the painting be ruined). The key reason is that Evelyn did not care about her painting. Students cite evidence from the story to support this reason: Evelyn left her painting outside, while Kelly carefully wrapped hers in a brown paper. So, students are building an argument supported with legitimate reasons and accurate evidence from the story. And yet, these reasons and evidence alone do not justify an inferential leap to the position that Kelly should not tell. Something is missing to warrant this conclusion. This is when the teacher steps in and tries to unearth the unstated assumption made by the students: "Are we then saying if Evelyn doesn't have respect for her work, then her work should not be protected?" (turn 16); "If she [Evelyn] does not care, then don't save it?" (turn 18); "But I am wondering what position are we connecting to?" (turn 20). It takes the teacher several turns to help students figure out what they are assuming about the relationship between Evelyn's lack of care for her work and Kelly's decision not to tell.*
Teacher (18)	So, if Evelyn cares about it, then save it; if she does not care, then don't save it?	
Daniel (19)	If Evelyn did care about it, she would not prop it against the school wall and go to play.	

continued

SPEAKER (TURN)	TRANSCRIPT	COMMENTARY
Teacher (20)	But I am wondering what position are we connecting to? . . . Because we have evidence that Evelyn does not care, we should not save the painting? Is that what we are saying?	
Rosa (21)	Partly, and the other part is if the person isn't going to follow the rules that were specifically told to them, and they are just not going to bother, then what's the point of trying to help them? She propped the painting against the school wall! If Evelyn is going to treat it like it means nothing, I guess everyone else should too. Because that's how much it means to you.	*Finally, in turn 21, Rosa explicitly states the missing link: "If Evelyn is going to treat it [the painting] like it means nothing, I guess everyone else should too." This link properly connects the reasons and evidence to the position, making an argument more complete, or the house more stable (see figure 5.4). Yet, this is also the statement that many other students find highly objectionable! In fact, we often notice that much of the disagreement in the discussions is related to hidden assumptions. This is why uncovering missing links is such an important part of effective facilitation.*
Several students (22)	I disagree! I disagree! I disagree!	

FIGURE 5.3

Argument house with a link missing

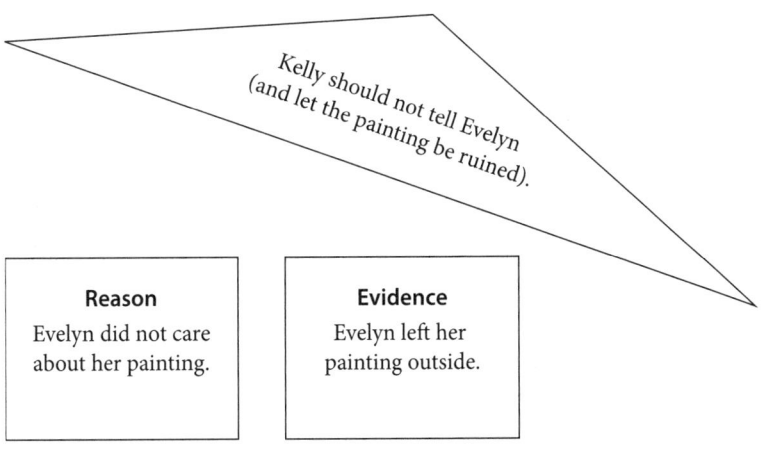

FIGURE 5.4

Argument house with a stated link

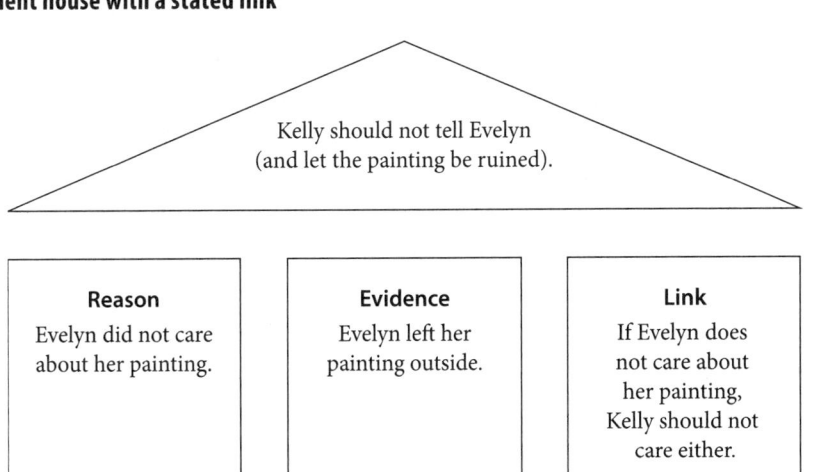

Consider again the discussion excerpt and figures 5.3 and 5.4: How was the teacher able to notice the missing link and find an effective way to prompt his students to recognize their assumptions? Although it is not evident from the excerpt, the teacher was carefully listening to students' arguments and engaging in the practice of Tracking the line of inquiry included in the ART. The video of this discussion shows the teacher quickly jotting down students' key ideas on a piece of paper. Working in real-time, the teacher was categorizing students' ideas into parts of an argument (i.e., position, reason, evidence, challenge, response to challenge) to get a sense of which parts were present, which were missing, and how they connected (or did not connect) to each other. The teacher also relied on his students to help with tracking by often asking them to clarify and summarize. Tracking the line inquiry is a complex skill, but you don't need to wait to perfect it before having your first discussion. As with any other skill, like dancing or cooking, you learn it by doing, with every discussion offering yet another opportunity to practice.

PLANNING WHAT TO DO BEFORE AND AFTER THE DISCUSSION

Here we discuss how to use the Discussion Planning Tool in figure 5.1 to plan for pre- and post-discussion activities. Turning to the pre-discussion section, we need to first determine how the students will read the story. Because "What Should Kelly Do?" is a short and simple text, independent reading just once should work for most students. Of course, you should always use your judgment to determine what, if any, supports and accommodations your students need.

When you are planning pre-discussion activities, the key principle to remember is to keep it simple. We want to encourage students to engage with the story, but we don't want them to think about it so much that they are tired of it. We want to pique their interest just enough so that they are eager to come to the discussion ready to think deeply about it. In the case of "What Should Kelly Do?," we recommend fairly straightforward activities, since the story is short and it does not place heavy demands on most students' prior knowledge. For example, having a one-minute pre-discussion with a peer, as illustrated in the transcript earlier in this chapter and in figure 5.1, can be sufficient to energize students for the upcoming discussion. Also, since the big question is already given in the title, you could have students choose a position and underline one or two sentences in the story that they can use to support it. Alternatively, students might illustrate their favorite part or draw a painting they would submit to the art contest described in the story. Remember, pre-discussion activities do not always have to relate to the big question; the goal is simply to help students build cognitive and affective connections to the text.

Regarding post-discussion activities, the main idea is to promote the transfer of argument skills practiced during inquiry dialogue to individual engagement in argumentation through listening, reading, speaking, or writing. The key principle to keep in mind with post-discussion activities is that "it is all about argument." The story about Kelly's dilemma ends abruptly, providing a perfect opportunity for students to finish it by writing an argument about Kelly's decision. For example, students can complete the following prompt: "Suddenly, things became clear to Kelly. 'I know exactly what I should do and why,' she thought to herself, 'I should . . .'"

You can further explain the task to students by using the following prompts:

- Remember to clearly state Kelly's position and support it with reasons and evidence.
- Remember also to think about how other people might disagree with Kelly and how she would respond to them.

If you don't have enough time for this activity, students could instead draw argument houses using the handout included in appendix E. If you wish, you can grade both of these post-discussion activities using some or all of the criteria from the scoring rubric presented in appendix F.

Appendix (Chapter 5)

What Should Kelly Do?[1]

"It's beautiful, whether you win first place or not."

That's what Mother said when Kelly showed her the painting she'd done for the school art contest. But Mother put it differently to Aunt Lois. "She really has talent, Lois," Kelly heard her say on the phone. "I'll certainly be disappointed if she doesn't win first prize."

Kelly would be disappointed herself, in a way. She was almost the best artist in the whole school. Almost. Of course, there was always Evelyn Fields.

When Evelyn felt like painting, she could turn out pictures that looked good enough to be on magazine covers, but she only painted when and what she wanted to. She had said over and over again that she couldn't care less about prizes and contests and rules.

The art teacher certainly cared about rules, though. "Last year," she said, "I spent half my time reminding students of the deadline and rounding up paintings on time. This year each person is responsible for his own painting. Anyone whose picture isn't in the office by nine-thirty Friday morning is out of luck."

On the day of the contest, Kelly, with her painting carefully wrapped in brown paper, waited on the school steps for the bell to ring. Evelyn arrived, propped a picture against the side of the school, and hurried over to the swings.

Kelly looked at Evelyn's picture. Evelyn certainly must have felt like painting this time, for the picture was the best she'd ever done—horses on the desert, and a fiery sun in the background casting a red glow over the entire landscape. Evelyn was sure to win first prize whether she wanted to or not.

Kelly could hardly hold back the tears. When the bell rang, she turned her picture in at the office and went to the fifth-grade room. The teacher assigned some arithmetic examples. Kelly broke her pencil on the first one, so she went to the sharpener by the window. As she was grinding away, some drops splattered against the glass. Kelly looked out and saw that it was raining. She saw something else, too.

There, right where Evelyn had left it, was the splendid horse picture. In five minutes, it would be too late for Evelyn to enter her picture in the contest, and Kelly would probably win. Kelly looked quickly at Evelyn, but the other girl was hard at work on a problem.

Well, she's got to learn to take care of her own things, Kelly told herself. The teacher said we were each responsible for our own painting, so Evelyn's responsible for hers. That's the rule. It's her tough luck if she doesn't win first prize.

But that wasn't the only problem. A few more minutes in the rain and the painting would be ruined. That would hurt Evelyn a lot more than losing the contest.

Kelly went back to her seat with her heart pounding. What should she do?

CHAPTER 6

Discussing "Ovatniah"

"Ovatniah" is a short story about a teenage girl, Marie, who lives with her mother in Seattle. This story was written by Roland Smith and published by Scholastic Storyworks in January 2014. We hope you can obtain and read the story before proceeding with this chapter. Briefly, the story is about a girl who has grown up removed from the traditions of her Alaskan ancestors; Ovatniah is her Eskimo name. During one summer, Marie's mother takes her to visit a remote village in Alaska, where Marie's grandmother lives. Marie's grandmother is a traditional ivory carver who specializes in carving old ivory from tusks preserved in the ice. At first, Marie does not seem to be interested in her ancestral culture, but she slowly connects with the traditions and values. She agrees to learn how to carve if her grandmother learns to play chess. As Marie learns to carve, she finds out about her culture from her grandmother, and her grandmother shows Marie a secret cave where the ivory is buried. Marie's mother, who has not shown any interest in the ancient traditions, wants to find out where the ivory is hidden so she can sell it to pay for her daughter's education. At the end of the story, Marie is confronted with the dilemma of whether to tell her mother where the ivory is buried: Marie and her grandmother are playing chess when Marie's mother walks in and notices Marie has been carving; her grandmother looks up at Marie and says, cryptically, "I believe it's your move, Ovatniah."

This story is ideal for helping promote inquiry dialogue. Marie is faced with a dilemma—a choice to be made—that invites students to weigh various values such as tradition, heritage, education, loyalty, truth, responsibility, and obedience to authority. There is an element of ambiguity about what is happening between Ovatniah, her mother, and her grandmother. Marie's strong character resonates with many students because of her striving for identity and the demands placed on her by her mother and grandmother. Some of the vocabulary may be a little challenging for struggling readers in fifth grade, and some students may lack the background knowledge needed to understand the geographical setting, the heritage and traditions of Eskimos, and the threats to their way of life. Other resources are readily available to help students build the necessary background knowledge, and the text can easily be integrated into a social studies unit on Native Americans.

PLANNING THE DISCUSSION

We begin by writing the title of the text and the grouping arrangement we will use. In this discussion, we plan to use a fishbowl with half of the class forming the inner circle, the fishbowl, and the other half forming the outer circle. The students in the inner circle will discuss the text, and those on the outside will be assigned the task of noting what is happening in the discussion. In this case, each student on the outside will be taking notes on the clarity of the discussion ("Do we understand what is being said and how it all fits together?") using the *Clarity* criterion in ART for Kids (see appendix C for details). The fishbowl arrangement is useful in the early stages of conducting discussions for developing the norms for inquiry dialogue or if you want to work with a smaller group but still involve all the students at the same time.

We begin planning with the launch in the middle section of the Discussion Planning Tool (see Figure 6.1).

We remind students of the general purpose of the discussion: to find the most reasonable or best answer to the big question. In this case, we use the phrase "best answer" but remind students what that means using the metaphor of a house: "our job is to reason together to find the best answer, and that means the one that makes the strongest possible house we can build." Next, we revisit the ground rules posted on an anchor chart at the front of the room. We have listed the same four rules as seen previously but also include the rule "We do not need to raise hands" to encourage a more open participation structure. For the specific focus of the discussion, we decide that students need to work on being clear in the language and structure of their arguments. This is the *Clarity* criterion for good argumentation listed in the ART. This focus is also reinforced by the use of the fishbowl in which students in the outer circles are asked to take notes on clarity.

FIGURE 6.1

Discussion Planning Tool for "Ovatniah"

Text: "Ovatniah"

Grouping: Fishbowl

PRE-DISCUSSION	DISCUSSION	POST-DISCUSSION
Reading: Read-aloud and buddy reading *Engaging with text:* Ask students to highlight words or phrases and then write comments or questions where they would like to "talk back to the text." Share with a partner. *or* Ask students to write eight words that best describe Marie's character. Then share the words with a partner to decide on two or three that best describe her. *or* Ask a student to take the role of Marie in the "hot seat." Other students pose questions to learn more about her character.	**Launch** *General purpose:* To find the most reasonable answer to the big question. *Ground rules:* • We do not need to raise hands. • We connect our ideas to what others say. • We look at the speaker. • We support our positions with reasons and evidence. • We challenge each other's ideas. *Specific focus:* Being clear in what is being said in our discussion. *Big question:* Should Marie tell her mother where the ivory is hidden? **Inquiry dialogue** *Position:* Yes, tell the mother. We have to do what our parents tell us. Marie needs to go to a good school. Marie can still learn to carve. *Position:* No, do not tell the mother. Marie needs to continue the tradition. Tradition is more important than education. Her mother can sell the ivory that Marie carves. *Talk moves:* How is this similar to . . . ? Would this be the same as . . . ? {Name} just offered another reason for. . . . So, it seems that we are torn between the values of tradition and of getting a good education. If someone were to argue against you, what might they say? **Closure** Did we make good progress toward answering the question? How did we do on being clear?	*Writing:* Ask students to write a paragraph completing the story in the form of a dialogue between Ovatniah and her mother. The dialogue should embody Ovatniah's position and reasons, as well as possibly a challenge from her mother. *and/or* Students act out the dialogue between Ovatniah and her mother in which Ovatniah states her argument and her mother responds.

The story raises several possibilities for a big question: "Should Marie tell her mother where the ivory is hidden?" "What should Marie do?" "Should Marie stay with her grandmother?" "Is Marie better off staying in Twin Rivers than returning to Seattle?" "Whose wishes should Marie honor?" "Is it ever okay to disobey your parents?" All these questions are contestable, authentic, and clear; they touch on issues of central importance to the story. Notice how these questions relate to the core themes such as the value of traditions in a modern world, identity, parent-child relationships, secrecy, trust, responsibility, obedience to authority, change, and loyalty. However, the questions "Should Marie tell her mother where the ivory is hidden?" and "What should Marie do?" will probably invite students to touch on more of these themes in the discussion than will the other questions. Notice, in particular, that the question "Is it ever okay to disobey your parents?" focuses on only a small set of themes (parent-child relationships, trust, responsibility, obedience to authority) and is worded in a general way that might not prompt students to use the text to support their positions. Also, the phrasing of the question, including the word *ever*, may be too categorical to result in genuine controversy. In the end, we decide to make "Should Marie tell her mother where the ivory is hidden?" the big question. As with "What Should Kelly Do?," it is a *should* question and is likely to invite students to think about the moral or ethical concerns surrounding Marie's dilemma.

The following introductory remarks come from a discussion a fifth-grade teacher had with her students about "Ovatniah." The students were seated in a fishbowl arrangement. The introduction was a little longer than usual because the focus was on clarity generally, and the teacher needed to remind students what this meant. She also needed to instruct students in the outer circle as to their task.

> **TEACHER:** Our goal, I want to remind you that we're not just sharing, our job is to reason together to find the best answer, and that means the one that makes the strongest possible house we can build. Remember our ground rules [pointing to the anchor chart at the front of the room]. Who would like read them? Nate?
>
> **NATE:** [reading from the chart] We do not need to raise hands. We connect our ideas to what others say. We look at the speaker. We support our positions with reasons and evidence. We challenge each other's ideas.
>
> **TEACHER:** Okay, thank you. Now one of the things we decided we need to work on is making sure we are clear in what is being said in our discussion. The

people in the outer circle today all have the sheet on *Clarity* [referring to the ART for Kids]. So I'm just going to read the questions out so the group in the middle knows also what we're looking for. We want to focus on these things. So when we're clear . . . *We explain our thinking clearly. We use words like* position, reason, evidence, *or* example *to explain what we mean.* So make sure you're telling us, "I disagree with her *example*" or "I have a different *position*" because it helps everyone track and follow things better. *We help each other clarify our ideas by asking follow-up questions.* So, if you're finding that you don't quite understand, it's good for you to ask a follow-up—you know, "Can you explain that more?" "What do you mean by . . . ?" *We connect what we are saying to what other people have said.* I think we're good as a group at that, so let's keep doing that. *We summarize what other people said.* So if you say, for example, "I agree with Alfredo when he said that the mother isn't being very kind." So, if you summarize just a little bit of what they said, then we know what you're connecting to. *We keep track of where we are in the discussion and where we're going.* Keep that in mind. How does what I'm going to talk about fit into the bigger discussion as a whole? Okay? [Talking to students in the outer circle] You're gonna watch for all these things for us and tell us whether we are doing a good job, okay. And I will try and keep track of things on my little paper here as well [referring to a blank sheet on her lap] . . . Our big question today is about Marie. Should Marie tell her mother where the ivory is hidden? . . . So, why don't you take thirty seconds to talk with your neighbor about some initial answers?
STUDENTS: [Students in inner circle talk in pairs for thirty seconds.]
TEACHER: Okay, start wrapping up. . . . Good. Who would like to start us off?

In the Inquiry dialogue section of the Discussion Planning Tool, it is useful to write down the positions students might take and possible reasons for and against each position. In the case of "Ovatniah," we expect that most of the reasons will revolve around value judgments that have to do with obeying one's parents and with the importance of tradition versus education in the modern world. It is also helpful to anticipate some of the talk moves you will use in the discussion. Because the focus of the discussion will be on clarity, we have listed some moves from the ART that foster clarity on figure 6.1. The group is quite good at connecting ideas, so we particularly want to focus on the other practices under clarity: clarifying meaning, labeling reasoning processes and parts of an argument, and tracking the line of inquiry. Because of the strong obligations many students feel toward their parents, we anticipate that students might all take the side that Marie should tell her mother. In preparation for this possibility, we might also be ready to ask: "If someone were to argue with you, what might they say?" or "Would this mean that Marie should be loyal only to her mother, and not to her grandmother, or even to herself?" These moves are useful to prompt students to consider an alternative perspective.

At the end of the discussion, during Closure, students should reflect on their progress, including both the processes and products of the discussion. In this example, the teacher uses the thumb gauge again to evaluate progress toward answering the big question, but she also takes this opportunity to point out a subtle assumption that students in the group were making. This assumption could be the target for discussion the next time the group meets.

> **TEACHER:** Let's think about the progress we made toward answering the big question. We can use our thumbs. Did we make good progress?
> [Students raise their hands to indicate progress.]
> **TEACHER:** It looks like most of you are saying . . . no or maybe? I agree. Let me take the floor for a bit. I think we're getting caught up in an assumption here. Everybody seems to be assuming that if Marie doesn't tell, then she gets to stay in Alaska. Is that a reasonable assumption here? We know that she wants to, right? The story says she's been thinking about it, right, she might want to. But is it safe to assume that Marie will be able to stay? . . . I think our thinking got bogged down by this assumption. So, when we pick up this discussion next time, one of the things we need to discuss is, is that a reasonable assumption? Is that true that she would be able to stay? Because if not, then we need to take our thinking in another direction. So, something to think about a little bit more next time.
> **ABBY:** Also, I think, I think we ignored some reasons. We talked about them, but I don't think we really thought about them much.
> **TEACHER:** I agree. That's something else we need to come back to.

As for evaluating the process, in line with the specific focus for this discussion, we need to allow plenty of time for students in the outer circle to evaluate how successful the group members were in being clear about what they were saying (the *Clarity* criterion).

> TEACHER: So, let's hear from our observers now. How did we do on being clear?
>
> ANDREW: I did number 5, *We summarize what other people said.* I gave you the lowest one.
>
> TEACHER: The big, frowny face? [referring to the scale on the ART for Kids sheet]
>
> ANDREW: Because only our teacher clarified what other people were saying. I feel like the kids should have clarified more what other people said.
>
> TEACHER: It's a good practice for all of us to get good at, right? Great.
>
> LISA: For number 2, *We use the words like* position, reason, evidence, *or* example *to explain what we mean*, I gave it the bad smiley face. Because, a lot of times, people said like, they stated a reason but they didn't, um, they didn't say their position so we had to like clarify it, and then, it's really confusing when people started going back and forth with reasons. I didn't . . . sometimes I got lost and couldn't tell what position they were on.
>
> TEACHER: So, would you want us to always first say "My position is . . ." or should we just say—
>
> LISA: [Interrupts] I think we didn't have *enough* of that because sometimes I got lost, not knowing what position people were on.
>
> TEACHER: Yeah, I agree. It was challenging, yeah.
>
> [Students in outer circle continue taking turns reporting on their ratings.]

ANALYZING AN EXCERPT OF DISCUSSION

In the excerpt shown in figure 6.2, we listen in on the same fifth-grade teacher and her students as they discuss "Ovatniah." Remember, the big question, which the teacher had written on the whiteboard, was "Should Marie tell her mother where the ivory is hidden?" We join the group mid-way during the discussion. As before, we suggest you read the entire transcript (column 2) before reading the commentary. Because the focus of the discussion was on clarity, look for the moves the teacher makes to help students be clear about what is being argued.

FIGURE 6.2

Excerpt of discussion of "Ovatniah" with commentary

SPEAKER (TURN)	TRANSCRIPT	COMMENTARY
Wendy (1)	I'd like to talk about what Jim said about how Marie's mother left at age 16. On page 22, the first paragraph says that the "Wasuli family had been ivory carvers for as long as anyone could remember, but the tradition had ended when Aanaq's only surviving child, Marie's mother, left Two Rivers at the age of 16." I think that Marie's mother is trying to make Marie mostly like her, and so that she wouldn't be like Aanaq. So that she'd be like her and be really successful, 'cause she wants to know where the ivory is so they'd both be successful in life. And she doesn't want her to stay there forever, probably, because she left at age 16, that probably means she didn't want to stay with Aanaq because she didn't want to carve; she didn't want to do that tradition, and I don't think she wants Marie to do it either.	*In turn 1, Wendy reads a sentence from the story and interprets that sentence to imply that Marie's mother did not care for her traditional way of life when she was young and, further, that she doesn't want Marie to follow the traditions either; she wants Marie to be like her. But Wendy also includes information suggesting that Marie's mother wants to know where the ivory is so that she and Marie can "be successful," presumably by selling the ivory. There are a lot of ideas and a lot of leaps of faith in Wendy's comments, and it is not quite clear how she wants to use this information.*
Teacher (2)	So connect this to the big question for me. What does that mean for the big question for you?	*Here, the teacher makes a clarifying move (ART practice 4, Clarifying meaning) to prompt Wendy to clarify how her ideas fit into the argument she is making.*
Wendy (3)	Marie shouldn't tell her Mom about the ivory because then her Mom will just use that for her and for her daughter.	*Wendy nicely states her position and supports it with a reason but doesn't quite make clear why it is bad for Marie's mother to use the ivory.*
Teacher (4)	And in a sense, are you telling me—I'm just wondering about this last piece—are you saying it's bad that Mom is trying to get Marie to be like her?	*The teacher realizes there is something missing and makes another move to clarify meaning (ART practice 4) using some of the ideas from Wendy's initial statement.*
Wendy (5)	I think it's bad because she should be who she wants to be. She shouldn't be what her mother wants her to be. She should be herself.	*Wendy finally clarifies why it would be bad for Marie's mother to use the ivory, making clear that Marie needs to forge her own identity.*

SPEAKER (TURN)	TRANSCRIPT	COMMENTARY
Teacher (6)	Okay.	
Helen (7)	I am going to bring up a point that was sort of talked about for a little bit of time, the point that she, Marie, has decided she doesn't really care about boarding school anymore. I disagree. I think kids have a tendency to just say stuff, and they don't really know what's going on in the background, and they don't know what's best for them yet. So, as a child, you want things that aren't the best for you. Maybe, for your birthday, you want like fifteen presents, and your parents only buy you five, and you're really disappointed, and you're angry at your parents, and then you just decide, "Wow, this is really, really not okay; this is not fair for me." But your parents are just doing what's best for you; they know what your life really means. So, I think that's the situation that Marie is in right now, because when it comes to your future and how you're gonna live and how you're gonna spend your life, a young girl who has her life ahead of her shouldn't be spending it like carving, at the age of, like in sixth grade. A girl in sixth grade shouldn't decide what she wants to do for the rest of her life, in a summer. I think everyone should really listen to their parents because their parents know what life is like in the real world, and their parents know what their child needs to live well in the future.	*Earlier in the discussion, the students had argued that Marie should not tell her mother where the ivory was hidden because she wanted to stay with Aanaq in Twin Rivers, quoting from the story that "She no longer cared about the boarding school in Seattle, or her friends back in Anchorage." Here, Helen challenges this reasoning. Helen argues that young children (at the age of Marie) are not capable of making informed decisions about their life and that they should be guided by their parents. In effect, she is saying that only parents know what is best for you. So, even though there is evidence from the text suggesting that Marie wants to stay and does not care about her life in Anchorage, Helen is arguing that Marie's wishes should not be taken into account when trying to decide whether or not she should tell her mother about the ivory.*
Teacher (8)	So, are you just saying that, in a sense you're saying . . . We gave the reason that she wants to stay; therefore, she shouldn't tell. You're saying that's not a good reason because our wants change when we're young, or our wants aren't always right?	*Here, the teacher revoices Helen's statement (ART practice 4) to make sure she understands what Helen said. Notice how the teacher phrases this as a question, giving Marie the space to accept or reject the teacher's interpretation.*

continued

SPEAKER (TURN)	TRANSCRIPT	COMMENTARY
Helen (9)	Yeah, and kids aren't exactly . . . they want things, but in the end, it's not the best idea.	
Teacher (10)	Okay.	
Helen (11)	And also, you can't live in the past; you need to focus on the future, 'cause for a young girl to be deciding that she wants to carve for the rest of her life, it's not the best idea. And her Mom probably has the right idea of doing something good with the money from the ivory.	*In turn 11, Helen adds another reason that Marie should tell her mother—because learning about the traditions of the past would not help Marie in her future.*
Teacher (12)	So it's not a good future for her?	*The teacher again revoices Helen's statement (ART practice 4) to clarify and distill Helen's contribution by focusing on its main idea: the negative implications for Marie's future.*
Helen (13)	Right.	*Helen confirms the teacher's interpretation.*
Nate (14)	I'd like to disagree with Helen because I know—	*Nate challenges Helen's argument although it is not yet clear what he is challenging.*
Teacher (15)	[Interrupts] About which part?	*The teacher prompts Nate to be specific about what part of Helen's argument he disagrees with (ART practice 6, Connecting ideas).*

SPEAKER (TURN)	TRANSCRIPT	COMMENTARY
Nate (16)	About what she said about your parents knowing what's right for you and you should go to the private school because you know what's going to happen in your life when it continues. I'd like to disagree with that point because kids want to have fun while they grow up, 'cause I don't wanna be, like, a kid who just studies and goes to a private school. I wanna have fun while I grow up. 'Cause you're not going to have this opportunity of having fun with your parents while they get older, and you become married. You're not going to have that time to share with them. And if you go to boarding school, you're gonna, like, miss 'em, you're not gonna have a good life, and you want to have fun and grow up with, like, friends and, like, an average kid; you want to be a nice kid and grow up, like I—	*Nate clarifies that he is challenging the assumption that only one's parents know what is best for you when you are young. He states that they may not understand the importance of having fun while young children are growing up. He makes an additional assumption that going to boarding school would not be fun. Notice that the teacher does not question this latter assumption.*
Winona (17)	[Interrupts] I would like to disagree with Nate's position because I agree with Helen—that your parents know what's best for you because they went through life and they know what it's like. And as Nate said that, like, they don't, and that's not true because they're your parents and they know how to raise you and, like, I mean, it's not like she's studying all the time, since she's in Alaska right now. If you were studying right now, you'd probably be at home with your books and stuff, but she's in Alaska with her grandmother carving ivory. So, I think that your parents do know what's best for you, but it's not like they want to keep you at home with no fun. [Students all talk at once.]	*Winona challenges Nate's idea and argues that parents do know what is best for their children. She also adds that Marie is in school and she is still having fun now, so doing what one's parents say does not exclude fun entirely. Notice how Winona readily connects her ideas (ART practice 6) with others in the group, by saying "I would like to disagree with Nate's position because I agree with Helen . . ." "as Nate said . . ."*

continued

SPEAKER (TURN)	TRANSCRIPT	COMMENTARY
Teacher (18)	Let's hold on one second. I just want to make sure that I'm clear, and maybe you can connect with me. What I hear we're doing is really just debating one of the reasons on the "don't tell" side, right? So we've said, we've said Marie should not tell because she's happy where she is now. And we're talking about this. And we're saying, well, it doesn't matter if she's necessarily happy because sometimes our parents know what's better than us, and our happiness is kind of fickle. And we're going back and forth about it, also saying that you should be able to be happy when you're young, I think, right? So part of this is just debating, I think, about this one reason and whether it's good, or whether we should ignore children's happiness as a good reason or not. So let's keep that in mind and make sure we connect to the big question as well. Because we're getting a bit lost. But I think that's what we've been doing.	*In turn 18, the teacher makes a tracking move (ART practice 7, Tracking the line of inquiry) to clarify where the group is in their argumentation and to clear up any confusion. The group seems to be working on the issue of whether Marie's happiness is a valid reason for deciding whether Marie should tell her mother where the ivory is hidden. The students are going back and forth on this and are not always connecting their reasons to their positions in response to the big question. The hope is that by the teacher's clarifying where the group is in the process of argumentation, the group will be able to make progress. Notice that the teacher uses words like* reason, side, *and* connect *(ART practice 5, Labeling reasoning moves and parts of an argument).*
Sian (19)	I disagree with Nate's position where he said that you have to have fun when you grow up. Because like Marie, if she thinks that boarding school is good, right for her, and if she thinks that's a way of her type of fun, then she should go. And you don't know if she's gonna be happy there or not, so we can't just make an assumption.	*Sian objects to Nate's argument, but she does this by challenging his assumption that going to boarding school would not be fun. The teacher could have challenged this same assumption earlier, but by waiting, she gave students the opportunity to come up with the challenge themselves. Note how Sian clearly labels her main objection: "We can't just make an assumption," showing meta-awareness of argumentation processes.*
Angela (20)	Kate, would you like to talk?	
Kate (21)	I agree with Sian, that um, because you don't know if they're going to be happy or not.	*Kate agrees with Sian's challenge saying that we cannot speculate as to whether Marie would be happy in boarding school.*

SPEAKER (TURN)	TRANSCRIPT	COMMENTARY
Gabe (22)	I want to talk about the reason if she's happy where she is. I think kids should be happy when they grow up, but I think what's more important than being happy is study, and getting smarter, and getting prepared for college, and for your life and your work. And I think it's more important to learn than to have fun.	*Gabe continues the line of thinking about Marie's happiness. He argues that education is more important than happiness (a value judgment), so Marie's happiness does not really count as a reason for not telling Marie's mother about the ivory.*
Teacher (23)	So you're challenging the fun part and saying an education is better?	*The teacher revoices Gabe's statement in terms of an explicit value judgment.*
	[Students all talking at once]	
Abby (24)	Kristin, would you like to talk? [opening her hand toward Kristin]	

In this excerpt, the teacher intervened often to ensure students were being clear about what they were saying and how they were contributing to the argument. She used a variety of talk moves to foster clarity. Notice that up until turn 18, the teacher intervened after almost every comment from students. After her tracking move (turn 18), however, she allowed the students to take more control of the discussion. It is interesting to note that, even after the teacher had summarized where the group was in their argumentation, the students were still interested in talking about Marie's happiness and whether it was important to think about it when deciding about the big question. Marie's happiness was an important issue for these students, and the teacher decided to let the inquiry follow their interests.

Another thing to notice is that many students offered long, elaborated explanations when articulating their ideas (see especially turns 1, 7, 16, 17). Students providing elaborated explanations of the reasoning behind their views is a feature of inquiry dialogue. Even though the teacher intervened often, she spoke less than students, did not dominate the discussion, and did not steer students toward a particular conclusion. Her strategically chosen questions were intended to advance the inquiry by asking students to clarify how their ideas connected with their positions and the ideas of other group members ("So connect this to the big question for me." "What does that mean for the big question for you?" "About which part?").

One other thing to notice is that two of the students (Angela and Abby in turns 20 and 24) asked students who had not spoken up until this point if they would like to contribute to the discussion ("Would you like to talk?"). Although not shown in this excerpt, earlier in the discussion the teacher paused to remind students to provide space for everyone to speak. As is evident in this excerpt, midway during the discussion, Angela and Abby took over the role of the teacher in managing turn taking. Inviting others to speak reflects respect for group members and is a hallmark of the community of inquiry we hope to build when engaging in inquiry dialogue (See Figure 1.1, "We make sure most of us are contributing most of the time" in "A community of inquiry").

PLANNING WHAT TO DO BEFORE AND AFTER THE DISCUSSION

Because "Ovatniah" might be a little challenging for readers, we suggest, even before the pre-discussion activities, beginning with a prereading activity to help build the background knowledge necessary for students to understand the story. For example, ask students what they know about Alaska, the Eskimos, and their culture. Show them where Alaska is located on a map and point out the Bering Strait and where the Yup'ik live in the southwestern part of Alaska, by the Bering Sea. Have them read a short informational text on twenty-first-century Eskimos, preferably one about the Yup'iks. You might want to connect the text to other material you have covered on Native Americans. You might also talk about students' own experiences learning from their parents or grandparents and of the importance of tradition, as well as its possible conflicts with the modern way of life.

For reading, we recommend students have at least two opportunities to be exposed to this story. Start with a read-aloud. As you read the story to the class, explain the meanings of the more challenging vocabulary in the story (e.g., ivory, mastodons, migrating). For the second reading, you could have the students pair up and engage in buddy reading so they can support each other.

You might consider several options for a pre-discussion activity. One option is "talk-to-the-text." In this strategy, as students read the story, they highlight words or phrases that make them wonder or pique their interest or remind them of things they know. The students then write comments or questions in the margins where they would like to talk back to the text. Next, they can work with a partner to share what they wrote.

Because Marie's character is so central to the story, another option is to ask students to write eight words that best describe her character. Then have students share the words with a partner to decide on the two or three words that best describe Marie. Yet another option is to use a process drama technique called hot seat. In this technique, you or one of the students takes on the role of Marie. Students then pose questions to "Marie" to learn more about her character (e.g., "Why do you want to go to boarding school?" "Have you changed as a person after being at Twin Rivers?"). "Marie" then would come up with plausible answers based on the information provided in the story. You may need to model this technique for students. Whatever you decide to do as a pre-discussion activity, remember to keep it simple. Students do not have to understand everything about the text before they come to the discussion; they need to know just enough to be able to the talk about it (and to want to!).

As with "What Should Kelly Do?," "Ovatniah" ends rather abruptly and on an ambiguous note. So you could use a similar post-discussion activity. Have students write a paragraph completing the story based on their position. The first sentence of each student's paragraph should embody Ovatniah's position statement (e.g., " I know you want to know where the ivory is, but I'm not going to tell you,' Ovatniah said to her mother"). In the rest of the paragraph, have students report the reasons Ovatniah gave to her mother. Remember, in a post-discussion activity, students have to be engaged in argumentation. They might even have the mother make a counterargument and have Ovatniah respond! Post-discussion activities are usually individual, but in the case of "Ovatniah," you could also have students act out the dialogue between Ovatniah and her mother (a speaking argument activity).

CHAPTER 7

Discussing "Hunting a Killer"

I n this chapter, we again examine how to support students' engagement in collaborative argumentation by discussing an entire lesson built around inquiry dialogue. This time, we use an informational text for the discussion. Research studies and policy documents, including the Common Core State Standards, advocate for the increased use of informational texts in elementary classrooms because these texts prepare students to become proficient readers of news articles, Internet-based sources, and content area materials.[1] Informational texts are particularly helpful for addressing the third criterion of quality argumentation: the *acceptability of reasons and evidence*. Because informational texts largely rely on verifiable facts, they offer multiple opportunities for students to use evidence to support their positions. Moreover, students can learn to critically examine text evidence by evaluating its quality, sources, and interpretations by peers during the discussions.

The informational text we use in this chapter is an article called "Hunting a Killer," written by Kristin Lews for the October 2012 *Scholastic Storyworks* series. We invite you to find this text and read it before continuing with this chapter. Briefly, it describes a real-life incident in which a hiker was found dead in Yellowstone National Park. The scientists and rangers had to decide whether the man was killed by a bear and under what circumstances. They conducted an autopsy and concluded that a female bear was guilty of killing the hiker. As a result, they decided to kill the bear. The rangers trapped the bear, killed her, and sent her cubs to spend the rest of their lives in captivity.

We prepare for the lesson by using the Discussion Planning Tool. We focus first on the inquiry dialogue and look closely at the launch, the big question, and the closure of the discussion. Next, we analyze an excerpt from the discussion of "Hunting a Killer," highlighting students' work with text evidence. We conclude with ideas for pre- and post-discussion activities.

PLANNING THE DISCUSSION

In figure 7.1, we begin by filling out the top portion of the Discussion Planning Tool with the name of the text and the choice of the grouping arrangement. For this discussion, we use a whole-class discussion. Compared to small groups, this type of grouping has an obvious advantage of having the teacher work with the entire class, thus making instruction more efficient. At the same time, such arrangement puts additional demands on the teacher, who now needs to follow and work with the arguments offered by many more students. To address this challenge, teachers sometimes enlist the help of one or two students whose task is to track and write the arguments offered by the group on the whiteboard for everyone to see. We come back to this strategy later in the chapter and illustrate its use in an actual classroom discussion of "Hunting a Killer."

For now, we turn to the middle section of the Discussion Planning Tool, the Discussion section. The general purpose of inquiry dialogue always stays the same: to find the most reasonable answer to the big question. We simply need to remind students of this purpose when we gather for the discussion. Next, we turn to the ground rules and reflect on whether we need to revise them. For example, after several discussions, students may no longer require a reminder to "support their positions with reasons and evidence" because this practice has become a habit of mind, or a regular pattern of behavior during the discussions. Alternatively, if we notice persistent problems with students interrupting each other, we may need to add a new ground rule: "Only one person speaks at a time." It is important that students continue to see ground rules as an active list of shared norms that enhance the quality of discussions. It is a good idea to periodically engage students in the review of the ground rules by asking questions such as "Are our discussions working? What problems have you observed recently? What can we do better?"

FIGURE 7.1

Discussion Planning Tool for "Hunting a Killer"

Text: "Hunting a Killer"

Grouping: Whole Class with Tracking Arguments on the Board

PRE-DISCUSSION	DISCUSSION	POST-DISCUSSION
Reading: Teacher read-aloud, followed by buddy reading *Engaging with text:* Students underline information that can help them decide about the fate of the bear. or Students use sticky notes to record their immediate reactions to the article.	**Launch** *General purpose:* To find the most reasonable answer to the big question. *Ground rules:* • Only one person speaks at a time. • We connect our ideas to what others say. • We look at the speaker. • We challenge each other's ideas. *Specific focus:* We use text evidence to justify our positions. *Big question:* Should the rangers have killed the bear? **Inquiry dialogue** *Position:* Yes, they should have killed the bear. The bear is guilty of killing a human. The bear may kill again. It might save other bears. *Position:* No, they should not have killed the bear. The bear only followed her instincts. We don't know if the hiker provoked the bear. People should assume the risks when they visit national parks. *Talk moves:* How do we know this? Is this true? Do we know this for a fact? Where is this information coming from? Is this a good source? **Closure** Students review the reasons and evidence listed on the board and identify statements that were challenged during the discussion.	*Speaking and listening:* Students conduct a mock trial of the bear. *Writing and reading:* Students pick a reason from the list on the whiteboard and write how to challenge it using available text evidence.

Next, we need to determine a specific focus for the discussion. Because informational texts offer additional opportunities to work with text evidence, our specific focus this time is to use evidence from text to justify positions. Note that when students refer to text during inquiry dialogue, they also get to practice questioning the quality of the evidence. For example, in "Hunting a Killer," the fact that the bear's "bloody paw prints" were found close to the body of a dead hiker is not, by itself, sufficient to conclude that the bear actually killed him: perhaps the hiker had died from something else. Later in the story, we learn that the scientists also conducted an autopsy on the hiker's body and decided that he died from being attacked by this bear. The later piece of evidence provides a stronger justification for concluding that the bear killed the hiker because it is based on a highly specialized medical procedure designed to determine the cause of death. By questioning and comparing evidence introduced by their peers, students learn to critically evaluate information based on its source, accuracy, relevance, and sufficiency. Needless to say, such skills are especially important in a contemporary world where fake information is often used to support unfounded conclusions and create divisions within societies.

Let's now turn to the big question. Remember that when you're trying to come up with a big question, one strategy is to think about major themes, concepts, controversies, conflicts, or tensions brought up in the text. You can also write down these themes in a form of "Theme A versus Theme B." For example, in the text "Hunting a Killer," some major themes are about animal rights versus human rights, instincts versus conscious decisions, protection versus destruction of nature, and intentions versus actions. Any of these themes can be developed into big questions. Here are some examples:

1. Is it fair for humans to kill animals?
2. Should animals have the same rights as humans?
3. Should animals have a right to their own territory?
4. Should the rangers have killed the bear?
5. Should we punish animals for following their instincts?
6. Should it matter why the bear killed the hiker?

Note that the preceding questions differ in terms of how general or specific they are. Questions 4 and 6 are more specific and more closely tied to the text. These questions are about the particular bear and the incident described in the story. The other questions are much broader, focusing on general rights and responsibilities of humans and animals. Both types of questions are suitable for inquiry dialogue, but each type is likely to elicit different argumentation practices from the students. More specific questions (4 and 6) are better suited for having students refer to "Hunting a Killer" and work with text evidence. On the other hand, the more general questions invite students to explore common assumptions about conflicts between humans and animals and use personal experiences and other sources of information to support their views. We recommend that teachers choose the big question depending on the specific focus for a given discussion.

Given our specific focus—the use of text evidence to justify a position—let's consider question 4: Should the rangers have killed the bear? Does this question meet the criteria for productive big questions? Is it contestable, authentic, central, and clear? For example, to test whether or not the question is *contestable*, we can try generating reasons for and against killing the bear. Examples of such reasons on both sides are listed in figure 7.1. Also, considering that our specific focus is on the use of text evidence, we can further examine the text of "Hunting a Killer" to see whether it affords the use of evidence on both sides of the issue. To do this, we can highlight sentences from the text that offer support for both "yes" and "no" positions. By thinking through possible answers to the big question and by examining the text, we will be better prepared to facilitate inquiry dialogue. In other words, it is helpful to reflect on relevant topics that are likely to be brought up during the discussion. In addition, it helps to revisit the ART criteria and practices that are relevant to the specific focus of the discussion. For our focus, we turn to ART Criterion 3, *Acceptability of reasons and evidence*, as well as facilitation practice 8 and related talk moves (see figure 7.1 and appendix A for details).

At the beginning of this chapter, we mentioned that teachers often ask their students for help with tracking arguments offered by the group. Let's visit a fifth-grade classroom in which a teacher uses this strategy when discussing "Hunting a Killer" with her students. As shown in figure 7.2, the teacher divided the whiteboard into three sections, representing common positions that often come up during inquiry dialogue.

Next, she explained the tracking strategy to her students:

So we are going to talk about whether they should have killed the bear like they did. The class is going to have a meaningful discussion about whether they should or

FIGURE 7.2

Tracking arguments for "Hunting a Killer"

Should the rangers have killed the bear?		
Yes	It Depends	No

shouldn't have. [The teacher points to the whiteboard.] We will be coming up with a "yes" position, with reasons and evidence for it, maybe "it depends," and a "no" position, with reasons and evidence. [The teacher turns to two students standing by the whiteboard.] And you are our trackers; you will be tracking our reasons and evidence. And at any point, when you don't understand what you've heard, you can jump in. Okay? Also, if you don't know what to write on the board because it's complicated or it's long, and you need help summarizing, making it shorter, also jump in and we will work on it together. Okay? [The teacher turns back to the class.] And we, all of us here, we want to keep looking at the board because, remember, in order to come up with the most reasonable answer, the best possible answer to this question, we have to figure out which of our reasons are strong and which ones we can challenge and make weaker. So we will work with the reasons and evidence that are up on the board, as well as add new statements to the board. Any questions?

This teacher's explanation demonstrates an effective way of applying key principles of engaging students in inquiry dialogue. First, the teacher gives greater control over the discussion to her students by sharing her responsibilities for tracking the group's arguments with them. She also engages students in a meta-level reflection about arguments and argumentation processes by having the two trackers classify the statements of their peers into different parts of an argument and by inviting the trackers to jump in and ask the group to explain more whenever they are confused about the statements offered by their classmates.

At several points during the discussion, as well as during Closure, the teacher used the tracking of arguments on the whiteboard to help her students evaluate their progress in finding the most reasonable answer to the big question. Here is what this teacher told her students during Closure:

> We are running out of time, so I'd like us to wrap up the discussion by taking a few minutes to look at the board. And I'd like everyone to look at all of the reasons and evidence we have on both sides and circle only the statements on the board that we challenged today. So this way we can see which statements are stronger, which are weaker, and which we maybe overlooked today. So, turn and talk to your peer for two minutes. Go through all the statements for each position and identify those that somebody challenged either with text evidence or based on the assumptions we were making. We are going to take two minutes on this. . . . [Students work in pairs for about two minutes.] So who would like to start? Do you want to pick out a reason that you have heard a challenge to during the discussion? [Several students raise their hands.]

This closure activity, which lasted for a total of eight minutes, provides students with opportunities to assess the progress made by the group and enables them to see inquiry as a process that advances forward to the most reasonable answer, even if it does not reach it in a given discussion.[2] By examining the summary of multiple reasons and evidence presented for each position, students can appreciate the breadth of ideas developed by the group during the discussion. The activity also alerts students to the importance of challenging each other's ideas in their search for the most reasonable answer. As students discuss stronger and weaker reasons and evidence, they can see that not all statements offered in support of either position are equally acceptable and that some statements would need to be eliminated because they did not withstand the challenges offered by the group.

ANALYZING AN EXCERPT OF DISCUSSION

In this section, we continue to follow the same fifth-grade teacher and her students as they discuss "Hunting a Killer." This time, we look at the middle part of the discussion, shown in figure 7.3. The first column in figure 7.3 includes the name of the speaker along with the corresponding turn number, the second column presents a transcript of the discussion, and the third column shows our commentary. As before, we suggest you read the entire transcript (column 2) before reading our commentary.

FIGURE 7.3

Excerpt of discussion of "Hunting a Killer" with commentary

SPEAKER (TURN)	TRANSCRIPT	COMMENTARY
Erica (1)	I think they should not have killed the bear because the bear was just trying to protect her cubs. And even if she weren't, it's still not right because . . . think about how many times we killed animals. Many people kill animals for their everyday lives because we eat animals. And think about how many times animals have killed people. It's way less. We kill many more animals. So it's not right that we are killing so much because that could impact the species because they can become extinct, or something like that. And it's just not right that we are killing so many animals that are innocent. Especially this bear because she was just trying to protect her cubs. She wasn't trying to hurt people. So it's not fair.	*In turn 1, Erica builds an elaborate argument for not killing the bear, using reasons and evidence from multiple sources. One of Erica's key points is about the motives of the bear. She explains that the bear "was just trying to protect her cubs. She wasn't trying to hurt people." In fact, the story contains no clear evidence about why the bear had attacked the hiker. In a more traditional classroom, it would be the responsibility of the teacher to question and correct Erica's misinterpretation. In contrast, during inquiry dialogue, the teacher first relies on her students to notice and challenge any problems with Erica's use of story evidence. In other words, the teacher does not intervene right away, giving her students an opportunity to work things out by themselves. It turns out that the teacher does not have to wait too long: in the very next turn, Lavina challenges Erica's interpretation, suggesting that the bear was "probably looking for a meal."*

SPEAKER (TURN)	TRANSCRIPT	COMMENTARY
Lavina (2)	I want to say the bear was not trying to protect her cubs. If it was, then the bear would not have been executed. It was probably looking for a meal, or something. And, say, a human kills another human. Most of the times, the human does not get executed. The human will probably go to prison. And the same thing should be done to a bear. If a bear kills a human, it does not make it right to kill the bear. They should just keep her, maybe, in a zoo, so she is away from people.	*In addition to disagreeing with Erica's interpretation of the bear's motives, Lavina offers a new reason for not killing the bear: since we don't typically kill people for committing a murder, we should also not kill this bear. During turns 3 through 10, the teacher asks Lavina to clarify her position and reasons, helps the group to follow Lavina's argument, and assists trackers with recording it on the board. Note that during this exchange the teacher checks back with Lavina two times (turns 7 and 9) to confirm that her ideas are accurately restated and captured on the board. These efforts by the teacher signal to all students in the group that their thinking is valued and that the teacher does not have a predetermined right answer in mind. Instead, the teacher is truly interested in what her students have to say about the big question and ready to work with their ideas.*
Teacher (3)	Okay, hold on. What's your position?	
Lavina (4)	I think it's not right for them to kill the bear.	
Teacher (5)	And you gave us a new reason. Which was . . . [The teacher turns to the whiteboard to address the two students who are tracking arguments on the board.] How are you doing on the new reason?	
Josh/ tracker (6)	Ummm . . . That she was not protecting the cubs?	
Teacher (7)	[to Lavina] Was that your reason?	
Lavina (8)	Well, no. . . . It's if a human kills another human, a human does not get killed.	

continued

SPEAKER (TURN)	TRANSCRIPT	COMMENTARY
Teacher (9)	So, we would not treat humans that way. Or, we don't kill people. [Josh is writing Lavina's reason on the board.] [The teacher turns to Lavina.] Right?	
Lavina (10)	Yes.	
Teacher (11)	And you are disagreeing with Erica's . . . reason?	*In turns 11 through 15, the teacher works closely with Lavina on the ART criterion 2, Clarity. She uses several facilitation practices from the ART, including Connecting ideas and Labeling reasoning processes and parts of an argument. As a result, Lavina figures out that she and Erica agree only on the position (i.e., the rangers should not have killed the bear). They disagree on the fact that the bear was protecting her cubs. This exchange allows Lavina and others in the group to develop an ear for the argument structure and to practice distinguishing between argument parts, such as positions and evidence. With the help of the teacher (i.e., "But you still agree with Erica's position?"), the students also engage in locating their own ideas in relation to the ideas of others.*
Lavina (12)	Her fact.	
Teacher (13)	Her fact. Okay. But you still agree with Erica's position?	
Lavina (14)	Yes.	

SPEAKER (TURN)	TRANSCRIPT	COMMENTARY
Teacher (15)	So we have some disagreement about the evidence from the text. So maybe we need to look at the text together. So let's look at our article. We have Erica who thinks that the bear was just trying to protect her cubs, and Lavina is saying that she wasn't. So is there anything in the text that tells us why the bear did what it did? [Several students raise hands.] So, just read from it, whoever wants to.	*In turn 15, the teacher makes a call to draw students' attention to the "disagreement about the evidence from the text." She invites the group to closely study the text in an effort to better understand the motives of the bear.*
Li (16)	It says . . . "As the days went by . . ."	*In the next several turns (16 through 24), students work together on finding and evaluating text evidence (ART Criterion 3, Acceptability of reasons and evidence). For example, in turn 18, Li cites the results of an autopsy that link the bear to the dead hiker. However, as pointed out by the teacher (turn 19), the autopsy results do not help us better understand the intentions of the bear: was she trying to protect her cubs, or did she attack the victim in order to eat him?*
Teacher (17)	Where are you? Can you point it out?	
Li (18)	Underneath, like, "The Inves-tigation Heats Up." The second paragraph. It's on page 7. . . . It said that, "an autopsy showed that the hiker had indeed died from bear-inflicted wounds." That kind of shows that the bear was hurting the human and killed the human.	

continued

SPEAKER (TURN)	TRANSCRIPT	COMMENTARY
Teacher (19)	So we know that the bear inflicted wounds on the human and killed the human. But we have disagreement about whether she did that because she was trying to protect her cubs or not. Is there any evidence in the text that tells us why the bear did what it did?	
Mark (20)	It did what it did, it says it on page 8. . . .	*In his turns 20 and 22, Mark offers another piece of evidence from page 8 ("i.e., she smelled something too good to resist: meat") to support the idea that the bear attacked the hiker in order to eat him. Another student, Sam, immediately detects a problem with Mark's use of evidence: the description on page 8 refers to a different episode that happened* after *the hiker had been killed.*
Teacher (21)	Page 8, everybody turn to page 8.	
Mark (22)	Under the "Verdict." "At the end of September the Wapiti Sow was leading her cubs along the Yellowstone River when she smelled something too good to resist: meat." So she was not protecting her cubs; she killed him because she was hungry.	
Sam (23)	I'd like to disagree with you on that. Because it was just the bison meat to trap her. They already knew that she was guilty.	*In turn 23, Sam challenges Mark's use of evidence, saying that it is not related to the killing of the hiker.*
Teacher (24)	So, the bear was attracted to the meat after she killed, right?	
Mark (25)	But if this happened here, it could have been the same the other time.	

Overall, this discussion about the motives of the bear illustrates many features of inquiry dialogue that support students' working with texts in the context of an authentic and meaningful task—deciding on the most reasonable and humane way of treating an animal. For instance, students carefully select parts of the text to read to the group not because they would be graded on doing so, but because they are trying to use textual evidence to support their position. This focus on searching for the most reasonable answer to a contestable question changes the activity from being a mindless and formulaic school task to authentic and goal-oriented work with the text.

The exchanges among Erica, Lavina, Mark, and Sam demonstrate well "the self-correcting principle" of a classroom community of inquiry, in which participants hold each other accountable for the quality of their arguments. When students misuse story evidence or engage in flawed reasoning, it is the responsibility of the entire group, not just the teacher, to critically examine and react to problematic statements made by their peers. In other words, the entire classroom community acts "as a safeguard against sloppy thinking. . . It is not that the group as a whole is incapable of making mistakes, nor that the majority opinion must rule, but that it is more likely that someone in a community will challenge what they deem to be unacceptable."[3]

Notice the discussion in figure 7.3 reveals a lot of confusion that students apparently had about the basic facts from this story. In a more traditional classroom, such confusion would likely go unnoticed or would be corrected solely by the teacher because students would not be given as much space to express what's on their minds. During inquiry dialogue, students address their confusion by engaging with each other's ideas, and as a result, they improve their comprehension of text.[3] Furthermore, they practice using effective reading and reasoning strategies, such as identifying, rereading, and questioning text evidence, to improve their understanding of the text.

The teacher in this excerpt speaks only about one-third of the time (229 words out of 655 total). Nevertheless, her involvement is ongoing throughout the discussion: she intervenes during eleven out of twenty-five turns. While giving greater control over talk to her students, the teacher in no way abandons her responsibility to insist on following the practices of quality argumentation. Until her students become fully independent in their ability to collaborate with each other, work with text evidence, and engage in rigorous argumentation, the teacher remains an important guide and a model of good thinking. Note that the teacher's comments during the discussion reveal not only her skills of facilitating a discussion but also her deep knowledge of the text "Hunting a Killer." While the students can and should work out their misconceptions about the texts during the discussion, the teacher needs to be one step ahead: well prepared to intervene and probe into *acceptability of reasons and evidence* whenever the students fail to engage in critical discussion of their readings.

PLANNING WHAT TO DO BEFORE AND AFTER THE DISCUSSION

"Hunting a Killer" might be a challenging article for some students to read because it is rich in detail and contains some advanced vocabulary (e.g., extinction, autopsy, carcass). For the reading, we suggest a teacher read-aloud followed by buddy reading, in which less and more fluent readers are paired to read the article aloud to each other.

For pre- and post-discussion activities, we can start by revisiting the specific focus for this discussion. Considering our focus on the use of text evidence, one pre-discussion activity could be to ask students to underline information in "Hunting a Killer" that would help them decide about the fate of the bear. For example, a sentence on page 7, which says that "an autopsy showed that the hiker had indeed died from bear-inflicted wounds," could be used to argue that the bear should have been killed. On the other hand, another quote from page 7, which states that "over the past 100 years, as humans have built more towns and highways, bear habitats have shrunk to 2 percent of the size they once were," could be used to argue that the bear should not have been killed. Note that the goal of pre-discussion activities—to encourage students' cognitive and affective engagement with text—can also be promoted by tasks that tap into students' personal connections to the story. For example, students can use sticky notes to record their immediate reactions to the article, especially since this text contains some disturbing details.

During post-discussion activities, the goal is to engage students in working with the arguments constructed during the discussion. One simple idea could be to have students respond to the list of reasons and evidence generated on the whiteboard with the help of the two trackers. For example, students can pick a reason from the list and write about a way to challenge it using available text evidence. Students can also respond to the list by noting the kind of information they would need to have to evaluate the acceptability of a given statement from the list. Also, if time permits, another activity could be to turn the classroom into a courtroom and hold a mock trial of the bear. Students can choose to play different roles, including the judge, the members of prosecution and defense teams, the jury, and even the witnesses. During the mock trial, students can present, listen to, and respond to arguments about the guilt or innocence of the bear to further sharpen their argument literacy skills.

CHAPTER 8

Discussing a Text Set About Sugary Drinks

In this chapter, we describe planning and conducting a discussion using a multi-modal text set: two informational articles and a video clip. Informational texts about controversial issues are ideal for promoting inquiry dialogue if they include rich detail and invite multiple interpretations. However, many nonfiction texts lack supporting information and offer justification for only one side of an issue or, at best, two sides as in a debate. Using a text set—two or more texts on a single topic—is a way of getting around this problem. Text sets encourage students to explore multiple perspectives and provide a rich source of text evidence. Students also have to consider the credibility of the different sources. Working with multiple texts aligns with the Common Core State Standards.[1] Comparing and contrasting information from two or more texts and then integrating and evaluating that information are important requirements of the Common Core. Making sense of information in diverse formats and media is also an important requirement.

The texts we feature in this chapter are all on the topic of sugary drinks. "So Long, Supersizes?" is the cover story written by Natalie Smith for the October 2012 *Scholastic News* magazine. The story is about the ban in New York City, led by then-mayor Michael Bloomberg, on the sale of sugary drinks larger than sixteen ounces. It describes the contribution of consuming sugary drinks to obesity and other serious health problems in the United States. It also mentions the perspective of critics who were not in favor of the ban; notably, it cites the arguments that the ban takes away individual freedom and that education is a better way of encouraging people to pursue a healthier diet. "Big Drinks Are Back" is a March 13, 2013, *Time for Kids* news article by Alice Park. It reports on the State Supreme Court's ruling striking down the ban on the grounds that it would be ineffective; according to the ruling, people can consume sugary drinks in many other ways. The video, titled "Proposed Soda Tax Divides California Residents," is from a 2014 *CBS This Morning* report. It discusses a vote in two California cities on legislation to introduce a tax on sugary drinks. You can find this video on YouTube, using the link www.youtube.com /watch?v=RMfLxeVcUBc. Other video clips address the New York City ban (e.g., www.youtube.com/watch?v=24sJe9H29NE), but the CBS report introduces another way of curbing consumption besides a ban on super-sized drinks.

As a multimodal set, these texts are ideal for promoting inquiry dialogue. Because they are about a controversial issue, include rich detail, and invite multiple interpretations, they have a high dialogic quality. Most students in the later elementary grades are familiar enough with the basics of taxation and legislation to understand the issues, making the texts accessible for most of them. The consumption of sugary drinks is relevant to students' lives, and most will readily engage with the topic. Each source presents different viewpoints for and against limiting the sale of sugary drinks. These viewpoints are expressed by nutrition experts, government officials, residents, and retailers. When working with this text set, students have the opportunity to consider the credibility of the different sources. They are also invited to reflect on the appropriate roles of government and of education in managing our lives, and the importance of social responsibility versus individual freedom.

PLANNING THE DISCUSSION

Figure 8.1 shows the Discussion Planning Tool for the sugary drinks text set. We will discuss the texts with a small group of students. Small-group discussion is easier to manage than whole-class discussion, and it helps foster independence on the part of students. In small-group discussion, students have more opportunities to contribute and take ownership of the talk.

Our planning for the discussion begins with the middle section of the planning tool. We remind students of the *general purpose* of the discussion—to find the most reasonable answer to the big question—and we revisit the *ground rules*. After several weeks of discussion, the rules should have become second nature for students, but it

FIGURE 8.1

Discussion Planning Tool for sugary drinks text set

Text: "So Long, Super Sizes?," "Big Drinks Are Back," "Proposed Soda Tax Divides California Residents" (video)

Grouping: Small group

PRE-DISCUSSION	DISCUSSION	POST-DISCUSSION
Reading: Independent reading and/or buddy reading of articles, followed by viewing the video. Students should read the articles and view the video at least twice. *Engaging with text:* On the second reading of the articles and viewing of the video, ask students to record information from all three sources on a note-catcher. Students record information supporting and opposing the sale of sugary drinks. Students can highlight the relevant information in the articles before entering it into the note-catcher.	**Launch** *General purpose:* To find the most reasonable answer to the big question. *Ground rules:* • We do not need to raise hands; we wait for a space to talk. • We connect our ideas to what others say. • We look at the speaker. • We support our positions with reasons and evidence. • We challenge each other's ideas. *Specific focus:* Acceptability (Using well-examined and accurate reasons and evidence) and Logical validity (Building strong arguments) *Big question:* Should sugary drinks be banned? **Inquiry dialogue** *Position:* Yes, they should be banned. People's health is more important than allowing them to drink soda. Obesity affects all of us. Soda is a major source of the sugar in our diet. *Position:* No, they should be taxed instead. People should have the freedom to do what they like. Banning sugary drinks will not solve the obesity problem. *Position:* It depends on the size of the drink: only super-sized drinks should be banned. It still gives people the freedom to drink soda. It might help people make healthier decisions about their diet. *Talk moves:* Do we know this for sure? Is that a good source? Is this always true? Why is that relevant? What follows from that? How does this relate to the big question? **Closure** Did we make good progress toward answering the question? How did we do on Acceptability? How did we do on Logical validity?	*Writing:* Ask students to write a public service announcement that argues for (or against) the sale of sugary drinks in their school. *or* Ask students to write a letter to the mayor of their town stating their position on sugary drinks and supporting this position with reasons and evidence. *Speaking/Listening:* Ask students to deliver the public service announcement in front of the class. *or* Have students in small groups create their own news video clips about the controversy over sugary drinks. Students can interview others about their views on the issue.

is useful to reflect on them periodically to see whether any of them need to be reinforced or added to help manage the group and support rigorous argumentation. We anticipate students will be eager to discuss the topic of sugary drinks, but we don't want them to have to raise hands to speak, so it might be helpful to remind students to wait for a space in the discussion to talk.

For this discussion, we will make the *acceptability* and *logical validity* criteria of good argumentation the *specific focus* for the discussion. We want students to use acceptable reasons and evidence in support of their positions, and we want them to be logical in the way they connect their positions, reasons, and evidence. To that end, we need to help students examine their reasons and evidence and to recognize and evaluate the stated, as well as unstated, links to their positions. Articulating reasons for our positions is, of course, a foundation for examining whether the connections between reasons and positons are logical, so we will need to be mindful that students provide reasons for their positions.

At first glance, it would seem there are a number of possibilities for a big question: "Is a ban on super-sized drinks a good way to curb obesity?" "Should super-sized drinks be banned?" "What is the best way to help people limit their consumption of sugary drinks?" "Are taxes a good way to reduce peoples' consumption of sugary drinks?" "Should the government be able to control people's drinking of soda?" It is important to keep in mind that we want students to draw from all three sources when supporting their positions. Some of these questions are oriented toward the articles about the New York City ban, whereas some are oriented toward the video about taxing sugary drinks; but some might do both. The question "Should sugary drinks be banned?" is general enough to prompt multiple positions based on all three sources. Although the question does not mention the size of the drink or the proposal to impose a tax on the sale of sugary drinks, it leaves open the possibility of a middle position beyond the two-sided "Yes, sugary drinks should be banned" or "No, sugary drinks should not be banned." Informed by the sources, students might adopt other positions: "Only super-sized sugary drinks should be banned," "Sugary drinks should be taxed rather than banned." This big question prompts students to explore the role of education in curbing obesity, the tensions between individual rights and government regulation, and other major themes arising from the texts.

The following introductory remarks come from a discussion of the text set in a fifth-grade classroom. This small group had nine students.

TEACHER: Remember our ground rules [pointing to the anchor chart on the wall]. One thing I would like us all to remember today is that we need to leave space for everyone to talk. There is no need to raise hands, but we need to make sure we don't interrupt each other too much. If someone is talking, just wait until there is space for you to jump in.

NANCY: Okay. [Other students nod in agreement.]

TEACHER: Thank you. Today we are going to focus on the *Acceptability* and *Logical validity* parts that we talked about before, not the *Diversity of perspectives* or *Clarity* parts. It doesn't mean they're not important. I just think we are pretty good at those. Acceptability is about: Are we using good information? Are we using the text to support our views? And remember *Logical validity* is about our reasons. Are we using reasons that support our views? Are they relevant? Do our positions really follow, right? Do we have any questions about these? [Students shake their heads "no."]

TEACHER: Okay. Let me give you the big question. Our big question is on the board. *Should we ban sugary drinks? Should we ban them?* Remember, we want to choose the position that is strongest. Really, what we are trying to do is figure out what is the strongest position. We can think about, for example, which one has more reasons. That's one way to think about it. Or which position has the strongest reasons. That's another way to think about it. So, let's take thirty seconds. Talk with your neighbor about your initial thoughts. Should we ban sugary drinks?

STUDENTS: [Students talk in pairs for thirty seconds.]

TEACHER: All right, let's wrap it up in ten, nine, eight, seven, six, five, four, three, two, one. All right. Who wants to start us off?

The teacher used a slightly different wording to remind students of the general purpose of the discussion ("Remember, we want to choose the position that is strongest. Really, what we are trying to do is figure out what is the strongest position"), and she did so at the end of the launch rather than at the beginning. She also gave the students a couple of ways of thinking about what makes the strongest positon or answer.

In the Inquiry dialogue section of the Discussion Planning Tool, we write down the positions students might take and possible reasons for and against the positions. Students might agree or disagree outright with banning sugary drinks, or they might add a qualification to the "no" position stating that no, sugary drinks should not be banned but should be taxed instead. Students might also take the position that only super-sized drinks should be banned. This is a separate position with a separate set of reasons supporting it. We expect that most of the reasons offered will revolve around value judgments about the importance of personal freedom, the right of the government to dictate what people can do, and the merits of education versus legislation for changing people's behaviors. The focus of the discussion is on giving acceptable reasons and evidence and on building strong arguments by making sure the connections between positions, reasons, and evidence are logical. To help maintain this focus, we list talk moves taken from the ART that help promote the acceptability of facts and values and the logical validity of arguments.

Remember, at the end of the discussion, during Closure, students reflect on their progress, both the processes and products of the discussion. In this example, the teacher has the students use the thumb gauge to evaluate their progress. In line with the specific focus for this discussion, the teacher asked students how well they thought they did on *Acceptability* and *Logical validity* criteria.

> **TEACHER:** How did we do on Acceptability? Let's use our thumb gauge. [Students raise their hands, with most thumbs in the middle position.]
>
> **TEACHER:** It looks like most of you are saying we did just okay. Can you tell us why you think that? Joe?
>
> **JOE:** Mostly what we were doing was just bringing up more reasons and more reasons and more reasons, rather than like challenging our reasons. And I think we could have used the text more.
>
> **TEACHER:** I think, yeah, let me talk about challenging for a second. I think it's an important skill for us and one that we need to practice maybe a little bit more. So we can disagree, if I'm a "no" and you're a "yes," it means we disagree, but it means we disagree on our position. But part of what we want to do too is disagree about reasons. So I can say, "I'm also a 'yes,' so I agree with your position, but I want to challenge your reasons." So, let's say we're building our houses; we have the "yes" house, and the "yes" is the roof and the bricks are the reasons. We want to build strong houses. We want to make sure all of our reasons underneath that position are strong and solid. So sometimes we can test these reasons by challenging them. And it doesn't mean we have a different position; it just means "I don't know if that one reason is really strong

enough for us to include here." And the text helps us with that too because text evidence is one of those kinds of bricks. So it's a thing we need to work on because I felt we were giving reasons and evidence for our positions but weren't necessarily scrutinizing other people's reasons and evidence. I mean in some cases we did, but we could do better with that. So, I like your point, Joe.

TEACHER: What about the *Logical validity*? How did we do on that part? Let me see your thumbs?

[Students raise their hands, most with their thumbs up.]

TEACHER: Why did you say good, Simone?

SIMONE: I thought everyone explained why they agree or disagree, and I thought we gave good reasons. They always tied in with the position.

TEACHER: And what about the progress we made toward answering the big question. Use your thumbs again. Did we make good progress?

[Students raise their hands to indicate maybe.]

TEACHER: It looks like most of you are saying . . . maybe. Why do you think that, Nancy?

NANCY: I think we ended up talking a lot about whether we should have the freedom to drink what we want or whether the government should be able to tell us what to do so we don't harm ourselves. So I think that was okay progress. Although, we didn't really answer that.

TEACHER: I agree. Part of the tension, the real tension here, is freedom to do what you want versus doing harm, right? So, is there a limit? Should there ever be a limit to be able to do what you want? It's a tough thing to think about. So, we could pick up on that next time.

ANALYZING AN EXCERPT OF DISCUSSION

Let's listen in on the discussion about sugary drinks that the fifth-grade teacher had with her small group of students (see the excerpt in figure 8.2). The big question the teacher posed was "Should we ban sugary drinks?" As in previous chapters, we suggest you read the entire transcript (column 2) before reading the commentary. As mentioned, the teacher tried to focus the discussion on *acceptability of reasons and evidence* and the *logical validity* of the arguments, although you also will see moves that focus on clarity. We join the group about a third of the way through the discussion.

FIGURE 8.2

Excerpt of discussion of sugary drinks text set with commentary

SPEAKER (TURN)	TRANSCRIPT	COMMENTARY
William (1)	I have another reason why we shouldn't ban. I think that most people who drink sixty-four-ounce drinks are sharing the drinks. So four people might share a sixty-four-ounce drink. So if we ban, we might have to pay a lot more to drink.	*In turn 1, William introduces another reason for not banning super-sized sugary drinks: people will have to pay more money. And the reason they will have to pay more money is that they share them with others.*
Teacher (2)	Why would we have to pay more? Tell me a little bit more.	*The link between paying more and sharing is not clear, so the teacher prompts William to explain the link (ART practice 11, Evaluating inferences).*
William (3)	Because we have to buy more cups.	*William explains that to share a drink, they will have to buy more cups, so they will need to pay more.*
Teacher (4)	Buy more of them, like buy six ten-ounces or something, so it would cost more? Okay. And you're saying . . . I'm not sure if we're getting it from the text, but you're saying: In cases when people buy sixty-four-ounce drinks, it's because they're sharing them?	*The teacher revoices the link to make sure she understood it correctly (ART practice 4, Clarifying meaning). Notice how the teacher flags that William is only assuming that people buy sixty-four-ounce drinks to share. Further, she points out that the basis for his assumption is not clear ("I am not sure we are getting it from the text"). Although she might have contested the acceptability of William's reason, she chose simply to make it visible to give students the opportunity to contest it (ART practice 8, Evaluating facts).*
William (5)	I think most people are.	
Teacher (6)	Okay.	

SPEAKER (TURN)	TRANSCRIPT	COMMENTARY
Adrian (7)	I just did the math, and if you buy four sixteen-ounce drinks, that's the same as a sixty-four-ounce drink, and that's a lot!	*Adrian points out that a sixty-four-ounce drink is a lot, no matter how it is divided up.*
Joe (8)	If you buy sixty-four-ounce drinks, it's for movie theaters and sports arenas. And that will take awhile. You're not going to have a seven-ounce drink for two hours at a movie.	*Joe introduces another situation in which buying a sixty-four-ounce drink is appropriate: if it is consumed over a long period of time.*
Adrian (9)	I know, but it's still pretty big to have a sixty-four-ounce drink. And sixteen times four is sixty-four. It's pretty big. It depends if it's for just one person.	*Adrian reiterates that a sixty-four-ounce drink is still a lot, especially if one person consumes it.*
Teacher (10)	Joe, are you just giving another instance where we need sixty-four ounces, and it's in cases where we're going to be there a long time?	*The teacher returns to Joe's statement to clarify what he said (ART practice 4, Clarifying meaning) and to ask how being in the movie theater or sports arena relates to buying sixty-four ounce drinks (ART practice 11, Evaluating inferences).*
Joe (11)	Yeah, you're not just going to have, like, a seven-ounce drink. Plus, at movie theaters, I don't think everybody does this, but most people do, I think they share sixty-four-ounce drinks for like a family of four.	*Joe affirms the teacher's interpretation and reiterates the other situation in which buying a sixty-four-ounce drink is appropriate: if it is for sharing with others.*
Heather (12)	Usually, when people buy large drinks, they don't finish them because they're so big. So it would be better if they buy just a sixteen-ounce drink, then they could buy another one, and then it wouldn't be wasted.	*Heather argues that people tend not to drink all of a super-sized drink, so it would be better to buy them in smaller amounts to reduce waste. But it is not clear how this relates to the big question.*
Teacher (13)	So, we're going fast; I need help. Is that an argument for "should ban" or "should not ban"?	*The teacher asks Heather how her statement relates to whether sugary drinks should be banned (ART practice 11, Evaluating inferences).*
Heather (14)	Should.	*Heather indicates that her reasoning is in support of the position that sugary drinks should be banned.*

continued

SPEAKER (TURN)	TRANSCRIPT	COMMENTARY
Teacher (15)	So, it's should. And what's the new reason? Because we waste?	*The teacher attempts to make visible what is happening and calls attention to what Heather was adding to the argument (ART practice 6, Labeling reasoning and parts of an argument). Note how the teacher does it in a way that still gives Heather control over the discussion.*
Heather (16)	Yeah. Because we waste when we buy large drinks.	*Heather confirms the teacher's interpretation.*
Teacher (17)	Okay.	
Nancy (18)	I think I kind of agree with Joe and Adrian, even though it's two different sides. Like, if you buy a sixty-four-ounce drink, you might waste a lot of the drink. But I also get that when Joe said that you wouldn't have a seven-ounce drink for like two hours of a movie or something. I feel like it should be in between, like sixteen. Also, they said that they have thirty-two ounces, but that's also a lot, so I think it should be like in the middle, in between, if you're going to a movie or sports arenas and stuff.	*Nancy offers what seems to be a compromise between Joe and Adrian's positions, suggesting that a middle-sized drink would be appropriate in situations that might involve sharing or long periods of time.*
Teacher (19)	I'm trying to figure out how this relates to the big question. Because Adrian has said sixty-four ounces is just too much, in general. He thinks it's just way too much sugar. But I hear some other people saying, if I have sixty-four ounces over three hours, is that still too much? Because I feel like we're now saying if we have sixty-four ounces over three or four hours, it's not that big of a deal. But it's still the same amount of sugar. So, I'm wondering how that connects to our big question?	*In turn 19, the teacher clarifies where the group is by summarizing the arguments (ART practice 7, Tracking the line of inquiry). A major argument being proposed is that there should not be a ban on sugary drinks if the drink is consumed over a long period of time. But the unstated assumption seems to be that consuming sugar over a long period of time is okay. The teacher tries to prompt the students to evaluate the acceptability of that unstated inference (ART 11, Evaluating inferences).*

SPEAKER (TURN)	TRANSCRIPT	COMMENTARY
Adrian (20)	Even if you're drinking sixty-four ounces like, at a baseball game, and it's a four-hour game, and you're sitting there the whole game, it's still too much because it's not like you're burning off the calories. You're not burning off calories off of the sixty-four ounces.	*Adrian challenges the assumption that consuming sugar over a long period is okay. This shows the importance of revealing unstated assumptions (as the teacher did in turn 19) because it allows the students to see their weaknesses and challenge them.*
Amanda (21)	Maybe if they made a ban on drinks only for restaurants or for places where you're not watching something, that would be so much better.	*Amanda seems to continue to believe that consuming sugar over a long period is okay and that the ban should be imposed only in certain situations.*
Jenny (22)	I want to add on to that because that ban won't really stop people from getting more sugar because you could just get another drink and keep on getting them, so it's not really going to do much good for people who really want the sugary drinks. And they could just get another one. And soda and sugary drinks aren't the only things with sugar in them. There's so many things with sugar that would not be banned. It won't really affect people that much.	*In turn 22, Jenny challenges her peers who argue for banning sugary drinks by saying that the ban would be ineffective in reducing people's sugar consumption. She asserts that people can still consume sugary drinks and that there are other dietary sources of sugar.*
Sam (23)	I think it's supposed to be a step to, like, stop people from drinking, um, consuming sugar.	*Sam, who has been quiet up until this point in the discussion, responds to Jenny's challenge that a ban would be ineffective. In a barely audible voice, he introduces the new idea that a ban would be one step toward reducing people's consumption of sugar.*
Teacher (24)	Can you say that again?	*The teacher, recognizing the value of Sam's contribution, asks him to repeat what he said to make sure everyone heard it.*

continued

SPEAKER (TURN)	TRANSCRIPT	COMMENTARY
Sam (25)	It's a step forward to stop people from consuming sugar.	*Sam repeats his statement more clearly. Note that he has not explicitly stated his position; nor is it clear, logically, why one measure toward reducing sugar consumption is a good reason for banning sugary drinks.*
Teacher (26)	So even if it doesn't stop everybody, it's a good step forward, and that's a reason for doing it?	*The teacher tries to help Sam by making his inference explicit (ART practice 11, Evaluating inferences), saying in effect that even if the ban does not stop everyone, it will at least stop some people; therefore, the ban should be imposed.*
Sam (27)	[Nods head.]	
Simone (28)	I want to say if you want to have those drinks, and you don't care if you're obese or not, then you should just have it because America can't tell you to not have the drinks you want. And you should be able to have it because everyone is an individual, so you can make your own decisions if you want to have those drinks or not. And it's your choice if you want to be healthy and not have all that sugar and the calories.	*Simone brings up the issue of freedom of choice as a reason for not imposing a ban. She argues that everyone is an individual, and if you are an individual in the United States, then you should be able to exercise freedom of choice. Therefore, there should not be a ban. Note that she is quite clear about her reason and how the reason connects to her position.*
Teacher (29)	So, even if you want to do something harmful to yourself, it's your choice?	*The teacher revoices part of Simone's argument, focusing on the most controversial part, in an effort to invite other students to react (ART practice 4, Clarifying meaning).*
Simone (30)	Yeah.	

SPEAKER (TURN)	TRANSCRIPT	COMMENTARY
Angie (31)	I want to say something from the video. . . . Even if you know that it's not good for you and you drink it, like a sixty-four-ounce drink, then you can get obese and then you can get diabetes, and then you need more health care and the government has to pay for people to take care of people in the world.	*Angie challenges Simone's argument by saying that people's freedom of choice as to what they drink negatively affects others because the costs of health care for the sick would have to be borne by the government.*
Teacher (32)	So, it doesn't just hurt the person; it costs the health-care system money to take care of that?	*The teacher again revoices Angie's challenge (ART practice 4, Clarifying meaning).*
Angie (33)	Yeah.	
Joe (34)	I would like to add on to what you've all said. It's like smoking. It's your choice. You know it's bad, but no one's stopping you; it's your choice.	*Joe comes to the defense of Simone's argument that people should have freedom to choose what they do, making an analogy between drinking sugary drinks and smoking cigarettes (a connection made in the video).*
Heather (35)	I disagree that people should be able to make their own choice because, with this ban, you could realize a lot easier that you shouldn't drink so much because now you could get diabetes and heart disease, and you could get really, really bad diseases. And I think that this ban might help people realize that.	*Heather argues for a ban on sugary drinks, supporting her position by saying that the ban will help people realize the health problems caused by excessive consumption of them.*
Teacher (36)	Is there anything in the text that helps us? I thought I read something about people's under-standing or . . . Because I think what we just said was: If you *know,* right, if you're aware of the decision and the consequences, then you should be able to make the decision. But I thought the last point was that some people might not know the consequences and the ban will help them realize that. So, is there any information we have here? I thought I read it, but maybe it was in the video?	*The teacher seizes on this opportunity to emphasize the acceptability criterion of good argumentation by prompting students to examine if there is any evidence in one of the sources that would support Heather's argument (ART practice 8, Evaluating facts).*

continued

SPEAKER (TURN)	TRANSCRIPT	COMMENTARY
Heather (37)	Oh, it says here [pointing to the first paragraph on the last page of the article "So Long, Super Sizes?"]: "People are not aware of how many calories they can consume by drinking beverages," says Alicia Calvo. . . . Calvo says the ban 'is helping educate people regarding portion sizes.'"	*The students and the teacher search for any relevant information, and Heather identifies a statement from a nutrition expert, reported in one of the articles, that supports her argument.*
Teacher (38)	Okay. So we have at least some information that people might not know the consequences of what they're doing by drinking these drinks and that the ban might help people learn about the health problems.	*The teacher connects the evidence to the arguments being discussed, stating that we cannot assume everyone is aware of the health problems associated with the consumption of super-sized sugary drinks and that the ban would help bring the issue to people's awareness. This provides a strong challenge to the argument that people should be able to exercise their freedom of choice—if they are not aware of the health risks, then how can they make the choice that is right for them?*

This excerpt shows a wide-ranging discussion on the pros and cons of banning sugary drinks. Students drew on all three sources when advancing their arguments, and they shared a variety of perspectives on the issue: they considered the issue of individual rights versus government responsibility, the role of the ban in educating people about the health risks of consuming large amounts of sugary drinks, and the effectiveness of the ban. They also proposed all sorts of qualifications on the ban— only for certain sizes, only in certain locations, only under certain circumstances. Although it might seem the teacher intervened frequently, she shared responsibilities for the flow of the overall discussion with the students (we chose this excerpt to illustrate the teacher's moves). Students had a lot of control over turn taking and ensured everyone had a chance to contribute. In terms of having students take more ownership of the talk, this was a very good discussion.

Half of the teacher's moves were focused on *acceptability of reasons and evidence* and the logic of the connection between students' positions and their reasons and evidence. The remaining teacher moves were to ensure clarity in the language and structure of the arguments. When examining acceptability, the teacher did so with a light touch, choosing to bring a contestable reason to the forefront to see if students would question it (turn 4) and gently encouraging students to refer to one of the sources to see if it provided support for a student's reasoning (turn 36). She might have contested students' beliefs that most people buy super-sized drinks when they want to share with others, but she chose to wait to see if the students would question this reasoning; as it happened, they did not.

Similarly, when examining the logic of the connections between positons, reasons, and evidence, the teacher was careful not to do so in a way that would be too forceful or disruptive. The students readily provided reasons for their arguments (ART practice 10, Articulating reasons), but it was not always clear how they were connecting their reasons and positions. For the most part, the teacher simply prompted students for the link (turn 10), asked them to make clear which position their reason connected to (turn 13), or made the link visible in her comments (turn 26). Only in turn 19 did the teacher contest an assumption the students were making.

PLANNING WHAT TO DO BEFORE AND AFTER THE DISCUSSION

We recommend having students read the articles first and then watch the video. The two articles are accessible for fourth- and fifth-grade students, and most students should have no difficulty reading them. We also recommend having the students read the texts at least twice before the discussion.

When you are dealing with multiple texts, the challenge is for students to integrate information from the different sources. As a pre-discussion activity, we suggest students use a note-catcher, a graphic organizer with separate spaces (boxes or circles) to record details from the respective texts (including the video) so that students can keep track of the information. Figure 8.3 provides an example.

On the second reading of the articles, students record in each empty space in figure 8.3 the points they read that support and oppose the sale of sugary drinks. Another option to help students integrate information from the various sources is

FIGURE 8.3

Note-catcher for sugary drinks text set

	Yes! Sugary Drinks Should Be Banned	No! Sugary Drinks Should Not Be Banned
"So Long, Super Sizes?"		
"Big Drinks Are Back"		
"Proposed Soda Tax Divides California Residents" (video)		

for them to take notes on a Venn diagram with two (for use with the two articles) or three (for use with all sources) intersecting circles. Students could record information that is common across the sources in the space where the circles intersect and information unique to each in the separate areas.

We encourage you to show the video twice: the first time for students to develop an overall understanding of the issue of imposing a tax on sugary drinks and the second time for students to take notes on the note-catcher. When showing the video, you might wish to pause it periodically for short bursts of discussion to help students identify and record specific facts they have heard. Most students should have some familiarity with the concept of taxes, but if not, providing a brief explanation during or after the video should suffice. Remember to keep any discussion to a minimum at this point, just to clarify any misunderstandings; we want to reserve discussion of the controversy over sugary drinks for the inquiry dialogue.

Several options would provide a good post-discussion activity. Students could write a public service announcement that argues for or against the sale of sugary drinks in their school. They could even deliver the announcement in front of the class. Another possibility is for students to write a letter to the mayor of their own town or to their senator stating their position on sugary drinks and their reasons.

Yet another possibility is for students, working in small groups, to create their own news video clips about the controversy over sugary drinks. The news item would need to explain the controversy and the arguments for and against the ban or tax on the drinks. Students could interview their peers who act out the roles of nutrition specialists, shopkeepers, restaurant or movie theater owners, and members of the public, about their views on the issues. Remember, post-discussion activities are all about argument. Whatever activity you choose, it should encourage students to examine the positions on the issue and the reasons and evidence that can be used to support the positions.

PART THREE

Moving Forward

CHAPTER 9

Choosing a Text for Inquiry Dialogue

In theory, in the hands of an expert facilitator, it should be possible to engage students in inquiry dialogue with any text. In reality, however, at least for most of us, a well-chosen text provides useful support for this practice. In this chapter, we offer guidelines for choosing a text for engaging students in inquiry dialogue. We start by outlining three characteristics of text that help promote inquiry dialogue. We then illustrate these features using several texts. We also describe a number of other texts you might use. We stress that successfully implementing inquiry dialogue does not hinge on using prescribed texts. The texts we describe are just examples of the kinds of texts that help promote inquiry dialogue. Our goal is to illustrate the important features to keep in mind so that you can choose your own texts.

The following guidelines and examples are based on our experience working with teachers. Unfortunately, there is only a little theory and research to help guide the selection of texts. We encourage you to try different texts and reflect on why some work and others do not. In the final analysis, a good text is one that lends itself to asking a big, contestable question that invites multiple responses from students.

WHAT MAKES A GOOD TEXT FOR INQUIRY DIALOGUE?

A good text for inquiry dialogue has a dialogic quality, is accessible to students, and has the potential to engage their interests.

Dialogic

A good text for discussion has a dialogic quality. Here, we use the term *dialogic* in the sense described by Mikhail Bakhtin, a Russian literary theorist and philosopher who wrote about texts and language.[1] For Bakhtin, texts are "utterances" just like any other utterances in a chain of communication; they are responsive to what was said or written previously and anticipate what might be said or written in the future. What's more, he argues that each text contains traces of many "voices" engaging in dialogue with each other. Meaning, for Bakhtin, resides in the dynamic interplay among the multiple voices "when different perspectives are brought together in a way that allows them to 'inter-animate' or 'inter-illuminate' each other."[2]

Of course, any text can be treated dialogically, but some texts lend themselves to more dialogic treatment than others. A text that is high in dialogic quality functions as a thinking device in that it opens up a space for discussion and the negotiation of ideas and meanings.[3] It is rich in conceptual content and deals with issues that lend themselves to multiple interpretations, perspectives, explanations, or opinions. A text that is high in dialogic quality is thought provoking and invites several readings. It taps into our fundamental values and commitments, and addresses issues of certain complexity that are worth discussing, such as moral or ethical values (e.g., fairness), questions about the human condition (e.g., friendship, honesty, compassion), or policy decisions (e.g., school uniforms, the concussion crisis in sports, self-driving cars).

Texts that deal with potential dilemmas, questionable decisions, or ambiguities are ideal for inquiry dialogue. Indeed, there is research evidence to suggest that texts that display such qualities (what researchers call "grist"), when used in conjunction with other tasks, increase students' ability to construct cogent and persuasive arguments in their writing.[4] Dilemmas, questionable decisions, and ambiguities all support multiple points of view and provide opportunities for students to weigh up reasons and evidence and, ideally, formulate the best or most reasonable solution or interpretation.

Accessible

A good text for discussion is accessible. It is one for which students have sufficient background knowledge to understand the topic and issues addressed. Background knowledge is key if students are to comprehend a text.[5] To engage in discussion, students do not have to understand every aspect of the text—deeper understanding will develop during the dialogue. But the content should be familiar enough so that the text is generally accessible to students. Imagine asking fourth-grade students in Ohio to read a story about the lives of immigrant, itinerant farmworkers in California (we have tried this!). The topic might be familiar enough for students in parts of California, but students in the Midwest might be puzzled as to why the workers and their families were there and what they were doing!

In terms of text complexity, it is okay to use texts that are a little more demanding than your students are used to reading. The text should be accessible to students, but it does not have to be completely accessible. The Common Core State Standards call for using texts at different points along a scale of complexity and for using more complex texts when appropriate.[6] Using a text that is more challenging in terms of vocabulary, language structure, or cohesion may actually help stimulate thoughtful discussion. Having students discuss a complex text is also a good way of showing students how they can read and problem-solve a difficult text together.

Engaging

A good text for discussion should engage students' interests. A text is engaging when the students can identify with the characters portrayed and their life circumstances. The topic should be relevant and of concern to students. Imagine giving fifth-grade students a text about the introduction of a flying machine in ancient China and asking them to discuss the dilemma this posed for the emperor and his way of life (we have done this too!)—an interesting dilemma, but the time and setting are far removed from our students' lives. Why would students care about the emperor and what he thought? Of course, even ancient texts can be made ageless and engaging with effective pre-discussion activities, so it is important to consider the relevance of the text during the planning stages.

In the next two sections, we illustrate these guidelines by describing examples of nonfiction and fiction texts that provide strong support for inquiry dialogue. For the sake of familiarity, we start with the article "Hunting a Killer."

NONFICTION

Lewis, Kristin. "Hunting a Killer." *Scholastic Storyworks* (October 2012): 4–8.
This article describes a real-life incident in which a man was found dead in Yellow Stone National Park. Scientists had to decide whether the man was killed by a grizzly

bear and under what circumstances. They conducted an investigation and, under a system of "bear justice," concluded that a female bear was guilty of killing the man. As a result, the bear was put down, and her cubs were sent to spend the rest of their lives in captivity.

This article addresses issues of animal versus human rights, justice, freedom, and responsibility. Because of the rich content and the far-reaching consequences of the bear's and the scientists' actions, the question as to whether the mother bear deserved to be put down is open to multiple points of view. Therefore, the dialogic quality is high. In addition, there is considerable text evidence to help students make reasoned conclusions. Students typically have much background knowledge to bring to the text, and they readily engage with the issues.

Tarshis, Lauren. "Deadly Hits." *Scholastic Storyworks* (January 2012): 4–9.
This article addresses the issue of the concussion crisis in sports by relating the experience of thirteen-year-old Zackery Lystedt who played in a middle school football game. Zack experienced a concussion during the game but continued to play. He suffered a brain injury, collapsed on the field, and endured months of rehabilitation in the hospital. His experience led to the Lystedt Law and similar regulations to protect young players from sports injuries and lent support to the alleged connection between concussions and brain disease among National Football League (NFL) players.

This article raises issues of individual freedom, responsibility, adult-child relationships, and culture, among others. The question "Who was responsible for Zack's injury?" allows students to consider multiple positions, ranging from Zack, to his coach, to his parents, to the NFL, to the media and sports culture at large. As such, the dialogic quality of this article is high. Students come to this text with considerable background knowledge about sports and sports injuries from their own experiences and the media. They readily relate to Zack's plight and to other events and characters in the article.

To have high dialogic quality, nonfiction texts about controversial issues must include rich detail and invite multiple interpretations. "Hunting a Killer" and "Deadly Hits" are perfect in this way. Unfortunately, many other nonfiction texts lack supporting information and offer justification for only one side of an issue or, at best, two sides as in a debate. Using two or more texts on a single topic (a text set) can help enhance the dialogic quality of the readings used to support inquiry dialogue. Text sets encourage students to explore multiple perspectives and provide a rich source of text evidence. Students also have to consider the credibility of the different sources. In addition, text sets can be multimodal. For example, in the case of the article about the concussion crisis, you might identify other media sources on the issue of concussions (e.g., a podcast about the growing number of concussions in youth soccer or an NFL commercial celebrating the tough actions of football players).

FICTION

Whitebird, Mary. "Ta-Na-E-Ka." *Scholastic Voice* (1973): 135–41.

"Ta-Na-E-Ka" is a short story, by Mary Whitebird, about an eleven-year-old American Indian girl, Mary. Mary must endure the ritual of Ta-Na-E-Ka, a test of individual survival in the forest to mark her transition from childhood to adulthood to become a warrior. Mary struggles with the relevance of the ritual in modern times while wanting to honor the traditions of her grandfather and her people. Instead of surviving in the forest, unlike her cousin, Mary spends the days of Ta-Na-E-Ka in the shelter of a marina at a nearby lake and then at a restaurant where she buys food from the owner.

The story raises issues of tradition versus modernity, respect for elders versus individual freedom, rules versus flexibility, as well as themes of coming of age, fairness, and inventiveness, among others. Mary's decision not to follow the rules laid down by her grandfather is questionable. Did she do the right thing? Should she have followed her grandfather's directives? Is it always important to follow tradition? Has she fulfilled the ritual and became a warrior? The richness of the content and the ambiguities in the actions of the characters render the text high on the scale of dialogic quality. Although the vocabulary and language of the text are challenging, the text is accessible in terms of the knowledge of American Indian culture needed to understand it. Likewise, the text is engaging because the moral and ethical issues confronting Mary are not that different from those confronting many children in their interaction with parents, teachers, and friends. So students in the upper elementary grades readily identify with the main character and her struggle.

Howe, J. "Victor." In Birthday *Surprises: Ten Great Stories to Unwrap*, edited by Johanna Hurwitz, 74–85. New York: Beech Tree, 1995.

"Victor" is a short story about a young boy, Cody, who is incapacitated in a hospital bed, just prior to his thirteenth birthday. Cody creates an imaginary world, inspired by the ceiling tiles in the hospital, to help him get through the illness. He refers to the world as "The Land Above" and invents characters that inhabit this world. A mysterious man named Victor, who visits Cody, tells him stories about what his life will be like when he grows up, and these stories give Cody the hope and strength to overcome his illness.

There is considerable ambiguity in the story about the character of Victor. Who is he? Is he an imaginary figure from The Land Above? Is he an old man wandering the hospital hallway? As a result, the dialogic quality of the text is high. The story is unusual in that the ambiguity revolves around the identity of one of the characters rather than a moral or ethical dilemma. It invites students to ponder the age-old questions of what is real, what is not, and how we can tell the difference. Students in fourth and fifth grade readily understand the story and are intrigued by Cody's illness and the character of Victor.

An additional consideration in choosing fiction text is the subgenre. Realistic fiction seems to yield more productive discussions than nonrealistic fiction. Realistic fiction describes a plausible series of events that could happen in the world in which we live. Nonrealistic fiction, on the other hand, describes events that could not occur in real life, but occur in some alternative universe, as in fantasy and science fiction. Discussing nonrealistic fiction can lead to lots of speculation, but it is difficult to engage students in reasoned, rigorous thinking when almost anything can happen. Texts in which authors anthropomorphize plants, animals, or other things (e.g., *Alice in Wonderland* by Lewis Carroll, *The Rabbit's Judgment* by Suzanne Crowder Han) present similar difficulties. Such texts may be highly dialogic, accessible, and engaging, but it is difficult for students to know what criteria to use when deciding on the most reasonable answer in such imaginary worlds.

OTHER TEXTS FOR INQUIRY DIALOGUE

Here we briefly describe other nonfiction and fiction texts that we have used and found to be helpful for promoting inquiry dialogue.

Nonfiction Texts

Modigliani, Laura. "Too Risky for Kids?" *Scholastic News* 5/6 (December 5 & 12, 2012): 4–5.
This article describes examples of young kids who have attempted to undertake extreme challenges such as climbing mountains, diving off cliffs, and sailing around

the world. It discusses whether children should be encouraged to engage in such activities given the physical risks and the emotional stress they pose for youngsters. Issues of individual freedom versus social responsibility are at the forefront. A number of other articles that touch on similar theme are suitable for upper elementary students s [e.g., "Extreme Teens." *Scholastic Scope* (May 6, 2013): 9–12; "Into the Death Zone: A Mount Everest Adventure." *Scholastic Storyworks* (February/March 2011): 4–8; "Too Young to Run?" *Scholastic News* 5/6 (September 30, 2013): 4–5]. The questions that these articles provoke are all along the lines of: Should young children be allowed to take on extremely dangerous challenges?

Modigliani, Laura. "Fashion Police." *Scholastic News* 4 (May 6 & 13, 2013): 4–5. This article visits the controversy over whether schools should have dress codes for students. It addresses issues of individual rights and freedom of expression versus the need for schools to maintain order and minimize distractions. Although the information in the article is sufficient to promote inquiry dialogue, it could usefully be paired with another piece on the pros and cons of school uniforms, such as "School Uniforms." *Scholastic Storyworks* (September 2011): 26–27. This *Storyworks* article introduces other issues to consider when regulating students' dress, including cost, safety, and comfort. As these articles themselves ask: Should students have the right to wear what they want to school? Should your school be telling you what to wear?

Mars One Text Set
Jones, Zach. "Move to Mars: Apply Now!" *Scholastic News* (April 30, 2013).
Davidson, Laura Leigh. "Are We Headed to the Red Planet?" *Scholastic News* (June 16, 2014).
Miller, Nancy. "First Human Colony Planned for Mars." *Teaching Kids News* (2015).
"The Mars 100—Mars One Astronaut Selection Round Three Trailer." YouTube video, 2:33. Posted by Mars One, February 15, 2015. https://www.youtube.com /watch?v=xxS7dCMBvSI.
Mars One, a private company, aims to send volunteer astronauts to Mars by 2023, pending funding from private investors. This mission will be accomplished at far less cost than that of a conventional government-run approach, but there is one catch—the company is offering only a one-way ticket! The technology to support a return flight to Earth is not yet fully developed and is very costly; a one-way trip to the red planet would be less expensive. This project has caught the imagination of

thousands of would-be astronauts who have volunteered to spend the rest of their lives on Mars. The first of two rounds of selection have been completed, and now one hundred Round 3 candidates remain. The final twenty-four people chosen would set up a colony. The project will be broadcast for a reality television program to help cover the costs. The promotional video in this text set expounds the virtues of the project for the survival of mankind and for the sheer inspiration it will provide to humanity; the articles provide a more practical perspective on the cost and the challenges that need to be overcome. Whether the project ever comes to fruition, the idea poses some interesting questions: Should people go on a one-way trip to Mars? Is this an appropriate use of money? Are the benefits worth the risks?

Fiction Texts

Adler, David A. "Don't Be an Uncle Max." In *Birthday Surprises: Ten Great Stories to Unwrap*, edited by Johanna Hurwitz, 34–43. New York: Morrow Junior Books, 1995.

"Don't Be an Uncle Max" is a short story about a young girl, Joanne, whose parents are unhappy with her for not doing her homework and for not taking her schoolwork seriously. Max is Joanne's uncle and a somewhat unconventional one at that; he is frequently out of work and moves around a lot, often living in exotic places. Joanne seems to idealize her Uncle Max, much to the consternation of her parents. Uncle Max has a habit of sending his favorite niece unusual gifts. For her birthday, he sends her a large, empty box from Alaska. In the box is a note that reads: "This box is filled with Alaska snow and lots of love." This story prompts questions such as: Is Uncle Max a good role model for Joanne? Should he have sent her an empty box for her birthday?

Heker, Liliana. "The Stolen Party." In *Mothers and Daughters: An Anthology*, edited by Alberto Manguel, 336–43. San Francisco, CA: Chronicle Books, 1998.

"The Stolen Party" is a short story about a young girl named Rosaura whose mother works as a housemaid for a wealthy lady, Señora Ines. Every afternoon, Rosaura and Señora Ines's daughter, Luciana, finish their homework together while Rosaura's mother cleans the house. Rosaura is invited to Luciana's birthday party though Rosaura's mother is reluctant to let her attend, fearing repercussions. Nonetheless, Rosaura insists on going to the party and helps out by serving food and drinks while also participating in the games and activities with the other children. As the children leave, Señora Ines presents each child with a small toy. But when it is Rosaura's time to leave, Señora Ines gives her money in payment for her help during the party. This story poses lots of questions around the themes of social class and friendship: Are Rosaura and Luciana friends? Should Rosaura have gone to the party? Should she accept the money?

Hughes, Langston. "Thank You, M'am." In *Short Stories by Langston Hughes*, edited by A. S. Harper, 223–226. New York: Hill and Wang, 1996.
"Thank You, M'am" is a short story about a teenage boy who attempts to steal the purse of an elderly woman as she is walking home at night. The elderly woman foils the theft and drags him to her home but does not call the police. Instead, she has him wash his face, and she heats up some food for them, all the while leaving the front door open. The woman asks the boy why he tried to steal from her, and he explains that he wanted to buy some blue suede shoes. The story ends with the woman giving the boy money for the shoes, sending him on his way, and closing the door. The story resonates with questionable decisions and ambiguity: Should the woman have reported the boy to the police? Should she have reacted differently? Did the boy deserve a second chance? Why did the boy not try to escape?

A FINAL WORD

Remember, our goal in this chapter is to illustrate what makes a good text for inquiry dialogue, not to prescribe set texts to be used. We offer these suggestions of articles and stories to illustrate the kinds of texts that promote productive dialogue so you can choose your own texts.

In the final analysis, a good text for inquiry dialogue is one that invites contestable questions that prompt a variety of interpretations and positions. To determine if a text lends itself to contestable questions, try to identify the major themes (e.g., justice) or tensions (e.g., animal versus human rights). Then generate questions for each theme or tension. You might also let the text speak directly to your own sensibilities; if something jumps out as problematic or questionable, pause and think about the larger issue underlying the text and try to construct a question around that issue. Once you have potential discussion questions in mind, test them to see if they are contestable by generating arguments on all sides. Consider whether the questions are asking for judgments to be made or call for a position to be taken and whether answering them will require inquiry (rather than guessing or speculation). Finally, try out the text and reflect on how well it prompted rigorous and collaborative argumentation and why it did (or did not) work.

CHAPTER 10

Moving Toward Student Independence

Teachers using inquiry dialogue aim to eventually become redundant! The whole point of engaging students in inquiry dialogue is that they become independent thinkers. Ultimately, we want students to develop their argument literacy skills to the point where they can apply them in other situations, without support of the teacher, such as when discussing complex questions with others, writing a persuasive essay, or reading a new text that contains arguments. In other words, we want the new ways of thinking and knowing that students learn during inquiry dialogue to become habits of mind that they use in any context that calls for engaging in argumentation. Helping students reflect on their talk (i.e., to become more metacognitive), engaging students in critical evaluation of their participation (e.g., by using the ART for Kids), and using post-discussion activities are all practices that help students transfer the skills and strategies of argumentation to new tasks and contexts, but there are additional ways to support students in becoming independent thinkers.

In this chapter, we discuss how to foster student independence. We begin by explaining the importance of gradually releasing responsibility for the discussion to students. Next, we describe three ways to foster independence: moving from whole-class to small-group discussion, moving from teacher-generated to student-generated questions, and stepping out of the dialogue to give students greater control over the flow of talk.

GRADUALLY RELEASING RESPONSIBILITY

As with any good teaching, one of the best ways to encourage independence and foster transfer is to follow the gradual release of responsibility model.[1] A diagram illustrating the process is shown in figure 10.1.

In the first stage, the teacher takes most of the responsibility for orchestrating the task, modeling what is involved and providing instruction. In the second stage, as the students gain more knowledge and skill, the teacher gradually cedes responsibility to the students, questioning and prompting the students, and modeling again as needed. In concert, the students gradually take up responsibility for the task, while the teacher provides support and guidance—scaffolding—when students have problems. In the third stage, the students practice the task with little support from the teacher. Hopefully, by this stage, the students have *internalized* the knowledge, skills, and strategies needed to perform the task and are capable of orchestrating much of it themselves. When the process is new to students or the task is very challenging, it is important to provide a lot of modeling and scaffolding. It is only when students

FIGURE 10.1

Gradual release of responsibility model

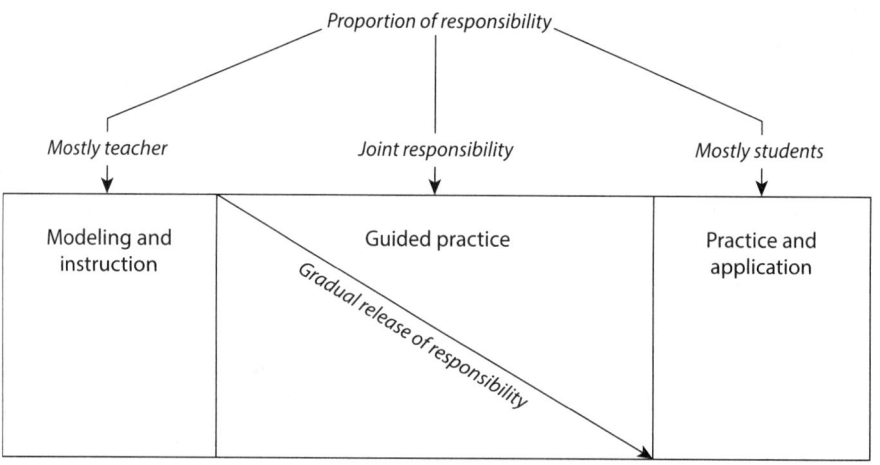

Adapted from P. David Pearson and Margaret C. Gallagher, "The Instruction of Reading Comprehension," *Contemporary Educational Psychology* 8, no. 3 (1983): 317–44.

become more adept at performing the task that the teacher should step back, provide less support, and let students assume more responsibility for the task.

Of course, scaffolding rarely disappears entirely. Good teaching is a constant dance between the teacher providing the lead and students taking up the task. As students become more expert, the teacher's job might be to up the ante, to step back in and encourage students to take on more of the task or more challenging aspects of the task. So, even as teachers remove the scaffolding for simpler materials and tasks, they are providing scaffolding, the support, for more difficult aspects of the task.

What does this gradual release of responsibility model mean for engaging students in inquiry dialogue? When conducting discussions, we, as teachers, can cede responsibility to students in various ways. We can use different grouping arrangements that allow students to take more ownership of the discussion. We can let students decide on the big question to be the focus of the discussion. And, within the inquiry dialogue itself, we can step back and let students take over the facilitation moves we have introduced.

INCREASING THE USE OF SMALL-GROUP DISCUSSIONS

A good way to foster independence on the part of students is to reduce the use of whole-class discussion and increasingly use small-group discussion. In the early stages of using inquiry dialogue, whole-class discussion is ideal to introduce students to this type of talk and to work on specific aspects of argumentation. When working with a whole class, we, as teachers, can readily bring up and explain different discussion practices (e.g., using ground rules), model different moves we would like our students to use (e.g., clarifying), and address weaknesses in students' argumentation (e.g., challenging others' ideas). Explaining and modeling with the entire class also make for efficient use of the teacher's time. What's more, because everyone has to be careful not to talk over each other and ensure everyone has a chance to participate, whole-class discussion has the added advantage of slowing down the discussion. This makes it easier for the teacher to facilitate and promote collaborative and rigorous argumentation.

However, in whole-class discussion, it is harder to have an open participation structure in which students can speak without a teacher or a classmate calling on them. Often, the teacher has to maintain a certain degree of control over turn taking to ensure things do not get out of hand and everyone has a chance to contribute. Students find it difficult to gain the floor in whole-class discussions and have fewer opportunities to participate. As in some of the examples featured in earlier parts of this book, one way of giving students control over turn taking in whole-class discussion is to have students raise their hands after a student has finished speaking and for the speaker to then nominate the next student to talk. But even this method of organizing student participation is not without problems.[2]

When we interviewed fifth-grade students about their experiences with inquiry dialogue, we learned that students struggled with getting the floor to speak during whole-class discussion: "What I liked least is that . . . like if I raised my hand, they would just keep calling to the person next to them or their best friends. . . . If you have your hand up a lot and they don't call you, then you just forget about it and don't say."[3] Students also complained that their classmates did not contribute enough to the discussions: "Only certain people talk. Like, I talked a lot and some other kids talked a lot too. But I did not hear many other kids' opinions, because they didn't raise their hand up. I think I would have liked to hear their opinions."[4] Even though students can benefit from inquiry dialogue as long as they are cognitively and emotionally engaged, either by speaking or actively listening, we believe it is harder to support students' active participation in whole-class discussion.[5] In large groups, for example, students are more susceptible to "social loafing," a well-documented reduction in engagement that can arise when students are working in groups.[6]

In small-group discussions, by contrast, it is easier to encourage an open participation structure. In other words, it is easier for the teacher to step back and give more control of turn taking to students. Also, some students feel more comfortable expressing themselves in small groups. Small groups make it easier for students to get the floor while also making it harder to loaf and hide behind other group members. By and large, students in small groups tend to have more control over the discussion and feel a greater sense of ownership.

Several research studies support these ideas. Research on interaction in small groups suggests that higher levels of productive student behavior are more likely under an *open participation structure* in which the teacher relinquishes control of turn taking and students can speak without being nominated by the teacher.[7] Moreover, the available evidence shows that the more students verbally participate in the discussion—giving detailed, elaborated explanations to others—the more they gain.[8]

Studies in which researchers have compared whole-class and small-group discussions confirm that small-group discussions yield greater benefits than whole-class discussion for students' learning.[9] In these studies, researchers argue that small groups provide more opportunities for students to speak, interact, and exchange different points of view. Many approaches to classroom discussion about texts use small groups or some combination of small-group and whole-class discussion.[10]

Teachers may conduct small-group discussions in various ways. One way is for the teacher to work with one group at a time while the rest of the students in the class do independent or center work. The independent or center work might include reading in preparation for an upcoming discussion or a pre-discussion activity. The teacher conducts discussions with each group in rotation over the course of the day or week. This is essentially the model used in guided reading.[11] Another way to work with a small number of students is to use a fishbowl with one group (the "fish") engaging in the discussion while the others outside the "bowl" are observing what happens during the discussion. A fishbowl is especially useful in the early stages of conducting discussions for developing the norms for inquiry dialogue and for working with a smaller group while still involving all students.

We are reluctant to recommend having students engage in peer-led discussions while the teacher circulates among the groups (as in literature circles). Effective facilitation of inquiry dialogue requires that teachers keep a road map of the arguments built by the students and choose facilitation moves that can improve the quality of the arguments. It would be hard for the teachers to decide on an effective facilitation move if they haven't followed a group's reasoning. Nonetheless, teachers we have worked with report some success having students discuss the text in peer-led groups while they are working with another group. The effectiveness of this approach hinges on choosing students for the peer-led groups who understand the text well and can work more independently than others. Students in those groups develop leadership skills in facilitating discussions and serve as models for others—yet another way to foster independence.[12]

How many students should make up a small group for inquiry dialogue? The best recommendation we can offer is the smaller the better, but they should not be so small as to limit the diversity of ideas necessary for productive discussions.[13] Experience—and some research—suggests groups of six to eight students work well. Research also suggests that mixed groups work better for engaging students in open-ended, collaborative tasks such as those involved in inquiry dialogue.[14] Working with groups of students that differ in terms of ability, motivation, gender, talkativeness, and other traits is a key ingredient for a successful discussion. The more diverse the group, the more likely it is that students will offer multiple positions and explore different perspectives together. More capable students can serve as models for less capable peers, who learn from observing more skilled ways of thinking and talking. And because the discussion is open ended—where the answers to big questions are neither obvious nor easy to find—the typically quieter or less advanced students are often the ones who come up with some of the most interesting insights during inquiry dialogue.

HAVING STUDENTS GENERATE BIG QUESTIONS

Another way to foster independence is to ask students to generate big questions about the text.[15] After having discussed big questions for some time, students will start to understand implicitly what makes a good big question for discussion and may be well positioned to take on the task of generating questions themselves. Having students as a group suggest questions and decide which question they would like to discuss encourages students to take ownership of the discussion and helps create a community of inquiry.[16] It also invites students to be thoughtful and critical about the texts they read and to think about which questions justify (or don't justify) further inquiry.

After students have read the story or article once or twice, ask them to each write a question they would like to discuss (this writing could be a pre-discussion activity). When the students come together, have them call out their questions while you write them on the board. Depending on the size of the group, you might have students share their questions in pairs to decide on the one they would like to ask before calling out their questions. Treat this exercise as a brainstorming activity; simply list as many questions as students would like to suggest and avoid editing the questions too much at this point. If students need prompting, the following may help:

- What questions does the text raise for us?
- What questions would be worth discussing?
- What did you find puzzling, confusing, or interesting?
- Do our questions cover all the important issues raised by the text?
- Do any of our questions suggest other questions we haven't asked yet?

- Can you think of a question that would highlight something different from what we have so far?

After recording the students' questions, work with them to decide which will be the big questions for discussion. Of course, choosing a big question to ignite discussion can be challenging because big questions need to be *contestable, authentic, central,* and *clear.* So you will need to support students and guide them in this process, at least initially. For example, you could guide them with the following questions:[17]

- Is that something we are likely to disagree about?
- Is there more than one answer to this question?
- Is that something we really want to know?
- Is this question about an important issue in the text?
- Does everyone understand this question?

If you notice some redundancy among the questions, or you consider some questions to be logically prior to others, you could pare them down by asking the following:[18]

- Are some of our questions about the same thing? Can some of them be combined?
- Is there a big question we could ask that would cover some or all of these questions?
- Do some questions assume we know the answers to other questions?

Deciding which question will be the big question for discussion will obviously involve some degree of negotiation and compromise among students, but it is important that they reach agreement if not consensus. Asking students to vote for each of the remaining questions, after rewording or paring them down, and proceeding with the majority vote is often useful.

If you find that students need even more help in generating questions that are appropriate for inquiry dialogue, then the following exercise in what makes a good big question might be useful.[19] After students have read the story "What Should Kelly Do?" show them the list of questions in figure 10.2 and ask them to group the questions into categories using whatever labels they would like to use (e.g., "open" versus "closed," "one right answer" versus "multiple answers," "important" versus

FIGURE 10.2

Questions about "What Should Kelly Do?"

1. What did the art teacher say about the rules of the competition?

2. What should Kelly do?

3. What did Evelyn paint?

4. What makes a painting beautiful?

5. Is it important to win a competition?

6. Does the text tell us that Kelly really wanted to win?

7. Are rules important?

8. Should Kelly tell or not tell Evelyn about her painting?

9. What would Evelyn think if her painting was ruined?

"not important," "answer in-the-text" versus "answer not-in-the text"). Students can do this exercise in pairs. It may be helpful to have them think about what they would need to do to answer each question.

Once students have put the questions into groups, ask them what labels they used and why. Discuss the different ways of categorizing the questions as a class. In doing so, ask students to think about which questions would be good for inquiry dialogue and why. It is okay if students have already discussed the question "What should Kelly do?" They can discuss why this made a good big question.

STEPPING OUT OF THE DIALOGUE

Yet another way we, as teachers, can foster independence is to metaphorically step out of the dialogue and gradually release responsibility for facilitating inquiry dialogue to the students. Remember, the goals in conducting inquiry dialogue are for students to collaborate with each other and to engage in rigorous argumentation. In the initial stages of conducting discussions, when students are still learning to engage in inquiry dialogue, we need to step in to model and support collaboration and strong reasoning. We do this by modeling productive ways of speaking and thinking using the kinds of talk moves illustrated in the ART. But eventually we want students to take a more active role in facilitating their discussions and to use the appropriate talk moves. This means that, over time, we need to hold back and see if students can assume more responsibility for orchestrating the discussion.

Finding the right level of involvement during inquiry dialogue is a constant balancing act. If we step in too much, we risk taking away ownership of the discussion from students. If we step back too soon, then the discussion can quickly become unproductive. We need to be sensitive to the level of the group's collaboration and reasoning—to develop an ear for talk—and reduce our support only when students demonstrate the skills for effective engagement in inquiry dialogue. If students are performing at a high level, then we do not need to step in as much. Of course, there will always be peaks and troughs in students' emerging capabilities over the year, and we cannot give up responsibility for encouraging collaborative and rigorous argumentation entirely; as students become adept at some aspects of quality argumentation, we need to introduce others. But over time, the level of teacher involvement should diminish.

To get a sense of this, let's look at an example. The following excerpt is taken from a small-group discussion in a fifth-grade class of a *Scholastic Storyworks* article titled "Should a Tiger Be Your Pet?" (February/March 2013, 24–25). The students had also watched a news video about their local zoo. The teacher and students were discussing the big question "Should people be allowed to have exotic pets?" The teacher began engaging students in inquiry dialogue in November, and this discussion took place in March of the following year.

> **AMY:** I'm kind of in the middle because, like Carla said, if you have enough money, then you should be able to keep the pet, but if you don't, um, they could be, like, all nice when they're smaller or when you first get them, and then they could automatically change and they could get all mean.
>
> **TEACHER:** How do we know that?
>
> **AMY:** Well, because when you see animals in the zoo and stuff, they don't, like, look mean, but when you see them in the wild, they look mean. So I don't see how it would change if you bought them.
>
> **JACK:** Um, I think that, you can have them as a baby, but you should give them to a zoo. Like, it says, on the second page, I'm pretty sure, it says about how

people, once their pythons get too big, they're just letting them out in the Everglades and the Everglades is getting ruined. So, I think that you shouldn't be able to own them if you can't keep them for the whole time.

JOHN: Well, if they give them to the zoo, then, like, on the video we watched, the Columbus Zoo only took, like, I believe six of them, because they didn't have enough room or any space to put more. So they'd have to, I think they'd also have to do special exams to get your exotic pets in the zoo.

JACK: But not all zoos are that full.

CARLA: Yeah, but I'm going to back up what Amy said, going back to what she said. She said that animals can change. Um, it says in here, um, somewhere it says [reading from the article] "But living with a wild animal can backfire." Because it says that "Every year there are reports of humans being bitten, mauled or even seriously injured by exotic pets."

TEACHER: Okay, so how does, what position is this supporting then?

CARLA: That we should get rid of it, so I'm kind of like in the middle.

AMY: So, what you are trying to say, Jack, is that you could raise the pet and then once they get bigger, you could give it back to the zoo?

JACK: Yeah.

Toward the end of the excerpt, Amy made a move to clarify what Jack had said a few turns earlier ("So, what you are trying to say, Jack, is that you could raise the pet and then once they get bigger, you could give it back to the zoo?"). Jack's utterance was not clear, and Amy revoiced his statement to ensure she and everyone else understood what he had said. In discussions earlier in the year, the teacher had often used the move "So are you saying that . . ." (ART practice 4, Clarifying meaning) to clarify students' contributions, and Amy appears to have internalized this move to the point that she can use it appropriately (and in her own way). Notice also, three turns prior to Amy's, that Carla used several talk moves from the ART. She connected with what Amy had said at the beginning of the excerpt (ART practice 5, Connecting ideas), she labeled her move to indicate she was providing support for Amy's opinion ("I'm going to back up what Amy said") (ART practice 6, Labeling reasoning moves and parts of an argument), and she cited evidence from the text (ART practice 8, Evaluating facts). In eleven turns, the teacher participated only twice. The teacher could see students were collaborating and arguing well, so she held back to let students manage this part of the discussion.

DECIDING WHEN TO RELINQUISH CONTROL

In this chapter, we have offered three pathways to fostering student independence by gradually releasing responsibility for the discussion to students. Figuring out when to relinquish control and how to do it are strategic decisions on the part of the teacher. Whole-class discussion is good for explaining, modeling, and working on different aspects of inquiry dialogue, but small-group discussion helps foster students' sense of ownership and increases their opportunities to participate. Well-crafted, teacher-generated, big questions help support a productive discussion, but student-generated questions give students practice questioning what they read and encourage students to feel more vested in the process of determining the most reasonable answer. Stepping into the dialogue is important for keeping the discussion on track and modeling productive ways of speaking and thinking during inquiry dialogue, but stepping out is essential if we want students to internalize the skills and strategies of argumentation. The best advice we can offer when deciding to relinquish control is to carefully observe and listen to students. It is only by developing an eye and an ear for strong collaboration and argumentation that we can know when students are ready to take on more responsibility for the discussion.

CHAPTER 11

Self-Study: How to Improve My Practice

Learning to become effective facilitators of inquiry dialogue takes time, practice, and careful reflection. To become better at facilitation, teachers benefit from structured opportunities to think about their own practice. This chapter describes how teachers can engage in self-study to examine their practice with the help of colleagues, technology, and assessment tools.

ENGAGING IN SELF-STUDY

Self-study is an established approach to professional learning that can help teachers improve their practice through reflection into their own classroom experiences.[1] As teachers, we often think about our past and future actions in informal ways, such as when pondering about how to respond better to a student's question while we're on the way home from work. Self-study takes these casual reflections to a new level: it makes them systematic, collaborative, and critical.[2] By *systematic*, we mean that during self-study teachers rely on an established system or a set of procedures designed to enhance their learning. By *collaborative*, we mean that teachers work closely with their colleagues to brainstorm solutions, learn from each other, and uncover the blind spots. And *critical* means that teachers are open to thinking about their practice in new ways, even if it involves revising long-held assumptions about what works in a classroom. As one educator explained, "I use the words self-study to mean critical examination of one's actions and the context of those actions in order to achieve a more conscious mode of professional activity, in contrast to action based on habit, tradition, or impulse."[3]

Self-study can be realized through a variety of activities, including reflection on our own facilitation and peer coaching. In this chapter, we describe these two activities in detail and offer strategies to help make teacher learning more productive, meaningful, and rewarding.

REFLECTING ON OUR FACILITATION

Research studies and professional development programs stress the importance of engaging teachers in a careful reflection on their own facilitation.[4] Luckily, modern technologies make recording and watching our own class discussions as effortless as pushing a button on a smartphone. While video recordings are now easily accessible, they are also so rich in information that we need to be strategic about selecting and analyzing the video to make sense of what we see and hear.

The strategies described here help make the study of your own videotaped discussions more systematic and effective. We have divided these strategies into three phases: selecting, analyzing, and planning. During the *selecting phase*, the teacher identifies segments for more in-depth examination, focusing on the strengths as well as the weaknesses of the discussion. During the *analyzing phase*, the teacher closely examines chosen segments and records new insights and discoveries about her practice. In the *planning phase*, the teacher determines a specific goal (or goals) to work on in the next discussion. Importantly, the teacher's enactment of this goal then becomes the subject of a new round of reflection. In other words, reflection is a cyclical process, during which the teacher selects a segment of practice, critically examines it, decides on a specific goal and related actions, tries out new actions in the classroom, and evaluates the effectiveness of these actions during the next reflection.[5]

Selecting Phase

We recommend that you work with the video as soon as possible after the video-recorded discussion. This will help you remember the general feel and context of the discussion, including what happened before and after the recording. Understanding the larger context can improve your ability to interpret what you hear and see on the video. To select informative segments for the analysis, try some of the following strategies:

1. View the entire video for a general sense of the discussion and write down time stamps for selected segments to come back to for later examination. The segments should represent both productive and problematic moments during the discussion. For example, you can time-stamp a segment when you or a student made a particularly useful comment that helped to advance the discussion. Also, following the key idea of being critical about your practice during a self-study, look specifically for segments that show difficulties, such as when the discussion stalled or became chaotic and incoherent.

2. Use the Argumentation Rating Tool (ART) as a guide for selecting video segments. For example, choose a particular practice (e.g., ART practice 4, Clarifying meaning) and find instances when you took the opportunity to effectively apply this practice. Also, look for the times when the opportunity to use the practice was missed yet using it would have helped improve the quality of students' argumentation.

3. Following the cyclical process of reflection, find the segments that show how you addressed or did not address the specific goals you set for yourself during the previous round of reflection.

4. If, after watching the video, you could not decide on a particular segment, simply choose any ten minutes of the discussion for further analysis or, if the time permits, examine the entire discussion.

Analyzing Phase

To make analysis of the discussion as productive as possible, we recommend always considering facilitation *in relation to students' argumentation*. The reason is that knowing when and how to intervene during inquiry dialogue requires that we first understand the strengths and weaknesses of the arguments that students are making. So, analysis of the discussion should combine evaluating the quality of students' argumentation with assessing opportunities to use a particular talk move that are either taken up or missed by the teacher. Following are specific suggestions for how to accomplish this:

1. Watch again the selected segment and track or reconstruct the development of students' arguments (i.e., positions, reasons, evidence, challenges, and responses to challenges). You may want to use the argument house template to help you with tracking. Review the facilitation practices and moves in relation to the reconstructed arguments. Ask yourself: How does this talk move help improve the quality of argumentation? Are there any missed opportunities for me to intervene? If so, what could I say and when?

2. Write down all the facilitation moves you made in a selected segment. Ask yourself: How do these moves relate to the quality of students' argumentation around the moves? What made me decide to step in here to ask the question? Or more generally, what is happening here? What do I see? What can I do differently?

3. Choose an ART criterion (e.g., *Clarity, Acceptability*) or a few specific facilitation practices from the ART (e.g., ART practice 4, Clarifying meaning, ART practice 8, Evaluating facts). Rate the segment on the criterion or practice, taking notes to support your score. Ask yourself: Why did I give myself this rating? What does my rating mean for the quality of students' argumentation? What could I have done to get a higher rating?

4. Transcribe selected segments of the discussion and use any of the strategies listed here. Working with transcripts helps us notice features of the talk and the quality of argumentation that are easily overlooked when watching a video.

5. Sample the entire video, using selected ART criterion or practice to focus your attention. Pause at different points in the video to reflect on what you just observed.

6. Consistent with the cyclical nature of reflection, examine any of your actions (or lack of actions) that would have helped achieve the specific goals you set for yourself in the previous round of reflection. Ask yourself: How well am I addressing my previously set goals? Am I being effective with my interventions? Am I missing any opportunities to intervene?

Planning Phase

In this final phase, we focus on setting and recording new goals to be tried out in a classroom and then assessed in a subsequent round of reflection.

1. Toward the end of the reflection, review your notes from the analyzing phase and think of a specific goal (or goals) to work on in your next discussion. You may also record your goals in the Closure section of the Discussion Planning Tool.

2. Maintain your notes, comments, and ART scores over multiple reflection sessions and review them as needed to track your progress.

PEER COACHING

We address this section to teachers who choose to act as coaches to their peers, thus supporting their colleagues and enhancing their own facilitation practices. Peer coaching adds an important dimension to the self-study process: it makes thinking about one's practice public and allows teachers to benefit from the knowledge, skills, and insights of their colleagues. According to research, coaching helps teachers improve practice, advance expertise, and develop self-efficacy, making it a common feature of professional development efforts.[6] In our own work with elementary school teachers, coaching was seen as one of the most beneficial ways to learn about facilitating inquiry dialogue.[7] Here is a quote from one of the teachers who worked with us:

> The coaching has been phenomenal. Watching the video with a coach and getting feedback on how I could have made a different move has helped me transfer that right into my teaching. It has also helped when I would watch the video by myself and feel like something had gone wrong, but didn't know what to do. Then I would show that to my coach and he would help me figure out what to do next time.

How to Conduct Peer Coaching

In a typical peer coaching session, a teacher meets with the coach for about forty minutes. The meeting should be scheduled to take place as soon as possible after the teacher's most recently videorecorded discussion. Typically, the coach and teacher sit side by side at a table in front of a computer. The computer is used to play the video of the discussion. The coach should come to the meeting equipped with the video of the teacher's discussion, two copies of the ART, and notes made from prior viewing of the video and from completing the three phases of reflection. The teacher should come to the meeting having watched the video of his discussion. The teacher might also complete the three phases of reflection and bring related notes to the meeting.

Note that the same three phases—selecting, analyzing, and planning—also apply to peer coaching. Furthermore, coaches can use the same strategies, with the only difference being that the coaches will apply these strategies to reflect on a videotaped discussion conducted by another teacher. For example, during the selecting phase, a coach identifies informative segments from a teacher's video to be discussed at the peer coaching meeting, focusing on both productive and problematic moments. During the analyzing phase, the coach considers the teacher's use of facilitation practices in relation to the quality of students' arguments and prepares questions to ask the teacher during the coaching session. During the planning phase, the coach develops tentative suggestions about the next steps for the teacher to take. These suggestions will be shared with the teacher during the coaching meeting.

To help make peer coaching a valuable experience for both parties, coaches should follow three key principles that underlie their engagement with teachers. First, it is important to recognize that coaching can be intimidating for some teachers because it puts them in a vulnerable position of exposing their actions to the critique of peers. This is why interactions between a coach and a teacher should clearly convey a sense of respect and collaboration. That is, the coach should emphasize collaborative language (e.g., using *we* instead of *you*), avoid discouraging comments, and focus on the joint goal of building better discussion practices. Second, to make the coaching sessions relevant to the teacher's needs, the coach should be responsive, allowing the content of the meeting to emerge from the teacher's questions and concerns. The coach might have ideas about what needs to be discussed at the meeting, but they should take a secondary position to the teacher's ideas, as long as the latter are germane to the topics of inquiry dialogue, facilitation, and argumentation. Ideally, the coach integrates the teacher's questions and concerns with her own judgments about the needed focus and topic of the meeting. Third, during the meeting, the coach should use every opportunity to model inquiry dialogue. For example, the coach should build on the teacher's comments, provide reasons and evidence for the given suggestions when possible, and explore the teacher's ideas or observations with additional questions and examples.

Figure 11.1 illustrates what happens during peer coaching with an excerpt from an actual meeting between a fifth-grade teacher and her coach. In this case, the teacher is only starting to learn about facilitating inquiry dialogue, whereas her coach is very experienced at this practice. The teacher and the coach had just finished watching a video clip from a discussion of "Deadly Hits," an article about a football player who suffered a serious concussion. Following one of the suggestions for analysis described earlier, the teacher and the coach had agreed to rate the discussion independently using the ART and then to discuss their ratings. We recommend you read the entire transcript in column 2 before reading the commentary. We also suggest you have the ART accessible to help you understand the references made by the teacher and the coach during the meeting.

FIGURE 11.1

Excerpt of peer coaching with commentary

SPEAKER (TURN)	TRANSCRIPT	COMMENTARY
Coach (1)	So, if we were going to rate on Diversity of perspectives (ART Criterion 1), what do you think you would be?	*Note that the coach invites the teacher to share her ratings first, before disclosing his own numbers. This gives the teacher more ownership and helps structure the discussion around her reflections on her practice.*
Teacher (2)	So, Diversity . . . um . . . I . . . maybe . . . Maybe a 5? 4 to 5.	*The teacher is hesitant about what her rating should be.*
Coach (3)	Yeah, yeah, I think it's 5. . . . Your big question is good, right? It's just that at some times, the students shift to a different question. And you kind of start restating their answers to that other question. So, it's focused on a couple of big questions here. If it would have stuck to the one question, which you did in the beginning . . . You were trying to bring them back, and they just kept kind of going away . . . But, yeah, I have you as a 5 here. You're not asking multiple questions. And the questions weren't "mixed in quality" [quoting from the ART]. You were still focused on getting students to do inquiry. So that's why it's completely a 5 for me.	*The coach enthusiastically supports the higher rating of the teacher (5) and goes on to explain the basis for his support. He starts by examining the discussion in relation to the ART practice 1, Centering on contestable questions. The coach points out that while the teacher chose a good big question, students ended up discussing two different big questions. The coach gently suggests that the teacher was not always successful at helping students maintain the focus on the big question ("they just kept kind of going away"). On the other hand, the coach observes that both questions gave students the opportunity to practice argumentation, so the teacher deserves a high rating of 5. Note how the coach quotes from the ART to justify his rating.*

continued

SPEAKER (TURN)	TRANSCRIPT	COMMENTARY
Teacher (4)	Okay, all right. So, the students . . . Maybe—I think a 5 for the students.	*The teacher agrees with the coach and switches her attention to examining students' actions in relation to practice 1 from the ART.*
Coach (5)	Yeah, it's to me, yeah . . . It's kind of on the line there, right?	*Turns 5 through 8 illustrate well the collaborative nature of peer coaching. In turn 5, the coach tentatively suggests that the students' rating on the ART practice 1 (Centering on contestable questions) may be somewhere between 5 and 6, and he invites the teacher to react ("It's kind of on the line there, right?").*
Teacher (6)	Right, like in the middle. 'Cause I think the students were sharing their perspectives. They were going a little bit more than agreeing with each other's views by giving their own. But I think they didn't go as far as they could have.	*The teacher picks up the coach's idea and explains why she agrees with him: while students sometimes managed to go beyond simple agreement with each other, "they didn't go as far as they could have."*
Coach (7)	Right, yeah. There were multiple perspectives, but maybe not so much "collaborative construction of arguments," right? So that's why it would dip to 5 for me. And at other times, I think they were just kind of saying, "I agree with so and so" and saying the same thing.	*The coach agrees with the teacher and clarifies why he also thinks students "didn't go as far." Although they offered multiple perspectives, they did not engage with each other's views. Again, the coach quotes from the ART to support his view.*
Teacher (8)	I agree. Yes, yes, a lot of that.	
Coach (9)	And did they share responsibilities?	*In turn 9, the coach is referring to the ART practice 2, Sharing responsibilities.*

SPEAKER (TURN)	TRANSCRIPT	COMMENTARY
Teacher (10)	Um . . . they did well with it. And this was the first time we tried the nominating [laughs]. Sometimes I was like, "All right, just pick. Like, you don't have to look around for your friend, just pick, like we talked about before. Just pick" . . . And I think for me . . . I think I'd be on the border of a 4 and a 5. I felt like I was trying not to steer the discussion and control it. But I don't know if I really did it. I don't know.	*The teacher's comment in turn 10 suggests that she has a friendly, trustful relationship with her coach. In a few sincere, humorous remarks, the teacher reveals how she felt about her students taking too long to decide who they wanted to nominate to speak. She is also openly doubtful about her attempt to release control over the discussion to her students.*
Coach (11)	But I feel like you did! I mean, there were times where you were doing a little steering. But, it was to relevant evidence . . . connected to what they were saying. It's not like you were trying to get them to the conclusion that you wanted. So, if anything, I think you're dipping over here into the 5. Maybe there's a little 4 going on there, but let's see. [Reading from the ART] This "largely controls the flow of the discussion." I don't think so—	*The coach reassures the teacher about her ability to share the control of the discussion with her students. Moreover, he helps the teacher see the difference between procedural versus substantive comments. That is, he suggests that although the teacher intervened in the discussion, her comments were used to support procedures of rigorous argumentation, rather than to lead students to a given answer. The coach also invites the teacher to reexamine her rating by referring back to the ART.*
Teacher (12)	I don't think I really . . . I don't think "largely" . . . I don't think so.	*In turns 12 through 14, the teacher and the coach collaboratively analyze the teacher's action by reading from the ART descriptions and sharing their opinions with each other.*
Coach (13)	And you didn't [reading from the ART] "mediate most interactions" between them.	
Teacher (14)	No.	
Coach (15)	So they manage turns, a few of them ask questions—	*In turn 15, the coach returns to examining students' actions in relation to the ART practice 2, Sharing responsibilities.*

continued

SPEAKER (TURN)	TRANSCRIPT	COMMENTARY
Teacher (16)	They did! They did need to elaborate more though. I would say maybe a 5 for the students there, because here it's saying like, [reading from the ART], "peer to peer exchanges are rare." But they were addressing each other, and they were commenting on each other's perspectives. So I think I'd give them a 5. I definitely don't think it's a 6.	*The teacher effectively uses the ART to explain the rating she have to her students.*
Coach (17)	I agree, and if we wanted to get to 6, we'd have to get into this [reading from the ART] "judging each other's answers." So, ultimately, part of what we want them to do is evaluating. And saying, "I can't agree with that. That's not reasonable" . . . So that's something to work towards.	*The coach agrees and uses this opportunity to clarify the requirements for the highest rating. In this way, the coach helps the teacher see what an ideal practice sounds like for her students, and he encourages the teacher to work toward that goal.*
Teacher (18)	All right, I'll take it.	
Coach (19)	Let's do one more, Discussing alternatives. [Reading from the ART] "Students consistently challenge each other's reasoning and respond to challenges."	*The coach suggests they analyze the discussion in relation to another ART practice (3, Discussing alternatives). He again quotes from the ART and gives the teacher the opportunity to discuss her ratings before turning to his own.*
Teacher (20)	I would give them . . . a 5 or a 6 for that. I think that the ones that were actually really verbalizing were giving reasons to why they thought the person was responsible. I mean, they could have given more . . . so maybe a 5?	*The teacher is again hesitant about her ratings. This, together with the fact that she is only starting to learn about this type of talk, indicates that the teacher is still building her understandings about what a successful (and a less successful) inquiry dialogue sounds like, especially in relation to specific practices outlined in the ART.*

SPEAKER (TURN)	TRANSCRIPT	COMMENTARY
Coach (21)	Yeah, I think I'm going to go with a 5 and the reason I'm 5 is because of that last exchange. Like, this is a high-level move because it's a response to challenge. It's like, "I think it's the coach for this reason. I disagree, the coach didn't know." And then Jeremy comes back and says, "Yeah, but he didn't have to know. Zack was down for five seconds and that's enough." So it's like the response, it's like "I recognize that you've given me a legitimate challenge. But I can fix it."	*The coach takes the opportunity to explain the rationale for his rating to the teacher. In this way, he helps the teacher improve her understanding of the practice and the criteria used to evaluate it. He uses specific quotes from the discussion to show the teacher what "high-level" argumentation sounds like. Note how the coach reconstructs the arguments made by the students to point out the function of the important part of good arguments, a response to challenge.*

The excerpt in figure 11.1 demonstrates many of the important principles of peer coaching, including the attention to trust, collaboration, and constructive feedback. The coach is consistently being respectful and generous in his communications with the teacher, while at the same time finding ways to suggest how and where she can improve her practice. Note that the ART ratings are not used to judge the teacher or to give her a grade. Instead, the ratings offer a starting point for an informed and collegial conversation about what happened in this discussion and what can be done in the future to advance the teacher's facilitation and students' argumentation. The teacher and the coach work closely with the ART, often quoting directly from the tool. This way, the teacher, who is at the beginning stages of learning about inquiry dialogue, can study the descriptions in the ART in relation to her own practice. Analyzing the differences between the ideal discussion (as described in the ART) and one's own classroom practice can help develop a meta-level awareness about the strategic use of language during inquiry dialogue.

Additional Options for Peer Coaching

Peer coaching focused on video analysis and reflection on teacher facilitation can also be supplemented with these alternative activities:

- *Coplanning.* The coach and the teacher coplan a discussion using the Discussion Planning Tool. This option might be useful when the teacher is seeking to use inquiry dialogue with texts from existing language arts, social studies, or science curriculum (e.g., a novel, textbook chapter).
- *Tracking argumentation.* The coach and the teacher work together to track the arguments being constructed by the students. The sole focus is the argumentation during the discussion instead of the facilitation moves made by the teacher. This option might be useful when the teacher wants to improve her ability to hear and distinguish different parts of arguments that are generated during a discussion.
- *In-class observations.* The coach observes the teacher's facilitation of inquiry dialogue in the classroom and provides feedback to the teacher immediately following the discussion. This option might be useful when the teacher needs more direct and immediate support than can be provided when reviewing the video of a recent discussion.
- Review of curriculum materials. The coach and the teacher review and discuss potential materials for incorporating inquiry dialogue in other areas of the curriculum (e.g., science, social studies, math). This option is useful to encourage the use of inquiry dialogue in other curriculum areas and to facilitate transfer of argument literacy skills to other contexts.

CHAPTER 12

Frequently Asked Questions

In this final chapter, we address questions teachers typically have about inquiry dialogue. Teachers who participated in our research and professional development program often asked questions as they were learning about and using inquiry dialogue in their classrooms. Some examples of teacher questions are, "At what age is it appropriate to introduce students to inquiry dialogue?" "How can I engage shy students and work with those who speak too much?" "How can I help students see flaws in their arguments without discouraging them from expressing their views?" We have organized the questions and our answers into two categories: general questions and questions about facilitating inquiry dialogue. Of course, these kinds of questions have more than one good answer, so it is always helpful to discuss them with your peers who are practicing the same methods. It is also important to keep in mind that the facilitation of inquiry dialogue—like every other kind of skilled practice, such as cooking, writing, or playing basketball—is, at least to some degree, a matter of personal style. Although expert facilitators rely on a shared set of general principles, you should not expect that the way you engage in this practice will mirror precisely the way anyone else does it.

GENERAL QUESTIONS

How do I explain the use of inquiry dialogue to my school principal or to my students' parents?

Engaging students in inquiry dialogue helps them develop argument literacy skills and gain a deeper understanding of the issues raised in the texts they read. These outcomes relate directly to the Common Core State Standards.[1] In fact, argument literacy skills are given special importance in the Common Core. For example, several standards require students to present reasoned opinions when speaking and writing, to listen carefully to the ideas of others, and to work with texts to connect authors' ideas and supporting details.

Inquiry dialogue provides a training ground for learning the argument literacy skills described in the Common Core. It makes the process of argumentation visible to students. As students discuss big, contestable questions with their peers, they observe, practice, and eventually internalize the skills of argument. Such skills are needed to develop a deep and nuanced understanding of the important questions raised by the texts. Students can also use argument literacy skills in other situations, such as when discussing a new issue or when reading and writing arguments.

Participating in inquiry dialogue about stories and articles also prompts students to carefully examine the information in the texts or, in other words, to engage in close reading. When working with text sets, students have to integrate information across texts and evaluate the credibility of the sources. Many teachers find it helpful to use multimodal texts to give students practice in integrating information across video, audio, and printed texts. Close reading, integrating information across texts, and working with multimodal texts are all skills required by the Common Core.

Finally, inquiry dialogue also serves one of the larger and more ambitious goals of education: preparing students to actively participate in our social and political democracy. Giving students the opportunity to exercise their curiosity, ask challenging questions, evaluate the credibility of reasons and evidence, figure out what they believe about important issues, learn from other students who think differently, make their thinking accountable to a community of their peers—these are the attributes of participatory citizenship, without which our democratic way of life cannot thrive. Engaging students in dialogue about important questions helps them see school as relevant to their lives and view themselves as intelligent, thoughtful people who take responsibility for their own thinking and learning.

How often should I use inquiry dialogue in my classroom to see improvements in students' argument literacy skills?

Unfortunately, today we still do not have research-based guidelines to suggest a specific number of discussions needed to see positive effects from students' engagement in inquiry dialogue. What we know from numerous studies is that students at all grade levels are not skilled at argumentation: regardless of age, students have problems with justifying a chosen position and working with alternative perspectives.[2] We also know that a typical classroom today offers few, if any, instructional opportunities for students to practice and learn argument literacy skills.[3] So, to support students' engagement in argumentation, we recommend that teachers use inquiry dialogue *as frequently as possible, but at least once per week* during the school year. Inquiry dialogue is directly aligned with contemporary theories of learning that view students as active meaning-makers and consider language to be fundamental for thinking and learning.[4] Researchers who have examined the benefits of discussions that share features with inquiry dialogue report many positive effects, including improved argument literacy skills, better comprehension of texts, advanced quality of persuasive writing, as well as deeper conceptual understanding of disciplinary concepts and enhanced social skills.[5]

Should inquiry dialogue be practiced only in certain school subjects?

As you become more comfortable with facilitating inquiry dialogue in language arts settings, we hope you will find ways to draw on its principles and practices when teaching in other subject areas of your school's curriculum. For example, when learning about indigenous societies in North America or solving a math problem, students could be invited to generate their own inquiry questions, conduct research into relevant reasons and evidence, formulate and defend their positions, and test them against those offered by others, including the conclusions presented in textbooks. These skills are important because argumentation drives the construction of knowledge in every discipline, from history to mathematics, and the accepted textbook facts represent the conclusions of arguments that survived the scrutiny by members of professional communities, such as historians or mathematicians. Engaging students in inquiry dialogue across subject areas gives them a chance to experience the kind of thinking that underlies disciplinary expertise and invites them to appreciate the public, contestable, and evolving nature of knowledge.

At what age is it appropriate to introduce students to inquiry dialogue?

Although this book is based on work with fifth-grade teachers and their students, this does not mean that teachers should wait until the upper elementary grades to begin engaging students in inquiry dialogue. Our focus on grade 5 simply reflects our most recent work with teachers. Research shows that even more advanced argument components, such as objections and responses to objections, can be found in the talk of preschool children.[6] Further, young students who are offered opportunities to practice argumentation can benefit from these experiences and enhance their argument literacy skills.[7] With careful attention to children's individual differences and interests, teachers can engage students in productive discussions of controversial issues from the first years of schooling.

Should I combine inquiry dialogue with other instructional methods?

Although we encourage the use of inquiry dialogue in the classroom, we also recognize the need for other instructional approaches that can support the goals of rational thinking and deep understanding. That is, we believe that teachers should be able to flexibly choose from a broad repertoire of strategies, including more traditional discourse styles such as recitation and exposition. For instance, even during inquiry dialogue, teachers sometimes need to ask students to recall simple facts (e.g., "Is there the right to travel in the US Constitution?" "What does the text say about the DNA evidence from the crime scene?"). Also, sometimes, teachers need to use exposition to explain to students the structure or parts of an argument. The use of these more traditional discourse styles is appropriate, especially if it is done in service of promoting well-informed inquiry. As with any other approach, the use of inquiry dialogue should not become restrictive. Instead, we encourage you to be strategic in choosing methods and approaches that are best suited to meeting specific pedagogical goals you set for your students.

Using inquiry dialogue requires a lot of expertise that I currently don't have. Do I need to learn everything before I conduct my first discussion?

In this book, we have emphasized the importance of acquiring specialized knowledge and skills to effectively facilitate inquiry dialogue. For example, we discussed the structure of arguments and the criteria for quality argumentation. These and many other topics presented in the book are likely to be unfamiliar to many teachers. The good news is that to begin your first discussion, you do not need to have all the relevant expertise in place. As with most things, expertise in facilitating inquiry dialogue develops as you engage in this practice. Research suggests that engaging in "approximations of practice," or in practice that resembles the ideal only in some respects, is an essential part of teachers' professional development.[8] For example, when starting to learn how to facilitate inquiry dialogue, you can first focus on just one or two facilitation practices presented in the ART (e.g., practice 4, Clarifying meaning; practice 5, Connecting ideas).

In other words, we encourage you to view each discussion as a new opportunity to experiment with your use of talk, even if it involves making and learning from your mistakes. With each new discussion and each opportunity to try additional talk moves and observe their impact on the quality of argumentation, you will become more comfortable with the process. And by engaging in a systematic reflection on your practice, you can identify the strengths and weaknesses of your discussions and come up with specific solutions to try next time.

QUESTIONS ABOUT FACILITATING INQUIRY DIALOGUE

Should I stay with the one big question, or is it okay go in a different direction?

During a discussion, students might stray from the original big question and start talking about other topics. These diversions are acceptable if they inform the group's thinking about the big question. For example, before addressing the big question about who was responsible for a player's concussion during a football game, students might need to figure out how much knowledge a coach had about this type of injury.

At the same time, inquiry dialogue should not turn into unfocused talk that leads nowhere. It is important for students to learn how to stick with one question long enough to delve deeply into the issues. If students get too far off track, we need to step in by questioning the relevance of new subtopics and anchoring the discussion back to the big question. We can do this using the ART practice 7, Tracking the line of inquiry. For example, we can ask students about the relevance of a new topic, "What does this mean for the big question? Where are we now?" If the group wanders into a new big question unintentionally, we can always point this out and suggest that the group reserve that question for another time and then use the tracking moves from the ART to return to the original big question.

How can I engage shy students and work with those who speak too much?

During inquiry dialogue, the entire group shares responsibility for addressing problems with collaboration and argumentation. So, the first step is to revisit the ground rules, invite students to reflect on how things are going, and come up with ways of improving the discussion. It is important that students understand that more-or-less even participation is not merely a matter of etiquette or even of fairness, but also of rigorous argumentation. When some people do not participate, the group as a whole is deprived of their unique questions, insights, and perspectives. It is also a good idea to reassure your students that tendencies to speak a lot or to speak very little in a group setting are as common among adults as among children, and there's nothing inherently good or bad about either tendency. It's just that when we practice inquiry dialogue, we want to make participation as even as possible, for the sake of supporting rigorous and collaborative argumentation.

In addition to revisiting and discussing the ground rules, we have found the following strategies to be helpful in managing students' participation:

- Use talking chips, where each student has a limited number of chips to spend on turns during the discussion. This strategy helps students monitor their participation in the early stages of learning how to engage in inquiry dialogue. But it should be phased out as soon as students have learned how to regulate their own behavior.
- Follow the "three before me" rule, in which each student has to wait for three turns before speaking again.
- Invite shy students to begin the discussion. Let those students know about this plan in advance.
- Give additional opportunities for shy students to speak. For example, at some point in a discussion, you could say, "I notice that some people haven't had a chance to say what they think today, so let's give them a chance to talk." Of course, students in the groups should also invite others to speak.
- Use a once-around strategy, in which students are invited to offer a new idea (or to pass) going once around the circle.
- Have students watch a video of a recent discussion and talk with them about their participation during the discussion (e.g., "Did everyone contribute?"). This can also be done using the ART for Kids.
- Have a student or a group of students (e.g., the outer circle of a fishbowl) track everyone's participation and report back to the discussion group. Again, this can be done using the ART for Kids.

- Ask students to pause and take three or five breaths between each contribution, to think about their ideas. If necessary, you might even ask for a minute of silence to give everyone time to ponder about what has been said so far. This strategy is particularly helpful when the talk has been fast-paced and complicated. It's good to explain to students that the purpose of silence is to give everyone time to reflect, slow down, and be with their own thoughts. At the end of the minute, you might ask to hear from someone who hasn't spoken yet.
- Speak individually (outside the group) to a student who talks too much during the discussion. Let that student know that you appreciate what he has to contribute and ask for help in making the participation more even-handed.
- Point out or mark the valuable contributions made by students who are reticent to speak.
- Invite students to journal individually about what they took from a discussion and ask shy students for permission to share something they wrote in their journal with the class before the next discussion.

It is a good idea to introduce these strategies as experiments and to ask the group to discuss whether a chosen strategy was effective at addressing a given problem. Also, because the goal is to have students share in the responsibility of regulating their participation, we need to be careful that we do not structure the discussion too much. Use these strategies only sparingly. Otherwise, they can stifle student excitement and make the experience with inquiry dialogue too formulaic. Notice that many of the strategies for engaging shy students also help students who tend to speak too much learn to regulate their behavior.

Nonetheless, despite our best efforts, some quiet students may still speak less than others in the group. Do not despair—there is more to participation than speaking. Research suggests that students will benefit from inquiry dialogue as long as they are cognitively and emotionally engaged in the discussion, either by speaking or by *actively listening.*[9] You can promote students' active engagement in a discussion in various ways. For example, you can work to support a "culture of active participation" during the discussions by establishing ground rules and drawing students' attention to them, periodically asking students to reflect on what's been said, having post-discussion activities that build on the content of the dialogue, and inviting students to journal about what they took from a discussion.[10]

Sometimes my students seem to be bringing up the same points, going around in circles. How can I reduce repetition during inquiry dialogue?

Some repetition may be helpful during a discussion. For example, when we ask students to summarize or paraphrase what has been said before, we slow down the discussion and help improve the clarity of the arguments made by the group. However, too much repetition may indicate that students are not building on or challenging each other's ideas. As a result, the discussion may stall and lose direction.

One way to address excessive repetition during inquiry dialogue is to use the ART practice 6, Labeling reasoning processes and parts of an argument. For instance, imagine that when discussing "What Should Kelly Do?" three students in a row provided similar examples of Evelyn not caring about the art contest. You can first react with less intrusive statements, by saying "So, you just gave us another example, right?" or "Is this the same example as Nicole gave us earlier or is there something new here?" to help students recognize the function of their contributions. If this intervention does not work, you can address the problem with repetition in a more direct way and give students a little push to move forward: "Okay, I think we now have enough examples to show that Evelyn did not care about her painting. So, how does that help us with answering our big question?"

You might also use the tracking move to make students aware that they are continuing to revisit the same issue in the discussion. For example, "It seems like we got stuck on whether Marie was happy in Twin Cities. Does anyone have a suggestion about how we can move forward?" Another strategy is to invite students to categorize the reasons being offered for or against a position by asking, "Can someone tell us how many different reasons have been given so far?" If the students can identify that in six previous turns, only two different reasons were given, you might next ask, "Can anyone give us a reason *different* from those two?"

Is it okay for students to use their personal experience to support their positions, or should they only use evidence from the text?

Students can use personal experiences during inquiry dialogue. Good arguments contain all kinds of support, including personal experiences, examples (and counterexamples), as well as evidence from the text and other sources, such as books, movies, or popular media. There is no need to restrict students to using the text as their only source of evidence, unless there are good reasons for doing so (e.g., giving students targeted practice with using textual evidence in preparation for an upcoming writing exercise or test). The important thing is that students learn to provide strong justification for their positions, while also recognizing the limitations of different kinds of support. For example, a personal experience could be powerful and convincing, but it may not hold true for everyone else. Alternatively, a quote from the text might be taken out context, so you might prompt students to check to see if their interpretation is accurate.

How can I help students see flaws in their arguments without discouraging them from expressing their views?

The responsibility for pointing out flaws rests with the entire group, not just with the teacher. So, first, give other students the opportunity to correct their peers. However, if no one in the group points out an error, and if you think it is important enough for making progress in the discussion, it is a good idea to ask a question about it, rather than to simply correct it. The ART includes many examples of the types of questions used to address problems with students' reasoning. For example, if a student makes a factual error, you might ask him to explain the basis for his statement (i.e., "How do we know this? Where in the story does it say that?"). You might also invite other students to react to a given statement (i.e., "Do others agree or disagree with Kevin's way of reading the text?").

Sometimes no one else in the group understands the error or can help correct it. Then you might need to make a stronger move, such as clarifying the meaning of a word or offering a counterexample. But again, try to do this in a way that doesn't take the intellectual work away from the students. Instead of simply telling students what to think, use moves from the ART to make the process of argumentation visible to students. It also helps if we, as teachers, have developed the habit of admitting our own errors in front of the students and of thanking them when they point our errors out to us. We need to model for our students that making mistakes and self-correcting is an important part of inquiry, even for experts or authorities in a discipline.

Is it okay if students say, "I am undecided" or "I am on the fence"?

Inquiry dialogue is not a debate, so students do not have to commit to one side of the issue. However, you should help students clarify their positions by asking them to explain their reasons and evidence on each side. As long as students can support their position of "being undecided," they don't have to choose sides. In fact, for many complex questions, the best position may be to maintain the tension between two sides and to delay making a judgment until more information becomes available. In today's world, where people often express strong opinions without carefully studying the issues, it is important to reassure students that suspending judgment until one is genuinely persuaded by compelling reasons and evidence is always a respectable choice. During closure, it may also be helpful to check back with students to ask whether they moved toward another position and to explain why.

What should I do when all students line up on the same side of the big question?

In an ideal world, a truly contestable big question should protect us from having students line up on the same side of the issue. However, in the real world, even the best questions may not immediately provoke enough disagreement among students, especially if most of them belong to the same cultural group. One strategy to address this problem is to alert students to the fact that they are all thinking in a similar way and then push for an alternative view. For example, using the ART practice 3, Discussing alternatives, you can say, "We now have three examples showing that Evelyn did not care about the art contest. Can someone give us an example that illustrates a different point of view?" Note that students do not need to accept alternative perspectives to carefully think about them and to make sure that they are not overlooking important considerations on the other side. For example, you might ask students, "Do any of you know people who think differently about this?" Or you can simply invite students to play devil's advocate by asking, "If someone just now knocked on our door and said they disagreed with you, what reasons might they give?"

It is also important to mention that disagreement among students can often be masked by the lack of clarity during the discussion. We often see students using the phrase "I agree with . . ." when in fact they are disagreeing or agreeing only partially with the previous speaker. One way to unearth such hidden disagreements is to prompt students to clearly relate their contributions to each other by using the ART practice 5, Connecting ideas, and asking such questions as "How are you agreeing with Rebecca? Which part are you agreeing with?"

At times, you might need to introduce an alternative viewpoint by saying, "Some people might disagree and say that Evelyn cared about the contest because she made such a beautiful drawing. How would you respond to these people?" The phrase "some people might say" (rather than "I think") removes your authority as the teacher and makes the statement more neutral so that the students can find it easier to disagree with it. Still, we recommend that you introduce alternative perspective only occasionally because doing so precludes students from coming up with their own ideas and takes away from their ownership of the discussion.

Do we need to arrive at consensus?

The goal of inquiry dialogue is to find the most reasonable answer to the big question. It is this goal that orients the discussion toward collaborative and rigorous argumentation.[11] Nonetheless, classroom discussions will often end not because the group came up with the most reasonable answer to the big question, but simply because the time is up. Also, some questions may have more than one well-justified conclusion. In this way, inquiry dialogue is more like the deliberations of the Supreme Court, which typically end in majority and minority opinions, than like the deliberations of a jury, in which consensus is forced. It may also be impossible to make any further progress without finding out more information from additional sources. In such situations, a push for consensus would not be in the best interests of encouraging reasonable decision making.

For these reasons, reaching a consensus is not necessary during the discussions. Instead, the goal is to help students realize that not all positions can withstand the scrutiny of the group, and that by engaging in inquiry, we can eliminate some reasons and positions and make progress toward answering the big question. Pointing out the progress the group has made is important in these situations. For example, during closure, you might ask, "How many different possible answers to the big question did we come up with today? Did we eliminate any of those answers as less reasonable? For the positions that we ended up with, how many reasons for and against each position did we come up with? If we continue this discussion next time, where would we begin?"

During inquiry dialogue, students may talk about highly sensitive and contentious beliefs about the world that come from their cultural or religious backgrounds. Should I avoid such topics?

Because students have more authority over the talk during inquiry dialogue, they may indeed turn to topics that have direct relevance to their lives but that may be challenging to discuss. For example, students might introduce topics that deal with the questions of race, gender, inequality, religion, or violence, and they may have opposing viewpoints about these questions. It is understandable that our initial instinct may be to steer students away from discussing these difficult topics. Yet, we, as teachers, need to remember that students will likely discuss these topics with each other on the playground, on the school bus, and elsewhere. So, by discouraging such topics in our classrooms, we are depriving students of the opportunity to engage with important questions in a supportive environment: an inquiry dialogue that is facilitated by a caring adult, has established rules for treating each other with respect, and is characterized by a shared commitment to exposing misinformation and flawed reasoning.[12] Also, if students don't have productive models for resolving disagreements around the issues that concern their lives, how else will they learn to talk and live with others who think differently from them? Ultimately, it is up to the teacher to judge whether a particular topic is appropriate. We hope that our common humanity, respect for each other, and the adherence to the practices of collaborative and rigorous argumentation can help turn the discussion of (almost) any topic into an instructive and rewarding experience for everyone.

Argumentation Rating Tool (ART)

Practice 1. Centering on contestable questions

	ADVANCING 6	5	DEVELOPING 4	3	NOT YET 2	1
Teacher	The teacher **centers the discussion on a big, contestable question** about the text or about an issue related to it. Other open-ended questions may be asked in service of the big question. Questions invite multiple perspectives and target higher-order thinking, involving students in critical evaluation and analysis of each other's arguments. Eventually, the teacher invites students to take part in generating big questions in relation to assigned readings. *Today, our big question is . . .* *Did uncle Jed live a happy life?* *Should girls and boys play together in team sports?* *What are some big questions we can ask about this story?*		The teacher asks **questions of mixed quality**, including some open-ended questions. Questions may be designed to steer students toward a certain interpretation of the text. **The teacher may shape the discussion** to emphasize predetermined "points-not-to-miss" during the lesson. *Have you ever been away from home? Now you can imagine how Chano felt.*		The teacher asks **basic test questions** about specific details from the text or facts known from other sources (*What? When? How many?*) These questions typically have only one correct answer. *What happens to Carlos next? The answer is on page 65.*	
Students	Students **consistently** engage in the **critical and collaborative construction of arguments** in relation to the big, contestable question. These questions invite multiple perspectives. As a result, students go beyond simple agreement with each other's views. For example, a reason given by one student is challenged by the next student. Eventually, students take part in generating contestable questions about their readings. *My question is "Was Victor real?"*		Students **occasionally** engage with open-ended, contestable questions. They often **share similar opinions and experiences**, rather than critically evaluate each other's arguments. **Disagreement is rare.** *This happened to me, too! I was visiting my aunt in Boston . . .*		Students respond to basic questions, often with short, disjointed, and unrelated statements. Students primarily **report about established, known facts.** *The story says Carlos got too close to a skunk and he got sprayed.*	

Practice 2. Sharing responsibilities

	ADVANCING		DEVELOPING		NOT YET	
	6	5	4	3	2	1
Teacher	The teacher **shares responsibilities for the flow of discussion with students.** She may start by modeling effective moves to support student argumentation, but eventually she intervenes only to support all students' participation and rigorous argumentation. In the long run, the teacher becomes just one of the participants in the group. *You can now nominate the next person, Sirine.* *How should we address the problem with interrupting each other?*		The teacher invites students to contribute although she **largely controls the flow of the discussion.** She often nominates students, prescribes topic choice, and shapes the discussion to align with a given perspective. She mediates most interactions between students and may try to steer the discussion toward predetermined conclusions. *Great idea, Josh. That's what I thought about Carlos too. Beth, you agree with that, right?*		The teacher **has exclusive control** over the flow of the discussion. She holds the floor most of the time and talks more frequently and longer than students. She nominates students, asks questions, initiates topical shifts, and evaluates the answers. The pattern of talk is teacher-student-teacher-student. . . . *Teacher: Robin, what's the name of the main character?* *Robin: Amy.* *Teacher: That's right.*	
Students	Students **take on multiple key responsibilities** for the flow of the discussion. **There is a clear sense of ownership.** Most students participate in managing turns (self-selecting or nominating others), asking questions, judging each other's answers, introducing new topics, and suggesting strategies to improve the quality of argumentation. Students give longer, elaborated responses, and they direct their answers to other students, rather than to the teacher. There are consecutive peer-to-peer exchanges uninterrupted by the teacher. *Jon: Well, I think the one responsible for Zack's injury would be the coach because he was the one who let Zack play. Andy?* *Andy: I disagree with Jon because it said in the passage that Zack thought that his team needed help, so he decided to go back in.* *Beatrice: Wait, I think people are only calling on their friends to talk, and that's not fair.*		There are **some opportunities** for students to take ownership of the discussion. These are limited and/or **involve only a few students.** Students' responses are generally directed to the teacher. Peer-to-peer exchanges are rare.		Students **speak much less than the teacher** and direct their answers to the teacher. Their responses are short, often consisting of one word or phrase. The communication follows a typical recitation pattern of teacher initiating question-student responding-teacher evaluating. *Teacher: He sees a nest, way, way, way up on a cliff. And he must have pretty good eyes because what does he see in the nest?* *Robert: Eagles.* *Teacher: He actually sees eaglets. Leo, what's an eaglet?* *Leo: Baby eagles.*	

#1. DIVERSITY OF PERSPECTIVES: WE EXPLORE DIFFERENT PERSPECTIVES TOGETHER

Practice 3. Discussing alternatives

	6 ADVANCING	5	4 DEVELOPING	3	2 NOT YET	1
Teacher	The teacher **prompts students to take into account missing perspectives** overlooked by the group, whenever students fail to consider alternative viewpoints. **Teacher questions are well focused**, inviting students to carefully examine their disagreements. *Which part are you disagreeing with?* *Let Molly respond to this.* *If someone disagreed with you, what would that person say to argue against you?* *So far, we haven't heard from anyone who never had a pet. I wonder if they think the same way.* *Is this the only explanation?* *We have a number of examples already. Can anyone offer a counterexample?*		The teacher makes an effort to invite multiple interpretations. However, he **may miss opportunities** to probe for alternative perspectives, especially when students' answers are consistent with the predetermined plan for the lesson. The prompts for alternative perspectives are overly general. There may be clear content boundaries for the discussion. The teacher **may constrain and refocus the discussion** in a predetermined direction. *Anybody else?* *Does anyone disagree?*		There are **few, if any, opportunities** for students to consider alternative points of view to the correct answer given in the text or by the teacher. *That's right, Rachel. And then what happened?*	
Students	Students **consistently bring up alternative viewpoints.** These multiple viewpoints are seriously considered and challenged by group members. *I disagree with Jeff because . . .* *Well, some people might say that he cheated when he ran across the lake.* *But, Don, what about that time in the story when . . . ?* *I disagree with all of you and think that he should tell because . . .* *I guess if someone disagreed, that person might say that . . .*		Students **occasionally bring up or explore alternative viewpoints.** Disagreement is rare.		Students **do not** bring up and discuss alternative viewpoints.	

#2. CLARITY: WE ARE CLEAR IN THE LANGUAGE AND STRUCTURE OF OUR ARGUMENTS

Practice 4. Clarifying meaning

	ADVANCING 6 5	DEVELOPING 4 3	NOT YET 2 1
Teacher	The teacher **asks students to clarify their ideas** and to restate each other's responses, whenever student statements lack precision. She closely paraphrases, revoices, and **distills student responses**, helping to highlight key ideas. The teacher often **follows up with a student** to make sure the paraphrasing is accurate. (*Is that what you were saying?*) *I hear you saying . . . Is that what you mean?* *Can someone else say what you understand his point to be? . . . Jose, is that what you meant?* *So are you saying that. . .?* *How are you using the word . . . ?* *Are you making a distinction between . . . and . . . ?* *What characteristics make someone "an adult" . . . ?* *How is cheating different from lying?* *How is this similar to . . . ? Would this be the same as . . . ?* *Okay, so it looks like we can't move forward without first clarifying what we mean by . . .*	The teacher **occasionally** checks for clarity and asks students to explain their answers. When paraphrasing, the teacher **may change the original meaning** of student answers to emphasize specific points that students should not miss. The teacher sometimes selectively adds or subtracts information from student answers to fit in with a predetermined purpose for the lesson. Questions are often **overly general.** *Is everyone following so far?* *Is this clear? Any questions?* *Can you explain more?*	The teacher may ask students to simply **repeat right answers.** Incorrect, incomplete, or unclear answers from students often remain unexamined. *Say it again, Jorge, so that everyone can hear the right answer.*
Students	Students **paraphrase their own and each other's answers,** offer definitions, give examples, and otherwise work to clarify meaning, whenever necessary. They check with each other to make sure the group understands the ideas accurately and completely. *What I think Jose was saying is that . . .* *Mirabai and I were using the same word to mean different things. . . .* *Hannah, I am confused. Could you say that again?*	Students **occasionally** paraphrase their own answers, but not those of their peers. Students reformulate their ideas to clarify what they mean, instead of repeating what they originally said. *What I meant was that nobody is responsible. It's an accident.* *What I was saying was . . .*	Students **do not** paraphrase answers. They may repeat correct answers about specific facts from the text. They don't have opportunities to clarify or reformulate more complex thoughts.

#2. CLARITY: WE ARE CLEAR IN THE LANGUAGE AND STRUCTURE OF OUR ARGUMENTS

Practice 5. Connecting ideas

	ADVANCING 6 / 5	DEVELOPING 4 / 3	NOT YET 2 / 1
Teacher	The teacher **clarifies the group's reasoning** by making visible the connections among students' ideas. The teacher prompts students to relate their ideas to what's been said by others **in specific ways.** He attributes student ideas and questions to specific speakers. This happens whenever students fail to build on or challenge each other's arguments. *Which part are you agreeing with?* *What is the difference between what you are saying and what Quincy said?* *How does this relate to what William said?* *Martin, do you want to respond to Kim?* *Kelly, you said you are disagreeing with Jon's point. How are you disagreeing?* *I don't see how your example supports Keisha's position. Can you explain more?* *How is this example relevant to what Marina said earlier about . . . ?*	The teacher allows students to give redundant answers that make the points already made by others. The requests for connections are often **overly general. The teacher misses opportunities** to connect students' ideas. *Anything else?* *Does anyone have something to add?* *Does anyone agree or disagree?*	The teacher **does not** relate student answers to each other. *Okay, the next question on page 12 is, "Why did Morgan run away from home?" Who can give us the answer?*
Students	Student **responses are interrelated** and connected to the ideas of others. The responses are chained together as **students react to each other's positions and justifications,** building on or challenging each other's reasoning. *As Jack said before . . .* *I disagree about one thing in what Brad just said . . .* *Jamilla's point might be true, but I have a different example. . . .* *What Omar said changes everything for me. Now, I think . . .*	Students **occasionally** relate their answers to the contributions of other group members. Often, these connections involve the sharing of similar opinions and personal experiences. Thus, the degree of simple agreement and repetition may be high. *Colleen's story reminds me of one time when I got lost in the mall.*	Students simply state their answers in a sequential fashion, essentially disregarding the input of others. Their answers **do not** relate to contributions already made in the discussion.

Practice 6. Labeling reasoning processes and parts of an argument

	ADVANCING 6 5	4 DEVELOPING 3	2 NOT YET 1
Teacher	The teacher **consistently makes visible the process of argumentation**. She **calls attention** to a variety of reasoning moves and parts of an argument used by the students and asks students to label their reasoning. The teacher does this whenever there is a need to clarify the structure of the arguments and the processes of argumentation. *Is this a reason for or against . . . ?* *Thank you, Irina, for helping Jordan clarify his position.* *Jack just offered another reason for . . .* *So, should I put this example next to Tyson's reason?* *Mathew just made an important distinction. Let's make sure it is not overlooked.* *So, are you questioning Ann's assumption?* *Rumi is now challenging your reason..* *Who can tell me what kind of move Ben just made?* *The last few examples all made the same point; can anyone give us an example on the other side, or a counterexample?*	The teacher **occasionally** uses labels for basic reasoning moves and argument elements offered by the students. *This was a very good reason, Dennis.* *Who can give an example of this?* *Is there any evidence of that in the story?*	The teacher **does not** comment on students' reasoning.
Students	Students **consistently label their own reasoning and argument elements** and otherwise reflect on the processes of group argumentation. They suggest strategies to move the inquiry forward. *I agree with your position, but I disagree with your evidence.* *This may be off topic, but I want to add another reason for . . .* *Wait, I am not clear about this. I need an example.*	Students **occasionally** label their reasoning and argument elements. *I agree with Katy.* *I have another example.*	Students **do not** identify reasoning and argument elements.

#2. CLARITY: WE ARE CLEAR IN THE LANGUAGE AND STRUCTURE OF OUR ARGUMENTS

Practice 7. Tracking the line of inquiry

	ADVANCING 6 5	DEVELOPING 4 3	NOT YET 2 1
Teacher	The teacher **summarizes or asks students to summarize the arguments** made by the group in relation to the big questions. She does this **to help students see a continuous and clear line of inquiry**—moving from the big question, to generating and testing possible answers, to then narrowing down to the most reasonable answer or answers. This is done whenever there is a need to clarify confusion, improve coherence, assess progress, or help advance the inquiry further. *Where are we now? Let's retrace what has been said so far.* *So, it seems that we are torn between the value of learning a lesson and the chance to win a competition.* *How many different positions on our big question have emerged so far?* *Can someone now list all the reasons we gave for and against this position? Are we ready to eliminate any of them?*	The teacher may summarize or ask students to **summarize key points** of the discussion (e.g., to emphasize a given point). The teacher **misses opportunities** to summarize or to ask students to summarize the arguments made by the group. *Sally, what do we know about the relationship between Carlos and Gloria? . . . So, do you see now why he wanted to impress her?*	The teacher **does not** summarize or ask students to summarize the arguments. She **may ask students to retell specific facts** and events from the text to test for basic knowledge and comprehension. There is **no ongoing line of inquiry** to which the students could relate their ideas. *Max, tell us what the conditions on the ship were like? . . . Good. Kim, now what did the sailors decide to do next?*
Students	Students ask for and/or offer **summaries of each other's arguments**, by stringing together **multiple strands of a discussion**. They direct attention back to the big question and help each other **follow the on-going line of inquiry**, keeping the discussion well focused and relevant. *I think what Lisa and Rob were saying is that . . . But then Derek disagreed and said that . . .* *Sounds like we are going around in circles. Can we go back to Alex's example of . . . ?* *We decided that Kelly should not tell on Evelyn because . . .*	Students **may summarize key points of the discussion** or restate their own opinion. However, students do not summarize the arguments made by the group. *I was saying that Carlos wanted to impress Gloria because he liked her. So, he got too close to the skunk.*	Students **don't summarize group arguments**. They may recall the events from the text, often in a sequential fashion. *First, he climbed the mountain to get the bird's feathers. But then his rope broke, and he got stuck up there.*

#3. ACCEPTABILITY: WE USE REASONS AND EVIDENCE THAT ARE WELL EXAMINED AND ACCURATE

Practice 8. Evaluating facts

	ADVANCING		DEVELOPING		NOT YET	
	6	5	4	3	2	1
Teacher	The teacher **prompts students to examine each other's use of factual statements.** Teacher questions address the basis or accuracy of information from the text, other sources, as well as students' interpretations of what has been said by other group members. The teacher does this whenever there is a potential issue with the acceptability of factual statements that students offer in support of their positions. *How do we know this?* *Is this true? Do we know this for a fact?* *Where is this information coming from? Is this a good source?* *Is it always true? Is this true everywhere?* *Can someone offer an example on the other side?* *Is this evidence strong enough, considering what's at stake?* *Is this what Amanda was saying?*		The teacher **occasionally** asks students to refer to the text or other sources to support their positions. There is little to no evaluation of acceptability of information. *Where do you see that in the text?* *Is there any evidence in the story for what you're saying?*		The teacher may simply reference the text when testing student knowledge of basic facts. The teacher **misses opportunities** to prompt students to use factual information to support their positions. *Let's turn to page 442.* *What is the name of the character in the picture?*	
Students	Students consistently discuss **the sources and accuracy** of information used to support their positions. They refer to text and other sources for evidence, **address the acceptability of information, and correct each other's misrepresentations.** *But that's not what the story said. Here, on page 15, it says . . .* *How do you know that students were allowed to leave the building during recess?* *But that's just one example!*		Students **refer to the text or other sources** to support their positions. However, there is little to no evaluation of acceptability of information. *In the story, it said that . . .* *My mom showed me a newspaper article about this the other night, and it said . . .*		Students **do not** refer to text or other sources of information to support their positions. They simply recall textual information, but they do not use it in their arguments.	

Practice 9. Evaluating values

	ADVANCING 6	5	DEVELOPING 4	3	NOT YET 2	1
Teacher	The teacher **prompts students to examine value statements, including moral principles, beliefs, norms, rules, or conventions.** She does this whenever there is a problem with the acceptability and sources of value statements offered by students in support of their positions. *Is this value more important than other values? Why? (e.g., Is it more important to tell the truth or to protect someone's feelings?)* *How important is this, compared to other things we talked about?* *Do we ALWAYS have to follow this rule? (e.g., Are there any situations when lying can be acceptable?)* *Does this rule ALWAYS work? Does it work for EVERYONE, or only for SOME?* *Is this ALWAYS true?* *What if everyone thought or acted this way?* *Who says this is the case? Should we trust what they say?* *Can both of the things you said be true at the same time?*		The teacher **occasionally** asks students to examine value statements that describe moral principles, beliefs, norms, rules, or conventions. However, she may either steer students to a given position or attempt to validate all points of view, instead of critically examining them. *Of course, everyone has the right to their own opinion.* *So, we see that every family handles this kind of thing in their own way.*		The teacher **does not** ask students to examine value statements that describe moral principles, beliefs, norms, rules, or conventions.	
Students	Students **consistently address the acceptability and sources of value statements** used to support positions advocated by the group. *But Jerry, why do we have to wait to vote until eighteen, like our parents? I think we should be able to vote now, especially about things for our school.* *This rule should be changed, because . . .*		Students **occasionally** articulate or examine value statements used to justify their positions, supporting them with further explanations.		Students **do not** articulate or examine value statements used to justify their positions.	

Practice 10. Articulating reasons

	ADVANCING 6 5	DEVELOPING 4 3	NOT YET 2 1
Teacher	The teacher **asks students to provide reasons**, examples, and evidence, whenever students fail to support their views. *What is your reason for saying that . . . ?* *What would be an example of this?* *Can you explain why you disagree?* *What makes you say this?* *What would count as evidence for that position?*	The teacher **occasionally** asks students to explain what they think and why.	The teacher **does not** ask students to explain what they think and why.
Students	Students **consistently and appropriately address the questions "Why?" and "How?"** They take public positions on the issue ("I think," "I believe," "I feel") and support them with reasons and evidence. **They make elaborated, lengthy contributions, explaining their thinking to others.** *I disagree with Johan. I don't think that it's the coach's fault because in the paragraph it says the coaches weren't trained at that time to know what brain concussion looks like. And brain concussions are invisible injuries; it says it in this story, so I don't find that it's the coach's fault. . . . Plus, Zack said he was fine, so how is the coach supposed to know?*	Students **occasionally** explain what they think and why, providing some support for and elaboration of their views. However, longer responses often consist of simple retelling of personal experiences or events from the story, addressing the question of what happened. *I can connect to this. Like, I was in my house once, and I thought no one was home, so I started singing and dancing, and the whole time my sister was at the door recording me, and I didn't know that.*	Students **do not** explain what they think and why. Their responses are brief and factual, often consisting of one word or phrase. *Carlos got too close to the skunk.*

#4. LOGICAL VALIDITY: WE ARE LOGICAL IN THE WAY WE CONNECT OUR POSITIONS, REASONS, AND EVIDENCE

Practice 11. Evaluating inferences

	6 ADVANCING	5	4 DEVELOPING	3	2 NOT YET	1
Teacher	The teacher **consistently** helps students recognize and evaluate stated and unstated links between evidence, reasons, and positions. She enhances the quality of reasoning by addressing the following issues, as necessary: *How does this relate to our big question?* *So, are you saying that if you know about concussion, then you are responsible?* *Why is this relevant here?* *Does this follow from what Katrina said?* *What's the link between that and your position?* *What follows from this?* *Do you think we're jumping to conclusions here?* *Is that reason enough to accept your conclusion? Is this a safe generalization?* *Are you assuming that . . . ?* *What are we assuming when we say . . . ? Is that a reasonable assumption?* *I am not sure I see how this relates to your position that . . .*		The teacher **occasionally** helps students recognize and evaluate links between evidence, reasons, and positions. However, these questions **typically relate to inferences that stem from the text**, rather than from students' arguments. *What do you think will happen to Carlos now?*		The teacher **does not** prompt students to recognize or evaluate inferences.	
Students	Students **consistently** articulate and evaluate the quality of inferences linking evidence, reasons, and positions. *Sally: This team is going to win the next game because they lost too many games already. (Sally's unstated link is "If you lost in the past, you are due to win soon.")* *Elena: I disagree. Just because a team has lost a lot of games recently, it does not mean it will win big soon. . . . (Elena questions Sally's unstated link.)*		Students **occasionally** articulate and evaluate the quality of inferences linking evidence, reasons, and positions. However, these statements **typically relate to inferences that stem from the text**, rather than from students' arguments. *If she were afraid of the boy, she would not have invited him to her house.*		Students **do not** articulate inferences or evaluate their quality.	

ART During Inquiry

Overview of Four ART Criteria and Eleven Practices

1. Diversity of perspectives	1. Centering on contestable questions	*Today our big question is . . .*
	2. Sharing responsibilities	*You can now nominate the next person, Sirine. How should we address the problem of interrupting each other?*
	3. Discussing alternatives	*Which part are you disagreeing with? Let Molly respond to this. Is this the only explanation?*
2. Clarity	4. Clarifying meaning	*I hear you saying . . . Is that what you mean? So are you saying that. . .?*
	5. Connecting ideas	*Which part are you agreeing with? How does this relate to what William said?*
	6. Labeling reasoning processes and parts of an argument	*Is this a reason for or against . . .? Thank you, Irina, for helping Jordan clarify his position.*
	7. Tracking the line of inquiry	*Where are we now? Let's retrace what has been said so far. How many different positions on our big question have emerged so far?*
3. Acceptability of reasons and evidence	8. Evaluating facts	*How do we know this? Is this true? Do we know this for a fact? Where is this information coming from? Is this a good source? Is it always true? Is this true everywhere?*
	9. Evaluating values	*Is this value more important than other values? Why? How important is this compared to other things we talked about? Does this rule ALWAYS work? Does it work for EVERYONE?*
4. Logical validity	10. Articulating reasons	*What is your reason for saying that . . . ? Can you explain why you disagree?*
	11. Evaluating inferences	*Does this follow from what Katrina said? What's the link between that and your position? What follows from this? Do you think we're jumping to conclusions here? Are you assuming that . . . ? Is that a reasonable assumption? Why is this relevant here?*

FOCUSING ON DIVERSITY OF PERSPECTIVES

We Explore Different Perspectives Together

Practice 1: Centering on Contestable Questions

- Today our big question is. . .
- What are some big questions we can ask about this story?

Practice 2: Sharing Responsibilities

- You can now nominate the next person, Sirine.
- How should we address the problem of interrupting each other?

Practice 3: Discussing Alternatives

- Which part are you disagreeing with?
- Let Molly respond to this.
- If someone disagreed with you, what would that person say to argue against you?
- So far, we haven't heard from anyone who never had a pet. I wonder if they think the same way.
- Is this the only explanation?
- We have a number of examples already. Can anyone offer a counterexample?

FOCUSING ON CLARITY
We Are Clear in the Language and Structure of Our Arguments
Practice 4: Clarifying Meaning

- I hear you saying . . . Is that what you mean?
- Can someone else say what you understand his point to be? . . . Jose, is that what you meant?
- How are you using the word . . . ?
- Are you making a distinction between . . . and . . . ?
- How is this similar to . . . ? Would this be the same as . . . ?

Practice 5: Connecting Ideas

- Which part are you agreeing with?
- What is the difference between what you are saying and what Quincy said?
- How does this relate to what William said?
- Martin, do you want to respond to Kim?
- What does this mean for our big question?
- Kelly, you said you are disagreeing with Jon's point. How are you disagreeing?

Practice 6: Labeling Reasoning Processes and Parts of an Argument

- Is this a reason for or against . . . ?
- Thank you, Irina, for helping Jordan clarify his position.
- So, should I put this example next to Tyson's reason?
- Mathew just made an important distinction.
- So, are you questioning Ann's assumption?
- Rumi is now challenging your reason.
- Who can tell me what kind of move Ben just made?
- The last few examples all made the same point. Can anyone give us an example on the other side, or a counterexample?

Practice 7: Tracking the Line of Inquiry

- Where are we now? Let's retrace what has been said so far.
- How many different positions on our big question have emerged so far?
- Can someone now list all the reasons we gave for and against this position? Are we satisfied with these reasons? Are we ready to eliminate any of them?

FOCUSING ON ACCEPTABILITY

We Use Reasons and Evidence That Are Well Examined and Accurate

Practice 8: Evaluating Facts

- How do we know this?
- Is this true? Do we know this for a fact?
- Where is this information coming from? Is this a good source?
- Is it always true? Is this true everywhere?
- Is this evidence strong enough, considering what's at stake?
- Is this what Amanda was saying?

Practice 9: Evaluating Values

- Is this value more important than other values? Why? (e.g., Is it more important to tell the truth or to protect someone's feelings?)
- How important is this compared to other things we talked about?
- Do we *always* have to follow this rule? (e.g., Are there any situations when lying can be acceptable?)
- Does this rule *always* work? Does it work for *everyone*, or only for *some*?
- Is this *always* true?
- Who says this is the case? Should we trust what they say?
- Can both of the things you said be true at the same time?

FOCUSING ON LOGICAL VALIDITY
We Are Logical in the Way We Connect Our Positions and Reasons

Practice 10: Articulating Reasons

- What is your reason for saying that . . . ?
- What would be an example of this?
- Can you explain why you disagree?
- What makes you say this?
- What would count as evidence for that position?

Practice 11: Evaluating Inferences

- Does this follow from what Katrina said?
- What's the link between that and your position?
- What follows from this?
- Do you think we're jumping to conclusions here?
- Is that reason enough to accept your conclusion? Is this a safe generalization?
- Are you assuming that . . . ?
- What are we assuming when we say . . . ? Is that a reasonable assumption?
- Why is this relevant here?
- I am not sure I see how this relates to your position that . . .

ART for Kids

DIFFERENT POINTS OF VIEW

Do we discuss different ideas together?

1. We talk about big questions that are important and tricky to answer.

2. We make sure most of us get a chance to speak.

3. We explore different points of view.

4. We challenge each other's ideas when we disagree.

5. We change our positions if there are good reasons.

What do you see or hear to support your ratings?

_____

_____

What can we say or do to improve the ratings?

_____

_____

CLARITY

Do we understand what is being said and how it all fits together?

1. We explain our thinking clearly.

2. We help each other clarify our ideas by asking follow-up questions.

3. We connect what we are saying to what other people have said.

4. We use words like *position, reason, evidence,* or *example* to explain what we mean.

5. We summarize what other people said.

6. We keep track of where we are in the discussion and where we're going.

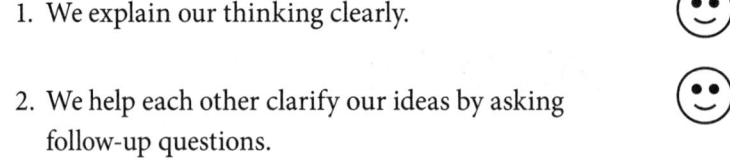

What do you see or hear to support your ratings?

_____

_____

What can we say or do to improve the ratings?

_____

_____

ACCEPTABILITY

Do we use well-examined reasons and evidence?

1. We make sure we use accurate information.

2. We refer to the text for evidence.

3. We question whether something is always true or true only some of the time.

4. We talk about how important some things are compared to others.

What do you see or hear to support your ratings?

_____

_____

What can we say or do to improve the ratings?

_____

_____

LOGICAL VALIDITY
Do we build strong arguments?

1. We explain why we agree or disagree.

2. We give relevant reasons and evidence for our positions.

3. We check to see if our reasons really lead to our positions.

4. We ask each other if we are assuming something that we really shouldn't.

What do you see or hear to support your ratings?

_____

_____

What can we say or do to improve the ratings?

_____

_____

Discussion Planning Tool:
Template

Text:

Grouping:

PRE-DISCUSSION	DISCUSSION	POST-DISCUSSION
Reading:	**Launch**	Speaking:
	General purpose:	
	Ground rules:	Listening:
	Specific focus:	
	Big question:	
Engaging with text:		
	Inquiry dialogue	Reading:
	Position:	
	Position:	
	Position:	
	Possible talk moves:	Writing:
	Closure	

Argument House: Template

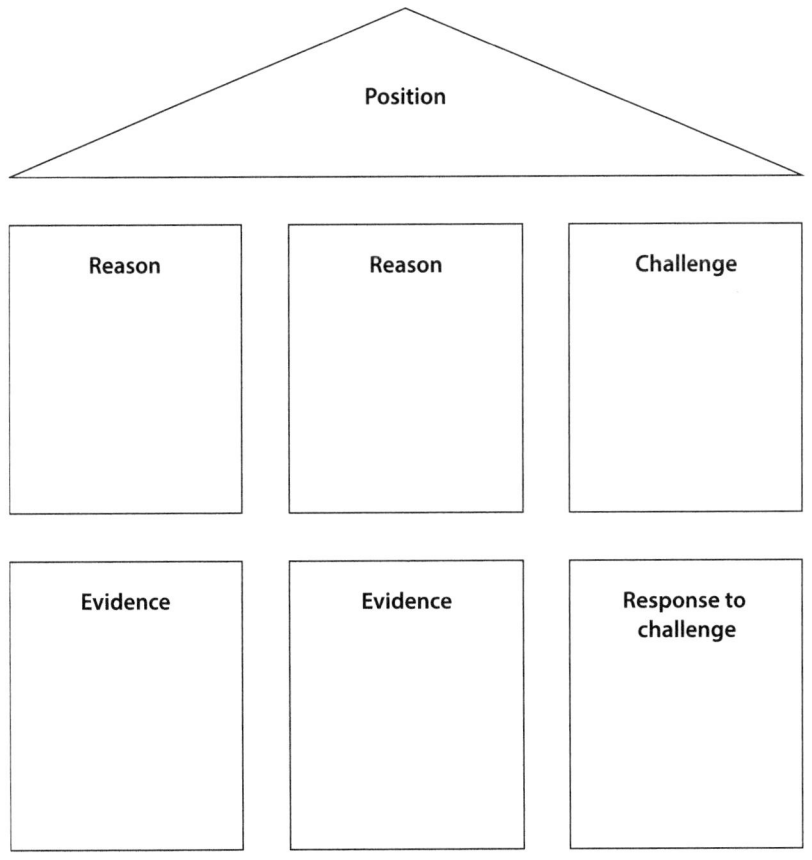

Writing Arguments: Scoring Rubric

Student ID _____

CATEGORY	4	3	2	1	SCORE
Support for chosen position	The writer provides a **clear position** that is **strongly supported** by reasons and evidence (e.g., there are more than four reasons or evidence). All reasons and evidence are relevant and accurate.	There is a **clear position** that is **moderately supported** by reasons and evidence (e.g., there are only two or three reasons or evidence, or not all reasons are relevant and accurate).	There is a **clear position** that is **not well supported** by reasons and evidence (e.g., there is only one reason, or none of the reasons is relevant and accurate).	The writer **does *not* take a position**, or does not directly address the question, or a position is *not* **supported** with reasons and evidence.	
Alternative perspective	The writer provides **more than one** reason or evidence for an alternative perspective. The writer **explains why** the chosen position is more reasonable than the alternative using accurate and relevant reason(s) or evidence.	The writer provides **only one** reason or evidence for an alternative perspective. The writer **explains why** the chosen position is more reasonable than the alternative, using accurate and relevant reason(s) or evidence.	The writer provides **one or more** reason(s) or evidence for an alternative perspective. **No explanation** is given as to why the chosen position is more reasonable.	The writer **does *not* provide** an alternative perspective. The argument is one-sided.	
Clarity	The essay has **clear** language and a coherent structure (e.g., position-support-alternative- restatement of position). The entire essay is well focused.	The essay has **reasonably clear** language and coherent structure. The majority of the essay is well focused (e.g., it may contain some irrelevant or inconsistent information).	**Only parts** of the essay have clear language and a coherent structure. The majority of the essay is *not* well focused (e.g., it may contain some irrelevant or inconsistent information).	The essay **does *not* have** clear language and a coherent structure. It lacks focus in addressing the question/prompt.	

Notes

Preface

1. Examples of such publications include Robert Ennis, *Critical Thinking* (Upper Saddle River, NJ: Prentice Hall, 1996); Trudy Govier, *A Practical Study of Argument,* 7th ed. (Belmont, CA: Wadsworth Publishing Company, 2010); Deanna Kuhn, Laura Hemberger, and Valerie Khait, *Argue with Me: Argument as a Path to Developing Students' Thinking and Writing* (New York, NY: Routledge, 2016).

2. Neil Postman, *The End of Education: Redefining the Value of School* (New York: Knopf, 1995); Matthew Lipman, Ann Sharp, and Frederick S. Oscanyon, *Philosophy in the Classroom* (Philadelphia, PA: Temple University Press, 1980), 73.

3. Lipman, Sharp, and Oscanyon, *Philosophy in the Classroom*, 73.

4. For example, National Governors Association Center for Best Practices, The Council of Chief State School Officers, *Common Core State Standards: Appendix A. Research Supporting Key Elements of the Standards* (Washington, DC: National Governors Association Center for Best Practices, Council of Chief State School, 2010); Partnership for 21st Century Skills, *A Framework for 21st Century Learning* (Washington, DC: P21, 2012); Abby Goodnough, "The Examined Life, Age 8," *New York Times,* April, 16, 2010; Deanna Kuhn, "Teaching and Learning Science as Argument," *Science Education* 94, no. 5 (2010): 810–24.

5. Gerald Graff, *Clueless in Academe* (New Haven, CT: Yale University Press, 2003).

6. National Governors Association Center for Best Practices, *Common Core State Standards*, 24.

7. Neil Mercer, Rupert Wegerif, and Lyn D. Mercer, "Children's Talk and the Development of Reasoning in the Classroom," *British Educational Research Journal* 25, no. 1 (1999): 95–111; P. Karen Murphy, Ian A. G. Wilkinson, Anna O. Soter, Maeghan N. Hennessey, and John F. Alexander, "Examining the Effects of Classroom Discussion on Students' Comprehension of Text: A Meta-Analysis," *Journal of Educational Psychology* 101, no. 3 (2009): 740–64; Alina Reznitskaya, Li-Jen Kuo, Ann-Marie Clark, Brian Miller, May Jadallah, Richard C. Anderson, and Kim Nguyen-Jahiel, "Collaborative Reasoning: A Dialogic Approach to Group Discussions," *Cambridge Journal of Education* 39, no. 1 (2009): 29–48.

8. National Governors Association Center for Best Practices, *Common Core State Standards*.

9. Deanna Kuhn and Wadiya Udell, "The Development of Argument Skills," *Child Development* 74, no. 5 (2003): 1245–60; Mercer, Wegerif, and Mercer, "Children's Talk and the Development

of Reasoning in the Classroom," 95–111; Christa S. C. Asterhan and Baruch B. Schwarz, "The Effects of Monological and Dialogical Argumentation on Concept Learning in Evolutionary Theory," *Journal of Educational Psychology* 99, no. 3 (2007): 626–39; Clark A. Chinn, Angela M. O'Donnell, and Theresa S. Jinks, "The Structure of Discourse in Collaborative Learning," *Journal of Experimental Education* 69, no. 1 (2000): 77–97.

10. Lipman, Sharp, and Oscanyon, *Philosophy in the Classroom*; Murphy, Wilkinson, Soter, Hennessey, and Alexander, "Examining the Effects of Classroom Discussion on Students' Comprehension of Text: A Meta-Analysis," 740–64; Reznitskaya, Kuo, Clark, Miller, Jadallahd, Anderson, and Nguyen-Jahiel, "Collaborative Reasoning: A Dialogic Approach to Group Discussions," 29–48; Ian A. G. Wilkinson, Anna O. Soter, and P. Karen Murphy, "Developing a Model of Quality Talk About Literary Text," in *Bringing Reading Research to Life*, ed. Margaret G. McKeown and Linda Kucan (New York: Guilford Press, 2010), 142–69.

11. Publications from this work include: Alina Reznitskaya and Ian A. G. Wilkinson, "Professional Development in Dialogic Teaching: Helping Teachers Promote Argument Literacy in Their Classrooms," in *Sage Handbook of Learning*, ed. David Scott and Eleanore Hargreaves (UK: Sage Publications, 2015), 219–32; Ian A. G. Wilkinson, Alina Reznitskaya, Kristin Bourdage, Joseph Oyler, Kathryn Nelson, Monica Glina, Robert Drewry, and Min-Young Kim, "Toward a More Dialogic Pedagogy: Changing Teachers' Beliefs and Practices Through Professional Development in Language Arts Classrooms," *Language & Education* 31, no. 1 (2017): 65–82; Alina Reznitskaya, Ian A. G. Wilkinson, and Joseph Oyler, "Supporting Teacher Spontaneous Use of Talk Moves During Inquiry Dialogue," in *Students' Spontaneous Use of Effective Strategies*, ed. Emmanuel Manalo, Yuri Uesaka, and Clark A. Chinn (Singapore: Routledge, in press).

Chapter 1

1. This and other excerpts in the book are taken from transcripts of video- or audiotaped interactions obtained as part of the research program "Dialogic Teaching: Professional Development in Classroom Discussion to Improve Students' Argument Literacy," described in the preface of this book. All student names were replaced with pseudonyms.

2. Hugh Mehan, *Learning Lessons* (Cambridge, MA: Harvard University Press, 1979).

3. Rosebud Yellow Robe, "Tonweya and the Eagles," in *McGraw-Hill Reading*, ed. by James Flood, Yan E. Hasbrouck, James V. Hoffman, Diane Lapp, Angela S. Medearis, Scott Paris, Steven Stahl, Josefina. V. Tinajero, and Karen D. Wood (New York, NY: McGraw-Hill School Division, 2001), 557–77.

4. Robin J. Alexander, *Towards Dialogic Teaching: Rethinking Classroom Talk*, 3rd ed. (York, UK: Dialogos, 2006); Arthur N. Applebee, Judith A. Langer, Martin Nystrand, and Adam Gamoran, "Discussion-based Approaches to Developing Understanding: Classroom Instruction and Student Performance in Middle and High School English," *American Educational Research Journal* 40, no. 3 (2003): 685–730; Christine Howe and Manzoorul Abedin, "Classroom Dialogue: A Systematic Review Across Four Decades of Research," *Cambridge Journal of Education* 43, no. 3 (2013): 325–56.

5. Deanna Kuhn and Wadiya Udell, "The Development of Argument Skills," *Child Development* 74, no. 5 (2003): 1245–60; Neil Mercer, Rupert Wegerif, and Lyn D. Mercer, "Children's Talk and

the Development of Reasoning in the Classroom," *British Educational Research Journal* 25, no. 1 (1999): 95–111; P. Karen Murphy, Ian A. G. Wilkinson, Anna O. Soter, Maeghan N. Hennessey, and John F. Alexander, "Examining the Effects of Classroom Discussion on Students' Comprehension of Text: A Meta-Analysis," *Journal of Educational Psychology* 101, no. 3 (2009): 740–64; Alina Reznitskaya, Li-Jen Kuo, Ann-Marie Clark, Brian Miller, May Jadallahd, Richard C. Anderson, and Kim Nguyen-Jahiel, "Collaborative Reasoning: A Dialogic Approach to Group Discussions," *Cambridge Journal of Education* 39, no. 1 (2009): 29–48; Christa S. C. Asterhan and Baruch B. Schwarz, "The Effects of Monological and Dialogical Argumentation on Concept Learning in Evolutionary Theory," *Journal of Educational Psychology* 99, no. 3 (2007): 626–39; Clark A. Chinn, Angela M. O'Donnell, and Theresa S. Jinks, "The Structure of Discourse in Collaborative Learning," *Journal of Experimental Education* 69, no. 1 (2000): 77–97.

6. Murphy, Wilkinson, Soter, Hennessey, and Alexander, "Examining the Effects of Classroom Discussion on Students' Comprehension of Text: A Meta-Analysis:" 761.

7. For example, Abby Goodnough, "The Examined Life, Age 8," *New York Times,* April, 16, 2010; Deanna Kuhn, "Teaching and Learning Science as Argument," *Science Education* 94, no. 5 (2010): 810–24; Matthew Lipman, *Thinking in Education* (New York, NY: Cambridge University Press, 2003); Partnership for 21st Century Skills, *A Framework for 21st Century Learning* (Washington, DC: P21, 2012).

8. Neil Postman, *The End of Education: Redefining the Value of School* (New York, NY: Knopf, 1995); Matthew Lipman, Ann Sharp, and Frederick S. Oscanyon, *Philosophy in the Classroom* (Philadelphia, PA: Temple University Press, 1980).

9. National Governors Association Center for Best Practices, The Council of Chief State School Officers, *Common Core State Standards: Appendix A. Research Supporting Key Elements of the Standards* (Washington, DC: National Governors Association Center for Best Practices, Council of Chief State School, 2010).

10. Ibid., 24.

11. Ibid., 24.

12. Ibid.

13. Ibid., 25.

14. Douglas Walton, *The New Dialectic: Conversational Contexts of Argument* (Toronto: Univeristy of Toronto Press, 1998).

15. Maughn Gregory, "Normative Dialogue Types in Philosophy for Children," *Gifted Education International* 22, no. 2–3 (2006): 160–71.

16. Ibid.

17. Susan Gardner, "Commentary on 'Inquiry Is No Mere Conversation,'" *Journal of Philosophy in Schools* 2, no. 1 (2015): 71–91.

18. Maughn Gregory, ed., *Philosophy for Children Practitioner Handbook* (Montclair, NJ: IAPC, 2008).

19. Alexander, *Towards Dialogic Teaching: Rethinking Classroom Talk*; Martin Nystrand, *Opening Dialogue: Understanding the Dynamics of Language and Learning in the English Classroom* (New York, NY: Teacher College Press, 1997); Rupert Wegerif, "Reason and Dialogue in Education," in *The Transformation of Learning: Advances in Cultural-Historical Activity Theory*, ed. Bert van Oers, Wim Wardekker, Ed Elbers, and Rene van der Veer Frontmatter (Cambridge, UK: Cambridge

University Press, 2008), 273–86; Rupert Wegerif, "A Dialogic Understanding of the Relationship Between CSCL and Teaching Thinking Skills," *International Journal of Computer Supported Collaborative Learning* 1, no. 1 (2006): 143–57.

20. Alexander, *Towards Dialogic Teaching: Rethinking Classroom Talk.*

21. Wegerif, "A Dialogic Understanding of the Relationship between CSCL and Teaching Thinking Skills," 146.

22. Gregory, *Philosophy for Children Practitioner Handbook*, 8.

23. Robin J. Alexander, *Essays on Pedagogy* (New York: Routledge, 2008): 110.

24. Ibid.

25. Lev S. Vygotsky, *Thought and Language (Newly Revised, Translated, and Edited by Alex Kozulin)* (Cambridge, MA: MIT Press, 1968).

26. Neil Mercer, *Words and Minds: How We Use Language to Think Together* (London: Routledge, 2000).

27. David Kennedy, "Developing Philosophical Facilitation: A Toolbox of Philosophical Moves," in *Philosophy in Schools: An Introduction for Philosophers and Teachers*, ed. Sara Goering, Nicholas J. Shudak, and Thomas E. Wartenberg (New York, NY: Routledge, 2013): 110–18; Lipman, Sharp, and Oscanyon, *Philosophy in the Classroom.*

28. Maughn Gregory, "A Framework for Facilitating Classroom Dialogue," *Teaching Philosophy* 30, no. 1 (2007): 59–84.

Chapter 2

1. Examples of scholarship on argumentation include the following: Robert Ennis, *Critical Thinking* (Upper Saddle River, NJ: Prentice Hall, 1996); Douglas Walton, *Argument Structure: A Pragmatic Theory* (Toronto: University of Toronto Press, 1996); Stephen E. Toulmin, Richard Rieke, and Allan Janik, *An Introduction to Reasoning* (New York, NY: Macmillan, 1979). Examples of instructional materials are as follows: Trudy Govier, *A Practical Study of Argument,* 7th ed. (Belmont, CA: Wadsworth Publishing Company, 2010); Maughn Gregory, *A Crash Course in Logic* (Lanham, MD: University Press of America, 1999); Jerry Cederblom and David W. Paulsen, *Critical Reasoning* (New York, NY: Wadsworth Publishing Compnay, 1996); Thomas A. Hollihan, and Kevin T. Baaske, *Arguments and Arguing: The Products of Human Decision Making* (Prospect Hights, IL: Waveland, 1973).

2. Gregory, *A Crash Course in Logic*, 1. The terminology used by Gregory has been slightly modified with the author's permission.

3. Jan A. Nielsen, "Dialectical Features of Students' Argumentation: A Critical Review of Argumentation Studies in Science Education," *Research in Science Education* 43, no. 1 (2013): 373.

4. Gregory, *A Crash Course in Logic,* 1. The terminology used by Gregory has been slightly modified with the author's permission.

5. Hollihan and Baaske, *Arguments and Arguing: The Products of Human Decision Making*, 294.

6. Gregory, "Normative Dialogue Types in Philosophy for Children," *Gifted Education International* 22, no. 2–3 (2006): 160–71; Sarah Michaels, M. C. O'Connor, Richard Sohmer, and Lauren Resnick, "Guided Construction of Knowledge in the Classroom: Teacher, Talk, Task, and Tools," in *Transformation of Knowledge Through Classroom Interaction*, ed. Baruch Schwarz, Tommy Dreyfus, and Rina Hershkowitz (London: Routledge, 2009), 105–29.

7. Gregory, *A Crash Course in Logic,* 1. The terminology used by Gregory has been slightly modified with the author's permission.

Chapter 3

1. Richard C. Anderson, Kim T. Nguyen-Jahiel, Brian McNurlen, Anthi Archodidou, So-Young Kim, Alina Reznitskaya, Maria Tillmanns, and Laurie Gilbert, "The Snowball Phenomenon: Spread of Ways of Talking and Ways of Thinking Across Groups of Children," *Cognition and Instruction* 19, no. 1 (2001): 1–46.
2. Susan Gardner, "Commentary on 'Inquiry Is No Mere Conversation,'" *Journal of Philosophy in Schools* 2, no. 1 (2015): 71–91.
3. David Kennedy, "Developing Philosophical Facilitation: A Toolbox of Philosophical Moves," in *Philosophy in Schools: An Introduction for Philosophers and Teachers,* ed. Sara Goering, Nicholas J. Shudak, and Thomas E. Wartenberg (New York, NY: Routledge, 2013): 110–18 ; Matthew Lipman, Ann Sharp, and Frederick S. Oscanyon, *Philosophy in the Classroom* (Philadelphia, PA: Temple University Press, 1980).
4. Nicholas C. Burbules, *Dialogue in Teaching: Theory and Practice* (New York, NY: Teachers College Press, 1993).
5. Alina Reznitskaya, Ian A. G. Wilkinson, Joseph Oyler, Kristin Bourdage-Reninger, and Ariel Sykes, "Using the Argumentation Rating Tool to Support Teacher Facilitation of Inquiry Dialogue in Elementary Language Arts Classrooms" (paper presented at the annual meeting of the American Educational Research Association, Washington, DC, April 8–12, 2016).
6. Examples of our own work are as follows: Alina Reznitskaya and Ian A. G. Wilkinson, "Professional Development in Dialogic Teaching: Helping Teachers Promote Argument Literacy in Their Classrooms," in *Sage Handbook of Learning,* ed. David Scott and Eleanore Hargreaves (UK: Sage Publications, 2015), 219–32; Ian A. G. Wilkinson, Alina Reznitskaya, Kristin Bourdage, Joseph Oyler, Kathryn Nelson, Monica Glina, Robert Drewry, and Min-Young Kim, "Toward a More Dialogic Pedagogy: Changing Teachers' Beliefs and Practices Through Professional Development in Language Arts Classrooms," *Language & Education* 31, no. 1 (2017): 65–82. Examples of other relevant articles include the following: Anna Soter, Ian A. G. Wilkinson, P. Karen Murphy, Lucila Rudge, Kristin Reninger, and Margaret Edwards, "What the Discourse Tells Us: Talk and Indicators of High-Level Comprehension," *International Journal of Educational Research* 47 (2008): 372–91; Lauren B. Resnick, Christa Asterhan, and Sherice Clarke, *Socializing Intelligence Through Academic Talk and Dialogue* (Washington, DC: American Educational Research Association, 2015); Laura Billings and Jill Fitzgerald, "Dialogic Discussion and the Paideia Seminar," *American Educational Research Journal* 39, no. 4 (2002): 907–41.
7. Alina Reznitskaya and Maughn Gregory, "Student Thought and Classroom Language: Examining the Mechanisms of Change in Dialogic Teaching," *Educational Psychologist* 48, no. 2 (2013): 114–33.
8. Alina Reznitskaya, Ian A. G. Wilkinson, and Joseph Oyler, "Supporting Teacher Spontaneous Use of Talk Moves During Inquiry Dialogue," in *Students' Spontaneous Use of Effective Strategies,* ed. Emmanuel Manalo, Yuri Uesaka, and Clark A. Chinn (Singapore: Routledge, in press); Reznitskaya, Wilkinson, Oyler, Bourdage-Reninger, and Sykes, "Using the Argumentation Rating Tool to Support Teacher Facilitation of Inquiry Dialogue in Elementary Language Arts Classrooms."

9. Laurance J. Splitter and A. M. Sharp, "The Practice of Philosophy in the Classroom," in *Studies in Philosophy for Children: Pixie*, ed. Ann M. Sharp and Ronald F. Reed (Madrid: Ediciones De La Torre, 1996), 285–314.

10. Maughn Gregory, "A Framework for Facilitating Classroom Dialogue," *Teaching Philosophy* 30, no. 1 (2007): 59–84.

11. Susan R. Goldman, M. Anne Britt, Willard Brown, Gayle Cribb, MariAnne George, Cynthia Greenleaf, Carol D. Lee, Cynthia Shanahan, and Readi Project, "Disciplinary Literacies and Learning to Read for Understanding: A Conceptual Framework for Disciplinary Literacy," *Educational Psychologist* 51, no. 2 (2016): 219–46; Jonathan Osborne, "Arguing to Learn in Science: The Role of Collaborative, Critical Discourse," *Science* 328, no. 5977 (2010): 463–66.

12. Splitter and Sharp, "The Practice of Philosophy in the Classroom," 285–314.

Chapter 4

1. We thank Kristin Bourdage for suggesting and contributing to the development of the Discussion Planning Tool.

2. Susan Gardner, "Commentary on 'Inquiry Is No Mere Conversation,'" *Journal of Philosophy in Schools* 2, no. 1 (2015): 71–91.

3. Maughn Gregory, "A Framework for Facilitating Classroom Dialogue," *Teaching Philosophy* 30, no. 1 (2007): 59–84.

4. Douglas Walton, *The New Dialectic: Conversational Contexts of Argument* (Toronto: University of Toronto Press, 1998), 522.

5. Gardner, "Commentary on 'Inquiry Is No Mere Conversation,'" 71–91.

6. Gregory, "A Framework for Facilitating Classroom Dialogue," 59–84.

7. Gardner, "Commentary on 'Inquiry Is No Mere Conversation,'" 71–91.

8. Alina Reznitskaya and Maughn Gregory, "Student Thought and Classroom Language: Examining the Mechanisms of Change in Dialogic Teaching." *Educational Psychologist* 48, no. 2 (2013): 114–33.

Chapter 5

1. E. H. Weiner, "What Should Kelly Do?" in *Unfinished Stories: For Facilitating Decision Making in the Elementary Classroom*, ed. E. H. Weiner (Washington, DC: National Education Association, 1980), 13–14. Reprinted by permission.

Chapter 7

1. National Governors Association Center for Best Practices, The Council of Chief State School Officers, *Common Core State Standards: Appendix A. Research Supporting Key Elements of the Standards* (Washington, DC: National Governors Association Center for Best Practices, Council of Chief State School, 2010); Nell K. Duke, V. Susan Bennett-Armistead, and Ebony M. Roberts, "Incorporating Information Text in the Primary Grades," in *Comprehensive Reading Instruction Across Grade Levels*, ed. Cathy Roller (Newark, DE: International Reading Association, 2002), 40–54.

2. Maughn Gregory, "Normative Dialogue Types in Philosophy for Children," *Gifted Education International* 22, no. 2-3 (2006): 160–71.

3. Laurance J. Splitter and A. M. Sharp, "The Practice of Philosophy in the Classroom," in *Studies in Philosophy for Children: Pixie*, ed. Ann M. Sharp and Donald F. Reed (Madrid: Ediciones De La Torre, 1996), 296.

4. P. Karen Murphy, Ian A. G. Wilkinson, Anna O. Soter, Maeghan N. Hennessey, and John F. Alexander, "Examining the Effects of Classroom Discussion on Students' Comprehension of Text: A Meta-Analysis," *Journal of Educational Psychology* 101, no. 3 (2009): 740–64.

Chapter 8

1. National Governors Association Center for Best Practices, The Council of Chief State School Officers, *Common Core State Standards: Appendix A. Research Supporting Key Elements of the Standards* (Washington, DC: National Governors Association Center for Best Practices, Council of Chief State School, 2010).

Chapter 9

1. Mikhail M. Bakhtin, *The Dialogic Imagination: Four Essays by M. M. Bakhtin*, ed. Michael Holquist, trans. Caryl Emerson and Michael Holquisted (Austin, TX: University of Texas Press, 1981); Mikhail M. Bakhtin, *Speech Genres and Other Late Essays*, ed. Caryl Emerson and Michael Holquist, trans. Vern W. McGee (Austin, TX: University of Texas Press, 1986).

2. Rupert Wegerif, "A Dialogic Understanding of the Relationship Between CSCL and Teaching Thinking Skills," *International Journal of Computer Supported Collaborative Learning* 1, no. 1 (2006): 146.

3. Yuri M. Lotman, "Text Within a Text," *Soviet Psychology* 26 (1988): 32–51.

4. Lindsay C. Matsumura, Richard Correnti, and Elaine W. Matsumura, "Classroom Writing Tasks and Students' Analytic Text-Based Writing," *Reading Research Quarterly* 50, no. 4 (2015): 417–38; Lindsay C. Matsumura, Elaine Wang, and Richard Correnti, "Teaching Tip: Text-Based Writing Assignments for College Readiness," *The Reading Teacher* 70, no. 3 (2016): 347–51.

5. Richard C. Anderson and P. David Pearson, "A Schema-Theoretic View of Basic Processes in Reading Comprehension," in *Handbook of Reading Research*, ed. P. David Pearson, Rebecca Barr, Michael. L. Kamil, and Peter B. Mosenthal (New York, NY: Longman, 1984), 255–91.

6. National Governors Association Center for Best Practices, The Council of Chief State School Officers, *Common Core State Standards: Appendix A. Research Supporting Key Elements of the Standards* (Washington, DC: National Governors Association Center for Best Practices, Council of Chief State School, 2010).

Chapter 10

1. P. David Pearson and Margaret C. Gallagher, "The Instruction of Reading Comprehension," *Contemporary Educational Psychology* 8, no. 3 (1983): 317–44.

2. Alina Reznitskaya and Monica Glina, "Comparing Student Experiences with Story Discussions in Dialogic vs. Traditional Settings," *Journal of Educational Research* 106, no. 1 (2013): 49–63.

3. Ibid., 55.

4. Ibid., 56.

5. Catherine O'Connor, Sarah Michaels, Suzanne Chapin, and Allen G. Harbaugh, "The Silent and the Vocal: Participation and Learning in Whole-Class Discussion," *Learning and Instruction* (in press).

6. Steven Karau and Kipling D. Williams, "Social Loafing: A Meta-Analytic Review and Theoretical Integration," *Journal of Personality and Social Psychology* 65, no. 4 (1993): 681–706.

7. Kathryn H.-P. Au and Jana M. Mason, "Social Organization Factors in Learning to Read: The Balance of Rights Hypothesis," *Reading Research Quarterly* 17, no. 1 (1981): 115–52.

8. Ian A. G. Wilkinson and Irene Y. Y. Fung, "Small-Group Composition and Peer Effects," *International Journal of Educational Research* 37 (2002): 425–47.

9. Lesley Mandel Morrow and Jeffrey K. Smith, "The Effects of Group Size on Interactive Storybook Reading," *Reading Research Quarterly* 25 (1990): 213–31; William Sweigart, "Classroom Talk, Knowledge Development, and Writing," *Research in the Teaching of English* 25 (1991): 497–509.

10. Sarah C. Lightner and Ian A. G. Wilkinson, "Instructional Frameworks for Quality Talk About Text: Choosing the Best Approach," *The Reading Teacher* 70, no. 4 (2017): 435–44.

11. Irene Fountas and Gay Su Pinnell, *Guided Reading: Responsive Teaching Across the Grades*, 2nd ed. (Portsmouth, NH: Heinemann, 2016).

12. We are grateful to Mrs. Courtney Ross for this suggestion.

13. Joyce Wiencek and John F. O'Flahavan, "From Teacher-Led to Peer Discussions About Literature: Suggestions for Making the Shift," *Language Arts* 71 (1994): 488–98.

14. Wilkinson and Fung, "Small-Group Composition and Peer Effects," 425–47.

15. Many ideas in this section are drawn from Maughn Gregory, ed. *Philosophy for Children Practitioner Handbook* (Montclair, NJ: IAPC, 2008).

16. Laurance J. Splitter and A. M. Sharp, "The Practice of Philosophy in the Classroom," in *Studies in Philosophy for Children: Pixie*, ed. Ann M. Sharp and Ronald F. Reed (Madrid: Ediciones De La Torre, 1996), 285–314.

17. Gregory, ed. *Philosophy for Children Practitioner Handbook*.

18. Ibid.

19. Our thanks to Dr. Joseph Oyler for this suggestion. See also Gregory, ed. *Philosophy for Children Practitioner Handbook*.

Chapter 11

1. Cynthia A. Lassonde, Sally Galman, and Clare Kosnik, ed., *Self-Study Research Methodologies for Teacher Educators, Vol. 7, Professional Learning* (Boston, MA: Sense Publishers, 2009).

2. Anastasia P. Samaras and Anne R. Freese, "Looking Back and Looking Forward: An Historical Overview of the Self-Study School," in *Self-Study Research Methodologies for Teacher Educators*, ed. Cynthia A. Lassonde, Sally Galman, and Clare Kosnik (Boston, MA: Sense Publishers, 2009), 3–19.

3. Anastasia P. Samaras, *Self-Study for Teacher Educators: Crafting a Pedagogy for Educational Change* (New York, NY: Peter Lang Publishers, 2002), xiii.

4. Mary M. Juzwik, Michael B. Sherry, Samantha Caughlan, Anne Heintz, and Carlin Borsheim-Black, "Supporting Dialogically Organized Instruction in an English Teacher Preparation Program: A Video-Based, Web 2.0-Mediated Response and Revision Pedagogy," *Teachers College Record* 114 (2012): 1–42; Linda Kucan, "Insights from Teachers Who Analyzed Transcripts of Their Own Classroom Discussions," *The Reading Teacher* 61 (2007): 228–36; Alina Reznitskaya and Ian A. G. Wilkinson, "Professional Development in Dialogic Teaching: Helping Teachers

Promote Argument Literacy in Their Classrooms," in *Sage Handbook of Learning*, ed. David Scott and Eleanore Hargreaves (UK: Sage Publications, 2015), 219–32.

5. Jo L. Brownlee, Gregory Schraw, Sue Walker, and Mary Ryan, "Changes in Preservice Teachers' Personal Epistemologies," in *Handbook of Epistemic Cognition*, ed. Jeffrey A. Greene, William A. Sandoval, and Ivar Bråten (New York: Routledge, 2016), 247–64.

6. Susan C. Cantrell and Hannah K. Hughes, "Teacher Efficacy and Content Literacy Implementation: An Exploration of the Effects of Extended Professional Development with Coaching," *Journal of Literacy Research,* 40 (2008): 95–127; Misty Sailors and Larry R. Price, "Professional Development That Supports the Teaching of Cognitive Reading Strategy Instruction," *Elementary School Journal,* 110 (2010): 301–22.

7. Alina Reznitskaya and Ian A. G. Wilkinson, "Dialogic Teaching: Rethinking and Positively Transforming Classroom Practice," in *Positive Psychology in Practice*, 2nd ed., ed. Stephen Joseph (Hoboken, NJ: John Wiley & Sons, Inc., 2015), 375–99; Reznitskaya and Wilkinson, "Professional Development in Dialogic Teaching: Helping Teachers Promote Argument Literacy in Their Classrooms," 219–32.

Chapter 12

1. National Governors Association Center for Best Practices, The Council of Chief State School Officers, *Common Core State Standards: Appendix A. Research Supporting Key Elements of the Standards* (Washington, DC: National Governors Association Center for Best Practices, Council of Chief State School, 2010).

2. Thomas M. McCann, "Student Argumentative Writing Knowledge and Ability at Three Grade Levels," *Research in the Teaching of English* 23, no. 1 (1989): 63–77; Mary L. Means and James F. Voss, "Who Reasons Well? Two Studies of Informal Reasoning Among Children of Different Grade, Ability, and Knowledge Levels," *Cognition and Instruction* 14, no. 2 (1996): 139–78; US Department of Education, Institute of Education Sciences, National Center for Education Statistics, "Reading 2011: National Assessment of Educational Progress (NAEP) at Grades 4 and 8," http://nces.ed.gov/nationsreportcard/pdf/main2011/2012457.pdf.

3. Robin J. Alexander, *Towards Dialogic Teaching: Rethinking Classroom Talk,* 3rd ed. (York, UK: Dialogos, 2006); Martin Nystrand, Lawrence L. Wu, Adam Gamoran, Susie Zeiser, and Daniel A. Long, "Questions in Time: Investigating the Structure and Dynamics of Unfolding Classroom Discourse," *Discourse Processes* 35, no. 2 (2003): 135–98; Christine Howe and Manzoorul Abedin, "Classroom Dialogue: A Systematic Review Across Four Decades of Research," *Cambridge Journal of Education* 43, no. 3 (2013): 325–56.

4. Gordon Wells, *Dialogic Inquiry: Toward a Sociocultural Practice and Theory of Education*, (Cambridge, UK: Cambridge University Press, 1999); Lev S. Vygotsky, *Thought and Language (Newly Revised, Translated, and Edited by Alex Kozulin)* (Cambridge, MA: MIT Press, 1968); Neil Mercer and Karen Littleton, *Dialogue and the Development of Children's Thinking: A Sociocultural Approach* (London: Routledge, 2007).

5. Deanna Kuhn and Wadiya Udell, "The Development of Argument Skills," *Child Development* 74, no. 5 (2003): 1245–60; Neil Mercer, Rupert Wegerif, and Lyn D. Mercer, "Children's Talk and the Development of Reasoning in the Classroom," *British Educational Research Journal* 25, no. 1

(1999): 95–111; P. Karen Murphy, Ian A. G. Wilkinson, Anna O. Soter, Maeghan N. Hennessey, and John F. Alexander, "Examining the Effects of Classroom Discussion on Students' Comprehension of Text: A Meta-Analysis," *Journal of Educational Psychology* 101, no. 3 (2009): 740–64; Arthur N. Applebee, Judith A. Langer, Martin Nystrand, and Adam Gamoran, "Discussion-Based Approaches to Developing Understanding: Classroom Instruction and Student Performance in Middle and High School English," *American Educational Research Journal* 40, no. 3 (2003): 685–730; Alina Reznitskaya, Li-Jen Kuo, Ann-Marie Clark, Brian Miller, May Jadallahd, Richard C. Anderson, and Kim Nguyen-Jahiel, "Collaborative Reasoning: A Dialogic Approach to Group Discussions," *Cambridge Journal of Education* 39, no. 1 (2009): 29–48; Christa S. C. Asterhan and Baruch B. Schwarz, "The Effects of Monological and Dialogical Argumentation on Concept Learning in Evolutionary Theory," *Journal of Educational Psychology* 99, no. 3 (2007): 626–39; Clark A. Chinn, Angela M. O'Donnell, and Theresa S. Jinks, "The Structure of Discourse in Collaborative Learning," *Journal of Experimental Education* 69, no. 1 (2000): 77–97; Lin, Tzu-Jung, Jing Chen, Seung Yon Ha, Elizabeth Kraatz, Irina Kuznetcova, Narmada Paul, Sungjun Won, and Eric M. Anderman, "The Influence of Collaborative Small-Group Discussion on Social Self-Efficacy and Class Relationships" (paper presented at the American Educational Research Association, San Antonio, TX, April 27–May 1 2017).

6. Ann R. Eisenberg and Catherine Garvey, "Children's Use of Verbal Strategies in Resolving Conflicts," *Discourse Processes* 32 (1981): 135–53.

7. Deanna Kuhn and Amanda Crowell, "Dialogic Argumentation as a Vehicle for Developing Young Adolescents' Thinking," *Psychological Science* 22 (2011): 545–52; Alina Reznitskaya, Richard C. Anderson, Brian McNurlen, Kim Nguyen-Jahiel, Anthi Archodidou, and So-Young Kim, "Influence of Oral Discussion on Written Argument," *Discourse Processes* 32, no. 2 & 3 (2001): 155–75; Mercer, Wegerif, and Mercer, "Children's Talk and the Development of Reasoning in the Classroom," 95–111; Murphy, Wilkinson, Soter, Hennessey, and Alexander, "Examining the Effects of Classroom Discussion on Students' Comprehension of Text: A Meta-Analysis," 740–64.

8. Pam Grossman, Christa Compton, Danielle Igra, Matthew Ronfeldt, Emily Shahan, and Peter W. Williamson, "Teaching Practice: A Cross-Professional Perspective," *Teachers College Record* 111, no. 9 (2009): 2055–100.

9. Kayoko Inagaki, Giyoo Hatano, and Eiji Morita, "Construction of Mathematical Knowledge Through Whole-Class Discussion," *Learning and Instruction* 8, no. 6 (1998): 503–26; Catherine O'Connor, Sarah Michaels, Suzanne Chapin, and Allen G. Harbaugh, "The Silent and the Vocal: Participation and Learning in Whole-Class Discussion," *Learning and Instruction* (in press).

10. The concept of "culture of active participation" was discussed by O'Connor, Michaels, Chapin, and Harbaugh, "The Silent and the Vocal: Participation and Learning in Whole-Class Discussion."

11. Maughn Gregory, "Normative Dialogue Types in Philosophy for Children," *Gifted Education International* 22, no. 2–3 (2006): 160–71.

12. Maughn Gregory, "Food for Thought," *The Occasional Paper Series of the New Jersey Network for Educational Renewal* 3, no. 2 (2005): 1–3.

Acknowledgments

We are indebted to our friend and colleague Dr. Maughn Gregory for sharing with us his expertise in argumentation and facilitation of inquiry dialogue and for providing insightful feedback on the manuscript of this book. We also would like to thank the colleagues and collaborators on our multiyear *dialogic teaching* project funded by the Institute of Education Sciences:

- Discourse Coaches: Kristin Bourdage and Joseph Oyler
- Research Associates: Kate Collins, Robert Drewry, Ariel Sykes, Hillary Kapa, Min-Young Kim, Sirine Mabrouk-Hattab, Alexandra Major, Kathryn Scott Nelson, Diana Purwaningrum, David Herren, and Sabrina Tejeda
- Project Managers: Monica Glina and Danielle Poling
- Advisory Board Members: Janice Almasi, Mary Juzwik, and Sarah Michaels

About the Authors

Alina Reznitskaya is a professor in the Department of Educational Foundations at Montclair State University. She has acquired expertise in educational psychology, quantitative research methodology, and psycho-educational measurement, and she teaches undergraduate and graduate courses on these topics. Dr. Reznitskaya conducts research on the role social interaction plays in the development of students' argumentation skills. She also designs and evaluates professional development programs that support teachers in their use of classroom talk to promote student learning. Dr. Reznitskaya's work has appeared in a variety of journals and edited books, including *Educational Psychologist, The Reading Teacher, Contemporary Educational Psychology, Cambridge Journal of Education, Elementary School Journal, Discourse Processes, Comprehension Instruction: Research-Based Best Practices,* and *Positive Psychology in Practice.*

Ian A. G. Wilkinson is a professor in the Department of Teaching and Learning at The Ohio State University. He has a background in educational psychology and research interests in cognition, instruction, and research methodology related to the study of literacy. Originally from Australia, Dr. Wilkinson has lectured and conducted research in Australia, New Zealand, and the United States. Dr. Wilkinson teaches courses on literacy learning and teaching, and conducts research on the impact of classroom talk on students' reading comprehension and the implications for professional development of teachers. He served as co-editor of *Reading Research Quarterly* from 2006 to 2012. His work has appeared in publications such as *Reading Research Quarterly, British Journal of Educational Psychology, American Educational Research Journal, Journal of Educational Psychology, The Elementary School Journal, Reading*

Psychology, The Reading Teacher, Learning and Instruction, Teaching and Teacher Education, the *Handbook of Reading Research*, the *Handbook of Research on Learning and Instruction*, and the *Handbook of Educational Psychology*.

Over the past several years, Drs. Reznitskaya and Wilkinson have worked with elementary school teachers to help them learn how to conduct classroom discussions that engage students in collaborative and rigorous argumentation. The research was sponsored by a grant from the Institute of Education Sciences, US Department of Education, with Drs. Reznitskaya and Wilkinson serving as coprincipal investigators.

Index